Solicitors and Money Laundering

101 871 726 9

SOLICITORS AND MONEY LAUNDERING

A Compliance Handbook

Second Edition

Peter J Camp LL.B Solicitor

The Law Society

Peter Camp, the author of *Solicitors and Money Laundering*, quotes extensively from the Law Society's official guidance in the text of this book. For the avoidance of doubt, the views expressed in this publication should be taken as those of the author.

Readers should note that the Law Society's official Money Laundering Guidance can be found at www.lawsociety.org.uk and represents the Law Society's views on this subject.

© Peter Camp 2007

ISBN 978–1–85328–593–6

Published in 2007 by the Law Society
113 Chancery Lane, London WC2A 1PL

Reprinted in 2007

Typeset by J&L Composition, Filey, North Yorkshire
Printed by MPG Books Ltd, Bodmin, Cornwall

Contents

Foreword

As Chair of the Serious Organised Crime Agency and a member of the Board of the Solicitors Regulation Authority, I am pleased to be invited to write the Foreword to this second edition of Peter Camp's *Solicitors and Money Laundering*, which provides updated guidance to solicitors on how the UK's money laundering legislation applies to them.

Organised crime and terrorism threaten the security and prosperity of the United Kingdom. The government is committed to reducing harm caused with all available tools. Tackling criminal finance provides opportunities to identify individuals involved in crime, to disrupt illegal activity and to deny criminals the rewards of their criminality. Effective collaboration between law enforcement, the private sector and legal and financial professionals is essential if those opportunities are to be maximised.

This book brings the picture up to date to the end of 2006, most notably in the light of the *Bowman* v. *Fels* Court of Appeal judgment and the Serious Organised Crime and Police Act 2005. It identifies risks to solicitors and professional advisers from exploitation by criminals and retains the key judgments from the first edition that 'the solicitors' profession is an ideal target for criminals' and 'a major reason why money launderers might target a solicitor's practice is the solicitor's client account'.

As experience grows of using the legislation, further amendments can be expected. The government has already given notice of its intention to seek parliamentary approval for amendments in the Serious Crime Bill, including the merger of SOCA and the Assets Recovery Agency. The continuing commitment of the international community to tackle criminal finances will also shape the UK response, as in the forthcoming Money Laundering Regulations 2007.

Peter Camp provides valuable and thorough guidance on the current state of the law and I am happy to commend this book to the profession.

Sir Stephen Lander
February 2007

Preface

This second edition of *Solicitors and Money Laundering: A Compliance Handbook* updates the previous edition by taking into account recent changes in legislation and case law.

The primary legislation, the Proceeds of Crime Act 2002, has been significantly amended in relation to its provisions on money laundering by the Serious Organised Crime and Police Act 2005. These amendments have been brought into effect over a number of months during 2005 and 2006. **Appendix A1** provides practitioners with extracts from the Proceeds of Crime Act as amended by the Serious Organised Crime and Police Act. The text of the handbook provides a detailed commentary on those amendments.

Solicitors' obligations under the money laundering legislation have also been considerably affected by the Court of Appeal's decision in *Bowman* v. *Fels* [2005] EWCA Civ 226. This decision has had a major impact on those solicitors involved in litigation (including the consensual resolution of issues in a litigation context). The decision also confirms that legal professional privilege is preserved in money laundering situations requiring solicitors to consider in detail the question of privilege before making external disclosures. These matters are also dealt with in depth in this second edition.

On 1 April 2006, the Serious Organised Crime Agency (SOCA) took over from the National Criminal Intelligence Service. The SOCA report forms and guidance on their completion are contained in **Appendix C4.**

As with the first edition, I have quoted extensively from the Law Society's guidance including new guidance on *Bowman* v. *Fels* and guidance for solicitors undertaking property work and private client work. However, the responsibility for the views expressed in the book remains mine and only where the context allows should these views be taken as being endorsed by the Law Society.

Peter Camp
January 2007

Table of cases

Table of statutes

Table of statutory instruments and European legislation

PART 1

Substantive Law

CHAPTER 1

Money laundering and the solicitors' profession: an overview

1.1 INTRODUCTION

In recent years, successive governments have taken steps to increase intelligence information regarding serious criminal activities. To this end they have introduced legislation which requires the disclosure of knowledge or suspicion of criminal activities. This legislation is aimed at those whose services may be used by the perpetrators of crimes, typically banks and other financial institutions and professional businesses such as solicitors and accountants. Failure to disclose can be a serious crime in itself. Initially the requirements to disclose were limited to crimes involving terrorism and drug trafficking (see the Prevention of Terrorism (Temporary Provisions) Act 1989 and the Drug Trafficking Offences Act 1986). However, in 1994, requirements to disclose a wider range of criminal activities (i.e. activities relating to indictable offences) were introduced by an amendment to the Criminal Justice Act 1988 contained in the Criminal Justice Act 1993. More recently, more draconian measures requiring disclosure were introduced in the Proceeds of Crime Act 2002 (PoCA 2002). Amendments have been made to PoCA 2002 as a result of the Serious Organised Crime and Police Act 2005 (SOCPA 2005).

In addition to the criminal law, regulation of businesses which potentially could be used by criminals was introduced with the Money Laundering Regulations 1993 (now the Money Laundering Regulations 2003, SI 2003/3075). Both sets of Regulations were introduced into UK law as a result of European Directives.

Where disclosure is necessary, the procedure is normally for disclosure to be made to the Serious Organised Crime Agency (SOCA). SOCA became operational on 1 April 2006 bringing together the National Criminal Intelligence Service (NCIS), the National Crime Squad and the investigative branches of HM Revenue and Customs and the Home Office Immigration Service. SOCA has as its core objective the reduction in the harm caused to the UK and its citizens by organised crime, including the trafficking of drugs and people. It works very closely with the revenue departments which continue to be responsible for tackling revenue and tax fraud. The agency has a UK-wide remit.

The solicitors' profession is an ideal target for criminals. Criminal property must be converted into apparently legitimate assets if it is not to be at risk of seizure by the authorities. Use of a solicitor's services to buy or sell property (real estate or business property) using the proceeds of crime or merely 'laundering' criminal proceeds through a solicitor's client account will potentially involve the solicitor in criminal activities. It is not possible for solicitors to argue that they did not know that their client was using their services in this way. The legislation imposes severe penalties on those who do not report when they know or suspect that they are involved with criminal property.

1.2   WHAT IS MONEY LAUNDERING?

The traditional view that money laundering simply involved 'cleaning dirty cash' (i.e. converting criminally obtained cash into clean money) is no longer appropriate. (One view is that the term 'money laundering' derived from the activities of Chinese laundries in Chicago in the hey-day of American organised crime.) 'Money laundering' encompasses a far wider range of criminal activities and today can be undertaken by the perpetrator of the original crime as well as by third parties on behalf of the perpetrator or others. It is an attempt to hide the proceeds of crime (by integrating such proceeds into other legitimate property or by confusing the audit trail) in such a way that the authorities cannot trace the proceeds back to the original crime.

There are three generally accepted stages to the money laundering activities of the criminal community:

1.   **Placement**: where cash is converted into non-cash assets.
2.   **Layering**: where several transactions are undertaken for no other reason than to confuse the audit trail between the original crime and subsequent proceeds.
3.   **Integration**: the final destination of the criminal proceeds.

Solicitors could find themselves inadvertently involved in any of these stages.

1.2.1   Placement

A large proportion of criminal property starts life as cash (this is particularly the case where drug trafficking is involved). The first thing the holder of such cash will wish to do is to convert the cash into a non-cash asset. It is increasingly difficult to pay large sums of cash into a bank account or through any other financial institution. The money launderer will therefore need to approach this in a more subtle way. Frequently this will involve a number of local cash businesses, for example taxi firms or retail shops. These businesses will regularly bank large amounts of cash and such deposits, being in the usual way of business, will not attract their banks' suspicion. If the money launderer can persuade owners of these businesses to bank some of the criminal cash at the same time as their own takings, substantial amounts of criminal money can be deposited in the banking system without suspicion being aroused. A cheque can then be drawn in favour of the criminal (or more likely some third party on behalf of the criminal) for the appropriate amount less, of course, the commission for providing this service.

Solicitors' involvement in placement is rare to the extent that it is unlikely that many solicitors will agree to receive large amounts of cash deposits. Clearly, if a client attempts to put the firm into funds for a transaction or for substantial costs using cash, suspicion should be aroused and steps should be taken to ascertain the legitimacy of funds. Where this proves to be impossible solicitors should act on their suspicion. However, it is possible that solicitors may be involved on the periphery. If, when acting for a cash business, a solicitor becomes aware of suspicious circumstances which point to the possibility of placement, he or she must take appropriate steps to avoid the risk of criminal liability. Further, solicitors asked to act on, say, a company formation, must be satisfied as to the commercial reason for the formation. Companies are frequently formed with a view to setting up bogus businesses in order that criminal proceeds can be laundered through those businesses.

1.2.2 Layering

Once any cash has been converted into a non-cash asset (e.g. a deposit account at a bank) the next stage in the money laundering activity is to ensure that the criminal property cannot be traced back to the crime. This stage is equally important for the criminal whose criminal property did not start as cash (e.g. where the crime involved fraud or the acquisition of non-cash assets illegally). As a result of PoCA 2002 provisions relating to confiscation and civil recovery of criminal proceeds (see **Chapter 8**) it is of particular importance to the criminal to ensure that any property he or she possesses cannot be traced back to the original crime. Civil recovery provisions mean that it is now necessary for the authorities only to discharge a civil onus of proof (i.e. on the balance of probabilities) in order to seek and obtain a recovery order. Criminal property is defined in PoCA 2002 as constituting a person's benefit from criminal conduct or representing such a benefit in whole or part, directly or indirectly (PoCA 2002, s.340). Consequently it does not matter how remote property is from the original crime; if the audit trail allows the authorities to trace the property back to the original proceeds of the crime (on the balance of probabilities) a recovery order may be granted. Layering is the attempt to ensure that this cannot happen.

Solicitors may frequently be involved inadvertently in the layering transaction. A firm's client account is ideal for layering purposes. If money can be passed through a client account and out the other side by a 'clean' client account cheque, this can amount to one step in the layering process. Obviously solicitors must be suspicious where potential clients ask that money be accepted into client account for onward transmission where the solicitor is not involved in any legal or commercial transaction on behalf of that client. The Solicitors' Accounts Rules 1998 provide additional guidance on the use of client account for non-legal purposes. Note (ix) to Rule 15 of the Rules states:

> In the case of *Wood and Burdett* (case number 8669/2002 filed on 13 January 2004), the Solicitors' Disciplinary Tribunal said that it is not a proper part of a solicitor's everyday business or practice to operate a banking facility for third parties, whether they are clients of the firm or not. Solicitors should not, therefore, provide banking facilities through client account. Further solicitors are likely to lose the exemption under the Financial Services and Markets Act 2000 if a deposit is taken in circumstances which do not form part of a solicitor's practice. It should be borne in mind that there are criminal sanctions against assisting money launderers.

Again, the criminal is more likely to use subtle means of passing money through client account, rather than an 'up front' request. Frequently solicitors are involved in abortive transactions and most of these will be legitimate. However, consider the following scenario. A solicitor is instructed by a new client. Appropriate money laundering verification procedures are followed (for details of these requirements, see **Chapter 9**). The client instructs the solicitor on a property transaction; the client is buying commercial property for consideration of in excess of £1million. The client explains that there is an urgency surrounding this transaction; the deal must be completed by a specified date or it is likely to collapse. The solicitor agrees with the firm acting for the vendor that, because of the deadline, the two firms will proceed on the basis of a simultaneous exchange of contracts and completion – not an uncommon procedure. A week before the planned completion date, the purchaser's solicitor is put in funds by way of a cheque or BACS payment. The funds cover the amount required to complete plus costs and disbursements including stamp duty. A day or two before the planned completion date the client telephones his solicitor and explains that there has been a hitch in the arrangements. For whatever reason given, the transaction cannot proceed to completion. Since no contracts have been exchanged there is no legal reason why the client cannot, at this stage, pull out of the deal. The client asks that the solicitor bills for the work done and returns the balance of the money held in client account. Is this a genuine abortive transaction or a successful layering exercise which has allowed the client to pass in excess of £1 million through the client account and out the other side?

Solicitors and their staff must be concerned about any deal which does not complete where substantial sums are placed in their client accounts before being returned to the client or a third party on behalf of the client. Solicitors must also question the commerciality of deals and after any appropriate investigation, act on any suspicion they may have. (For further examples of layering, see **Paragraph 1.3**.)

1.2.3   Integration

The final stage in the money laundering exercise is integration – the final destination for the criminal proceeds. After passing the funds through a number of layering transactions, the criminal should be fairly confident that funds are now unlikely to be traced back to the original crime. He or she is now ready to invest the funds in a legitimate investment which will give a legitimate return and, for all intents and purposes, allow the appearance of non-criminal wealth.

The authorities have indicated that they believe that much of the criminal funds invested in the UK end up in commercial property. The UK commercial property market is an ideal final destination for criminal funds sourced from both the UK and abroad. There is the potential for capital growth as well as rental income. Inevitably, if funds are invested in commercial property, a solicitor is involved in the conveyancing. This involvement can bring the solicitor within the scope of the criminal law.

However, commercial property is not the only asset used as the final destination for criminal funds. Some funds will be invested in genuine business deals (company acquisitions, corporate finance, partnership finance, or joint ventures). Any asset purchase or funding deal could potentially involve a firm in the money laundering exercise.

1.3   HOW ARE SOLICITORS INVOLVED?

It should be clear from the above, that solicitors could be involved in any or all three stages in a typical money laundering exercise. The following paragraphs expand on the details of a solicitor's potential involvement indicating that there really is no common area of practice that is not at risk. A departmental checklist can be found in **Chapter 12**.

1.3.1   Advice

It is clear from the substantive law that a solicitor need not be in possession of cash or other criminal property in order to run the risk of involvement in money laundering. One of the more dangerous offences from a solicitor's point of view is that of 'arrangements' contained in PoCA 2002, s.328 (for full details and commentary on this section, see **Chapter 2**). This section provides that an offence is committed if a person:

> enters into or becomes concerned in an arrangement which he knows or suspects facilitates (by whatever means) the acquisition, retention, use or control of criminal property by or on behalf of another person.

Thus a solicitor who gives advice knowing or suspecting that the advice facilitates the acquisition of criminal property could be guilty of this offence which carries a maximum punishment of 14 years' imprisonment. Tax evasion is a crime. In February 1999, Jack Straw MP (the then Home Secretary) said, 'Tax evasion offences are criminal offences . . . The [money laundering] legislation . . . does not treat them in any special way . . .' If a solicitor gives advice to a client which assists in a client's legitimate tax avoidance this is acceptable (and, indeed, a normal activity for solicitors). If, however, the advice facilitates tax evasion such advice could lead to a charge under PoCA 2002, s.328.

1.3.2   Use of client account

A major reason why money launderers might target a solicitor's practice is the solicitor's client account. For all intents and purposes a client account is like a bank account. Any use of client account for other than a legitimate underlying legal purpose should give rise to suspicion. Solicitors must be careful not to mistake what appears to be a legitimate use of client account with improper use leading to money laundering. As noted above, those intent on money laundering will use subtle means to avoid a solicitor's suspicion. A solicitor delivers a bill of costs to a client following the successful completion of a transaction. The client sends a cheque in payment of the costs. Sometime later, the same sum is received into the solicitor's client account by way of a BACS transfer. The payment comes from a third party who informs the firm that they have agreed to pay the client's costs associated with the transaction. One way or another, the solicitor will have to return the overpaid costs to the client or third party – money has been passed through client account and out again on a genuine client account cheque.

Particular care must be taken when a solicitor is asked to act as a stake-holder (i.e. holding money in client account on behalf of a third party until the happening of a specified event). This is an everyday occurrence in conveyancing transactions and where the property or other transaction appears genuine, no great risk will occur. However, if the instructions are such that the solicitor is only being asked to act as stakeholder without involvement in the underlying transaction, this should give rise to concern and appropriate enquiries should be made to check the legitimacy of the transaction. Solicitors' undertakings or guarantees are particularly useful to criminals. If they can persuade their victims to part with funds against the undertaking of a solicitor 'to hold the funds to the order of' the victim until the happening of a specified event, the victim is more likely to readily part with the funds.

Solicitors and their cashiers must at all times be vigilant to the possible misuse of client account. Unusual transactions and transactions involving the movement of funds through client account where, for whatever reason, there is no underlying legal transaction should be considered carefully and, if necessary, reported internally in accordance with the firm's procedures (for details of such procedures, see **Chapter 11**).

1.3.3 Purchase or sale of property/assets

Either as part of the layering exercise or as the final destination for criminal proceeds, property purchase or sale can form part of a money laundering exercise. If a client is involved in providing false information to a bank or building society as part of a mortgage transaction, the loan becomes criminal property (the proceeds of mortgage fraud). The property purchased with the mortgage funds becomes criminal property. When the property is sold, the proceeds of sale become criminal property. If the proceeds of sale are used to purchase another asset, that other asset becomes criminal property. If the asset is used as security to borrow money, that money becomes criminal property. The definition of criminal property is wide enough to catch all these items (for full details of the definition, see **Chapter 2**). A solicitor's involvement in any of these activities could risk involvement in money laundering if the solicitor knows or suspects that criminal property is involved.

Conveyancing and property lawyers are clearly at risk. The Law Society has issued specific guidance for solicitors undertaking property work (December 2005) – see **Chapter 12** and **Appendix B3**. However, the risk is not limited to real property transactions. Transactions involving shares, other securities and investments could equally give rise to risk of money laundering.

1.3.4 Hiding behind corporate or other vehicles or devices

Criminals involved in the laundering of criminal proceeds will frequently wish to avoid the use of their own names (particularly in the light of the identification procedures set out in the Money Laundering Regulations (see **Chapter 9**)). Consequently they are likely to seek to hide behind a corporate identity or seek to distance themselves from the transaction through the use of trusts or powers of attorney. Solicitors instructed to create companies or draft trust deeds or powers of attorney are clearly at risk of involvement in money laundering where such vehicles are being used for criminal purposes. Equally, solicitors instructed to act as directors, trustees or donees under a power of attorney where there is no commercial or other reason for the appointment may find themselves acting as a front for criminals.

1.3.5 Drafting documentation

A major need for any successful money launderer is the ability to move funds from one account to another or across one frontier to another jurisdiction. To do so through the legitimate banking system, an apparently genuine reason for the transfer of the funds will have to be found; a reason which will satisfy the suspicions of the bankers involved. If the launderer is able to produce genuine documentation prepared by a reputable firm of solicitors his or her task will be made much easier.

Loan documentation, drafted by solicitors, can be used as a reason for the transfer of funds – funds paid to discharge the loan or funds received to discharge a loan.

1.3.6 Confidentiality and privilege

Money launderers will frequently make use of a solicitor's services in the mistaken belief that any information given in the course of a solicitor's retainer is confidential and sometimes subject to the concept of privilege. They believe that a solicitor is prohibited from disclosing information received in the course of practising as a solicitor. Consequently any suspicion (or knowledge) of a criminal purpose will, they believe, not be passed on to the authorities.

It is undoubtedly true that such an obligation applies in both a solicitor's duty in law and in professional conduct. Lord Denning MR stated in *Parry-Jones* v. *The Law Society* [1969] 1 Ch 1:

> as between solicitor and client there are two privileges. The first relates to legal proceedings – commonly called 'legal professional privilege'. . . . The second privilege arises out of the confidence subsisting between solicitor and client. . . . The law implies a term into the contract whereby a professional man is to keep his client's affairs secret.

The money laundering legislation has made serious inroads into the duties of confidentiality and privilege. First, the definition of legal professional privilege for criminal proceedings has been codified by the Police and Criminal Evidence Act 1984 (PACE). Section 10 of that Act provides:

(1)   . . . items subject to legal privilege means:

   (a)   communications between a professional legal adviser and his client or any person representing his client in connection with the giving of legal advice to the client;

   (b)   communications between a professional legal adviser and his client or any person representing his client or between such an adviser and any other person made in connection with or in contemplation of legal proceedings and for the purposes of such proceedings; and

   (c)   items enclosed with or referred to in such communications and made:

      (i)   in connection with the giving of legal advice; or

      (ii)   in connection with or in contemplation of legal proceedings and for the purposes of such proceedings they are in possession of a person who is entitled to possess them.

(2)   Items held with the intention of furthering a criminal purpose are not items subject to legal privilege.

PACE, s.10(2) provides that items are not to be considered as privileged where they are held 'with the intention of furthering a criminal purpose'. The House of Lords in *R* v. *Central Criminal Court* ex p. *Francis* v. *Francis* [1989] 1 AC 346, held that the 'intention' in PACE, s.10(2) did not have to be the solicitor's intention. Provided someone had the intention to further a criminal purpose, items held would not be privileged.

Secondly, PoCA 2002 requires solicitors to disclose their knowledge or suspicions of a client's involvement in money laundering in certain circumstances (either by way of a defence or by way of an obligation). PoCA 2002 provides that such disclosures made by a solicitor in accordance with the requirements are 'not to be taken to breach any restriction on the disclosure of information (however imposed)' (see s.338 and **Chapter 2**). However, the Court of Appeal in *Bowman* v. *Fels* [2005] EWCA Civ 226 stated:

> There is nothing in the language of [PoCA 2002] to suggest that Parliament expressly intended to override legal professional privilege ... Much stronger language would have been required if [PoCA 2002] could be interpreted as bearing a necessary implication that legal professional privilege was to be overridden.

Privilege, as it applies to money laundering scenarios, is a complex topic. It is covered in **Chapters 4** and **5** of this book and Chapter 4 of the Law Society Guidance (as amended) (see **Paragraph 1.4** for details of Guidance).

1.4   LAW SOCIETY GUIDANCE

A number of criminal offences contained in PoCA 2002 (notably s.330 and 331 – see **Chapters 5** and **6**), the Terrorism Act 2000 (notably s.21A – see **Chapter 5**) and the Money Laundering Regulations 2003, SI 2003/3075 (reg. 3(3) – see **Chapter 9**) all provide that:

> In deciding whether a person committed an offence ... the court must consider whether he followed any relevant guidance which was at the time concerned:
>
> (a)   issued by a supervisory authority or any other appropriate body;
> (b)   approved by the Treasury; and
> (c)   published in a manner it approved as appropriate in its opinion to bring the guidance to the attention of persons likely to be affected by it.

A supervisory body, for these purposes, includes the Law Society.

The Law Society has issued Guidance to the solicitors' profession (*Money Laundering Guidance: Professional Ethics*, Pilot Edition, January 2004). The Guidance has been significantly amended in the light of *Bowman* v. *Fels* by the replacement of the original Annex 3 to the Guidance. The *Bowman* v. *Fels* guidance is reproduced in **Appendix B2**. Extracts from the main Guidance document appear throughout the text of this book and in **Appendix B1**. The Law Society's Guidance is described as a 'pilot' and has not been submitted to the Treasury for approval. The Society has acknowledged that much of the legislation is new and untested. It is seeking comments from members of the profession on the Guidance and in the light of experience and feedback from the profession it will then consider whether to seek Treasury approval for subsequent editions. Consequently, the courts are not technically required to take the Guidance into account. However, as stated in the Guidance, a court 'may still take it into consideration' in deciding whether an offence has been committed.

In addition to the main Guidance, the Law Society has also issued specific guidance: *Anti-money laundering guidance for solicitors undertaking property work* (December 2005) and *Anti-money laundering guidance for solicitors conducting private client work* (February 2006). These are reproduced in **Appendices B3** and **B4**.

1.5 CONCLUSION

It should be clear from the above that solicitors are at risk from inadvertent involvement in money laundering. The risk arises from the type of transaction solicitors are frequently involved with and from the fact that a criminal charge can follow from a solicitor's suspicion – it is not necessary for a solicitor to know that his or her client is involved in criminal activities. PoCA 2002 contains a number of obligations relating to a solicitor's possible involvement in money laundering activities. It is no longer possible for solicitors to 'turn a blind eye' to a client's potential criminal transaction. Any suspicion must be acted upon and the firm must ensure that adequate safeguards and systems are in place requiring all partners and members of staff to be aware of the dangers of inadvertent involvement and to understand the detailed requirements of the legislation.

CHAPTER 2

Criminal offences: arrangements (PoCA 2002, s.328)

2.1 INTRODUCTION

The Proceeds of Crime Act 2002 (PoCA 2002) received Royal Assent in June 2002. PoCA 2002 is a substantial Act and contains many provisions outside the scope of this book. Part 7 of PoCA 2002 deals with money laundering offences. Part 8 contains the offence of prejudicing an investigation. These provisions replace previous money laundering offences contained in the Criminal Justice Act 1988 (as amended by the Criminal Justice Act 1993), and the Drug Trafficking Act 1994. Part 7 came into force on 24 February 2003. Various parts of PoCA 2002 have been amended by the Serious Organised Crime and Police Act 2005 (SOCPA 2005). In particular, SOCPA 2005 has made amendments to Part 7 of PoCA 2002 some of which came into force on 1 July 2005 and others on 21 February 2006 and 15 May 2006. In addition, the Terrorism Act 2000 contains further money laundering offences relating to terrorist property (these offences are dealt with in **Chapters 3** and **5**).

There are five criminal offences dealt with in PoCA 2002, Part 7. These are:

- **Section 327**: concealing.
- **Section 328**: arrangements.
- **Section 329**: acquisition, use and possession.
- **Sections 330, 331 and 332**: failure to disclose.
- **Section 333**: tipping off.

Of these five offences, the offences contained in ss.327–8 (the money laundering offences) are, perhaps, of greatest risk for solicitors. The offence of 'arrangements' (s.328) has the greatest potential scope for solicitor's involvement. This offence is dealt with in this chapter – subsequent chapters deal with the other offences.

The offence in s.328 is not new. Similar offences were to be found in the amended Criminal Justice Act 1988 (applying to the laundering of the proceeds of indictable offences), and the Drug Trafficking Act 1994 (applying to the proceeds of drug trafficking). However, PoCA 2002 brings these offences into one statute and makes some subtle but important changes to the way this offence applies.

2.2 THE OFFENCE

Section 328 provides:

> A person commits an offence if he enters into or becomes concerned in an arrange-
> ment which he knows or suspects facilitates (by whatever means) the acquisition,
> retention, use or control of criminal property by or on behalf of another person.

The offence is a serious one with severe penalties available to the courts for
those found guilty. Under PoCA 2002, s.334 the penalty on summary conviction is imprisonment for a term not exceeding six months or a fine not
exceeding the statutory maximum or to both, or on conviction on indictment,
to imprisonment for a term not exceeding 14 years or a fine or both.

There are a number of points that can be made concerning this section.

*A person commits an offence if he enters into or becomes concerned in
an arrangement . . .*

A solicitor is commonly going to enter into or become concerned in an
arrangement as a result of the retainer between the solicitor and client. In
many cases, it will be the client who 'enters into' the arrangement and the
solicitor will merely be 'concerned in' the client's arrangement. This will,
however, be sufficient to bring the solicitor within the wording of the section.

The Court of Appeal in *Bowman* v. *Fels* [2005] EWCA Civ 226 has
excluded certain activities from the definition of 'arrangement' for the purposes of s.328. The excluded activities are described as 'litigation from the
issue of proceedings and the securing of injunctive relief or a freezing order
up to its final disposal by judgment' (para.83 of the judgment). The judgment
states that legal proceedings are a state-provided mechanism for the resolution of issues according to law. Parliament, according to the judgment,
cannot have intended that proceedings or steps taken by lawyers in order to
determine or secure legal rights and remedies for their clients should involve
them in 'becoming concerned in an arrangement which facilitates the acquisition, retention, use or control of criminal property', even if they suspect
that the outcome of such proceedings might have such an effect (para.84 of
the judgment).

The exclusion also covers consensual resolution of issues in a litigious
context. The Law Society has suggested that the logic of the exclusion in
relation to litigation and consensual resolution must apply the exclusion
to Alternative Dispute Resolution (ADR) (see paragraph 2.5 of the Law
Society's Guidance on *Bowman* v. *Fels* – **Appendix B2**). However, consensual
arrangements entered into independently of litigation (i.e. in a transactional
matter) will still be within the scope of s.328, as will sham litigation created
for the purposes of money laundering.

In the case of *P* v. *P* [2003] EWHC Fam 2260, Dame Elizabeth Butler-Sloss, P. suggested that the act of negotiating an arrangement would equally amount to being 'concerned in' the arrangement. The Court of Appeal's judgment in *Bowman* v. *Fels* provides support for the proposition that *P* v. *P* can no longer be regarded as good law in this respect and (at para.67) states: 'To enter into an arrangement involves a single act at a single point in time; so too, on the face of it, does to "become concerned" in an arrangement, even though the point at which someone may be said to have "become" concerned may be open to argument'.

The Law Society have extended their guidance on *Bowman* v. *Fels* to trans-actional work. The Society acknowledges that whilst the judgment does not seek to lay down definitive guidance on issues of interpretation outside litigation, it does provide support for a restricted understanding of what amounts to an arrangement in transactional work. The guidance suggests that:

- entering into or becoming concerned in an arrangement involves an act done at a particular point in time;
- a person does not enter into or become concerned in an arrangement under s.328 and no offence is committed until such an arrangement is made; and
- no preparatory or intermediate step taken in the course of transactional work which does not itself involve the acquisition, retention, use or control of property will constitute the making of an arrangement under s.328.

Solicitors may be involved in preparatory steps which may bring the arrange-ment into existence but ultimately a criminal offence will only have been committed if the arrangement does exist and, in the present (not the future), the arrangement has the effect of facilitating money laundering. Until an arrangement under s.328 exists, the solicitor can continue with any prepara-tory steps relating to the transaction without committing an offence. However, if the solicitor considers that the preparatory steps will inevitably lead to an arrangement and the solicitor would become concerned with that arrangement, the solicitor must either cease acting (so as not to become concerned in the arrangement) or seek a defence (usually by way of an authorised disclosure (see **Chapter 4**)).

. . . which he knows or suspects . . .

The section introduces a double test of knowledge or suspicion. First, it is necessary for the prosecution to show that the alleged offender knew or sus-pected that the arrangement would facilitate the acquisition, retention, use or control of criminal property. Secondly (as noted below), the definition of 'criminal property' for these purposes requires that the alleged offender knows or suspects that the property constitutes or represents the benefit (directly or indirectly) from criminal conduct.

Knowledge should not cause a problem when interpreting this section. If a solicitor knows that the arrangement will facilitate money laundering then the solicitor risks a criminal conviction if no steps are taken to avoid liability. Difficulties can arise when a client admits to the commission of a crime (for example, tax evasion). The solicitor may withdraw from the matter and thus will not be concerned in the arrangement. However, in this situation, a solicitor may still have an obligation to report under PoCA 2002, s.330 (see **Chapter 5**) but the concept of privilege may provide a defence.

Suspicion is a more difficult concept. Some people are more suspicious than others. What will amount to suspicion for the purposes of this statute? Any unusual transaction must be considered suspicious until enquiry has allayed that suspicion. Transactions that should give rise to concern and therefore should be investigated include:

- **Unusual settlement transactions**

  Consider the circumstances where, on an asset purchase, less funds are required on completion than expected by reference to the contractual provisions. Clients may excuse this by indicating that they have paid a direct deposit to the vendor. This typically indicates a possible mortgage or loan fraud. The property (i.e. the asset being purchased) is being overvalued for security purposes. The genuine price paid is the lesser amount.

- **Unusual instructions**

  The key to avoiding criminal liability is to know the client and know the typical transactions expected to be undertaken in the firm. Accepting instructions in a matter which is outside the normal type of work undertaken by the firm should give rise to a risk assessment – enquiries should be made to ensure that this is a legitimate transaction and one that the firm has competence to undertake.

  For example, a small traditional firm specialising in private client work should be suspicious if a new client requires the firm to act on a complex commercial transaction involving significant values. If the remuneration offered seems too good to be true, it probably is! Criminals wishing to launder money might take the (often erroneous) view that a small firm has less sophisticated money laundering procedures in place. Equally, larger commercial firms should be suspicious where commercial clients instruct them on private client matters beyond the scope of their normal work. Even if they have staff who are competent (or who could gain competence) the question should always be asked: 'Why are we being instructed?'

- **Secretive client**

  The Money Laundering Regulations 2003, SI 2003/3075 (see **Chapter 9**) require solicitors to obtain evidence of identity for most new clients. A client who is unwilling or unable to produce such evidence should give rise to concern. To continue to act without such evidence may put the firm in breach of the regulations and the lack of such evidence without good reason may give rise to suspicion that any arrangement might facilitate the acquisition, retention, use or control of criminal property. It is good practice to apply the identification procedures to all new and existing clients even if this is not strictly required by the regulations. By doing so, a solicitor is going somewhere towards allaying suspicion. Without such evidence, the authorities' case for showing suspicion is made easier.

Equally, it is necessary to consider identification of corporate and trust clients – in most cases going beyond the simple task of satisfying the firm that the company or trust fund exists. It is too easy for launderers to hide behind such vehicles so the identification procedures should be applied to those controlling the appropriate vehicle (i.e. the directors/shareholders of a company or the trustees/beneficiaries of the trust fund). Details of the requirements relating to client identification and recommended procedures are contained in **Chapter 9** and **Chapter 11**.

- **Cash transactions**

In a solicitor's practice, large cash transactions are usually rare and as such should give rise to concern. These might involve sale or purchase transactions involving cash or large sums of cash used to discharge the solicitor's costs. Of course, the use of cash in any transaction is not unlawful. Of itself, a client proposing to use cash does not give rise to an illegal act. However, it must put the solicitor on notice that the transaction might be one involving 'placement' (see **Chapter 1**) and as such the solicitor should not proceed unless he or she is satisfied as to the legitimacy of the transaction.

In some ethnic communities, cash is still the preferred currency for business transactions. Solicitors acting for members of such communities may be satisfied that a cash transaction is the norm. However, in most circumstances the use of large sums of cash should give rise to a sensible concern.

Many firms impose a cash limit (i.e. a maximum sum that can be accepted in cash). Frequently this is set at £500 but some firms have set a limit as low as £250.

Where cash is legitimately used, solicitors should refer to guidance in the Solicitors' Accounts Rules 1998 (SAR). The Law Society's 'Guidelines: Accounting Procedures and Systems' are contained in Appendix 3 SAR. These state (Guideline 3) that 'the firm should have procedures for identifying client money and controlled trust money, including cash, when received in the firm, and for prompt recording the receipt of the money . . .'

In earlier guidance ('*Complying with the Solicitors' Accounts Rules: A Practical Guide*' published by the Law Society, 1996) the following was stated:

Receipt of Cash

When cash is received from a client, particularly a large amount, consideration should always be given to the Money Laundering Regulations.

Any cash receipts should be counted in the presence of the client by the relevant fee earner and another member of staff. Care should be taken to check for any forged bank notes.

A receipt should be issued to the client and the client's signature should be obtained. A copy of the receipt should be retained on a central file. A posting slip should then be completed in the same manner as for cheques but should specify that the sum was received in cash. The cash, together with the posting slip, should immediately be passed to the accounts department for banking that day.

Withdrawal of cash

The following points should be considered when withdrawing client's money in cash:

- A posting slip should be completed in duplicate by the fee earner. The original should be passed to the accounts department and the copy retained on the client's file. The posting slip should indicate why cash is required.
- The fee earner should seek the client's written authority to make a withdrawal by cash and a copy of that authority should be passed to the accounts department and retained on a central file.
- The cash should be counted by the fee earner in the presence of the client/ recipient and another member of the firm.
- A signed receipt should be obtained and a copy passed to the accounts department for retention on a central file.
- Particular attention should be paid to security when withdrawing cash from the bank.
- It is a breach of the Accounts Rules to have client petty cash, as all client's money should be held in a client account at a bank or building society. Petty cash will usually be required only in respect of office expenditure, though it may be used to pay disbursements on behalf of a client, e.g. oath fees.

- **Suspect territories**

  The definition of criminal property includes, in certain cases, property derived from overseas transactions (see below). Consequently solicitors should be satisfied as to the source of any funding used as part of transactions and in particular should be aware of the dangers of receiving funds from overseas suspect territories.

  Some countries worldwide have lower levels of regulation than others. Particular care must be taken when any party to the transaction is based in or moves money from or to such countries. The Financial Action Taskforce was formed in 1989. It is an intergovernmental body with members from 31 countries and the European Commission. It publishes and updates a list of non-co-operative countries and territories ('NCCTs'). This list can be accessed by logging on to the following website: **www.fatf-gafi.org**

. . . facilitates (by whatever means) the acquisition, retention, use or control . . .

The arrangement (where a solicitor 'enters into or becomes concerned in an arrangement') must be such that the solicitor knows or suspects that it facilitates the acquisition, retention, use or control of criminal property. This is a very wide concept. Previous legislation (e.g. the Criminal Justice Act 1988 as amended) simply referred to the act of facilitating the retention or control of criminal property. PoCA 2002 extends this to now include 'acquisition and use'.

All of the examples given in **Chapter 1** could be said to be facilitating the acquisition, retention, use or control of criminal property. The use of the words 'by whatever means' ensure that the act of facilitation could be undertaken by a solicitor by placing money in client account; by transferring funds; by acting on the purchase/sale of property; or, as noted previously, simply by giving advice.

. . . criminal property . . .

Section 340(3) defines criminal property. Property is criminal if:

(a) it constitutes a person's benefit from criminal conduct or it represents such a benefit (in whole or part and whether directly or indirectly), and
(b) the alleged offender knows or suspects that it constitutes or represents such a benefit.

Section 340(2) defines criminal conduct as that which:

(a) constitutes an offence in any part of the United Kingdom, or
(b) would constitute an offence in any part of the United Kingdom if it occurred there.

The first point to note from this definition is that criminal property can be the benefit (however small) of a crime or it can (directly or indirectly) represent the benefit of a crime. The property does not have to be the original criminal proceeds. As a result of this definition, if cash is stolen, it is criminal property. If the stolen cash is used to buy an asset, the asset will be criminal property. If the asset is used as security to obtain a loan, the loan will become criminal property.

Section 340(5) provides that a person benefits from conduct if he obtains property as a result of or in connection with the conduct. Property includes (s.340(9)) money; all forms of property real, personal, heritable or moveable; or things in action and other intangible or incorporeal property. Further, property is obtained by a person if he obtains an interest in it, which is defined in relation to land as any legal estate or equitable interest or power and in relation to other property as including references to a right (including a right to possession) (s.340(10)).

Where a person receives a pecuniary advantage as a result of conduct he is taken to have received a sum of money equal to the value of the pecuniary advantage for the purposes of these provisions (s.340(6)).

The benefit must have derived from criminal conduct. The previous legislation limited this to benefit from indictable offences (i.e. serious criminal offences), drug trafficking and terrorism offences. PoCA 2002 does not replicate this restriction. Any criminal act which gives rise to a benefit can form the basis of a money laundering offence.

Further, the criminal conduct need not have occurred in the UK. As can be noted from the definition in s.340(1), the conduct will be criminal if it would have constituted a crime if it had occurred in the UK. Originally, there was no requirement in the statute that the conduct must constitute a crime in the jurisdiction in which it occurred.

This led to the so-called 'Spanish bullfighter' problem. The argument was made that any legitimate income earned by a bullfighter in Spain would amount to criminal property in the UK. Bullfighting in Spain is legal, but it is a criminal activity in the UK. Anyone who, with knowledge or suspicion, facilitated the retention, control etc. of this income could be guilty of an offence.

However, SOCPA 2005 provides for a defence where the accused knows or believes on reasonable grounds that the criminal conduct was not unlawful in the place where it occurred. This amendment came into effect on 15 May 2006 (see **paragraph 2.3** for details).

Overseas criminal property (i.e. the benefit of overseas crime) cannot form the basis of a money laundering offence if the conduct undertaken overseas is not a crime in the UK. An obvious example would be a sum of money sourced from an overseas jurisdiction where money was removed from the jurisdiction in breach of that jurisdiction's exchange control regulations. Since the UK does not currently have exchange control regulations, the activity of removing the funds from the overseas jurisdiction would not constitute a crime if it had occurred in the UK. It may be, however, that a client who is willing to breach overseas exchange control regulations might be prepared to breach other obligations. Solicitors should carefully consider all the surrounding facts before determining that a client in breach of overseas exchange control regulations does not give rise to concern.

One problem associated with this definition relates to the proceeds of tax evasion. As noted above, UK tax evasion is a criminal offence and as such can give rise to money laundering. What about the proceeds of overseas tax evasion? Can such proceeds form the basis of a money laundering charge if such proceeds are brought into the UK?

There appears to be a divergence of views on this. Some commentators take the view that the proceeds of overseas tax evasion should be treated in exactly the same way as the proceeds of UK tax evasion. However, others take the view that the offence concerned should be defined by reference to the overseas tax authority. In this case the activity will not be a UK crime if it had occurred in the UK. For example, it is undoubtedly a crime in the US to evade US taxation. If the definition of the crime includes the specific victim (i.e. the US tax authorities) the evasion of US tax would not be a crime in the UK if it had occurred in the US.

Solicitors should, however, err on the side of caution. Until such time as the courts give a definitive interpretation of overseas criminal conduct for these purposes it would seem sensible to act upon any knowledge or suspicion of such overseas activities and follow the appropriate procedures to avoid personal liability.

Finally, in relation to the definition of criminal property, it should be noted that PoCA 2002 makes it clear (in s.340(4)) that it is immaterial for the purposes of the definition:

(a)   who carried out the conduct;
(b)   who benefited from it;
(c)   whether the conduct occurred before or after the passing of this Act.

. . . by or on behalf of another person.

To be guilty under PoCA 2002, s.328, the accused must facilitate the acquisition, retention, use or control of criminal property 'by or on behalf of another person'. This offence is not aimed at the original perpetrator of the crime but at some other person who assists in the laundering of the criminal property of the perpetrator or other person.

However, in the context of a solicitor's practice, this does not mean that a solicitor can only be guilty of an offence where the act of facilitation is done for or on behalf of the solicitor's client. In most cases, the risk of committing this offence will arise from a client retainer in circumstances where the client is acting suspiciously. Since knowledge or suspicion is a necessary element of the crime, it follows that such knowledge or suspicion is most likely to arise in relation to the client's conduct from information received in the course of acting for a client.

In some cases, a solicitor may be acting for an innocent client but nonetheless, his or her actions could facilitate the acquisition, retention, use or control of criminal property by the person on the other side of the transaction. Completing the transaction in these circumstances could give rise to liability under PoCA 2002, s.328. Take, for example, a solicitor acting for a lender of money (a bank or building society) but not acting for the borrower. The lender's solicitor acquires certain information in the course of acting that gives rise to a suspicion that the borrower has given false information as part of the borrower's loan application. To continue to completion without taking appropriate steps could be facilitating the acquisition of criminal property by the borrower. The false information relied upon by the lender could bring about a loan or mortgage fraud; the loan itself could therefore be criminal property.

This particular point is worth making to clients and members of staff who might find a solicitor's money laundering procedures to be burdensome and unhelpful. Clients should be notified that the procedures are not simply designed to ensure that a solicitor is not involved with money laundering. A good system is designed to ensure that innocent clients are not inadvertently dragged into a money laundering investigation as a result of other parties to the transaction who might have criminal intent.

2.3 DEFENCES

Section 328(2) provides for a defence where the accused makes an authorised disclosure in accordance with the provisions of PoCA 2002, s.338. Since the defence under s.338 applies equally to the offence of concealing (s.237 – see **Chapter 3**) and to the offence of acquisition, use and possession (s.329 – see **Chapter 3**), details of the defence are to be found in **Chapter 4**.

Disclosure in accordance with s.338 is by far the most important and relevant defence for solicitors. However, there are four further defences specified in the section.

First it is a defence that the accused intended to make a disclosure under s.338 but had a reasonable excuse for not doing so (s.328(2)(*b*)). Although there is currently no judicial definition of what would amount to a 'reasonable excuse', solicitors should note that neither the duty of confidentiality nor legal professional privilege provide a reasonable excuse for these purposes. *Bowman* v. *Fels* has confirmed that common law legal professional privilege (LPP) is not overridden by s.328. However, the Law Society's guidance (para. 7.12 – see **Appendix B2**) suggests that where LPP applies this will prevent a solicitor from making a disclosure unless the client provides a waiver of privilege. If the client refuses, the solicitor should withdraw from the transaction and thus not become concerned in an arrangement. The Society's guidance does not suggest that it would be proper in these circumstances to become concerned with the arrangement but to use s.328(2)(*b*) as a defence against a failure to disclose.

Secondly it is a defence that the act (i.e. the prohibited act of facilitation) 'is done in carrying out a function [the accused] has relating to the enforcement of any provision of [PoCA 2002] or of any other enactment relating to criminal conduct or benefit from criminal conduct'.

Thirdly a new defence has been added by SOCPA 2005 following an amendment that was brought into force on 15 May 2006. The new s.328(3) provides that an offence is not committed under s.328 if the accused:

- knows or believes on reasonable grounds that the relevant criminal conduct occurred outside the UK; and
- the relevant criminal conduct is not unlawful under the criminal law of the place where it occurred and is not of a description prescribed by order made by the Secretary of State.

The Proceeds of Crime Act 2002 (Money Laundering: Exceptions to Overseas Conduct Defence) Order 2006, SI 2006/1070 is the Order referred to in the amendment and lists the criminal offences for which the definition of 'criminal conduct' remains unchanged. The offences listed are those which are punishable by imprisonment for a maximum term in excess of 12 months if committed in the UK unless the benefit arises from an offence under:

- the Gaming Act 1968;
- the Lotteries and Amusements Act 1976; or
- ss.23 or 25 of the Financial Services and Markets Act 2000.

As a result of this Order, the position regarding criminal property sourced from abroad has not changed greatly. Solicitors faced with overseas money or assets must first apply the basic definition of 'criminal property'.

- Is this money or are the assets derived from an overseas activity which would have been a criminal offence if it had occurred in the UK? If the answer to this question is 'no', the property will not be 'criminal property'. If the answer is 'yes', a further question must be asked.
- Are there reasonable grounds for knowing or believing that the activity was not unlawful under the criminal law of the country where the activity occurred? If the answer is 'no', the property will be 'criminal property' as defined by PoCA 2002. If, however, the answer is 'yes', the solicitor must further consider the offence in the UK.
- Is the offence punishable in the UK for a maximum term of in excess of 12 months? If the answer is 'yes' and the offence is so punishable, then despite the fact that the activity abroad is not an offence in that country, the property will be 'criminal property' (unless the offence is one of those specified and contained in the Gaming Act 1968, the Lotteries and Amusements Act 1976 or the Financial Services and Markets Act 2000). If the answer is 'no', the property will not be criminal property.

Fourthly, a defence has been added by SOCPA 2005 for deposit-taking bodies where the body operates and maintains an account and the criminal property is of a value less than the threshold amount. The threshold amount is determined in s.339A and is currently £250 (although the section provides for circumstances where this sum can be increased). This particular amendment came into force on 1 July 2005 but as solicitors are not deposit-taking bodies, this amendment is unlikely to affect them.

CHAPTER 3

Criminal offences: other money laundering offences

3.1 INTRODUCTION

Although the offence involving arrangements is likely to have a significant impact on solicitors, there are two other money laundering offences contained in the Proceeds of Crime Act 2002 (PoCA 2002), both of which involve criminal property (as defined). Section 327 of PoCA 2002 creates the offence of 'concealing etc.' and PoCA 2002, s.329 creates the offence of 'acquisition, use and possession'. Both these offences could give rise to difficulties unless solicitors take appropriate action to avoid risks. Both offences carry the same penalty on conviction as that applicable to 'arrangements', i.e. on summary conviction, imprisonment for a term not exceeding six months or a fine not exceeding the statutory maximum or both, or on conviction on indictment, imprisonment for a term not exceeding 14 years or a fine or both.

In addition to these two offences, a further money laundering offence is contained in the Terrorism Act 2000, s.18. Details of this offence are included at the end of this chapter.

3.2 CONCEALING ETC: THE OFFENCE

Section 327 of PoCA 2002 makes it an offence to:

- conceal criminal property;
- disguise criminal property;
- convert criminal property;
- transfer criminal property;
- remove criminal property from England and Wales or from Scotland or from Northern Ireland.

PoCA 2002 also makes it clear (s.327(3)) that for these purposes concealing or disguising criminal property includes concealing or disguising its nature, source, location, disposition, movement or ownership or any rights with respect to it.

Solicitors are likely to be at risk from this offence where money is held in client account and is subsequently transferred to a client or third party. Potentially, there is an overlap between this offence and the offence of 'arrangements' – transferring funds could amount to an arrangement facilitating the use of criminal property. The offence does not specifically refer to the need for the acts to be carried out with knowledge or suspicion. However, since the requirement of the offence is to conceal etc. criminal property and the term 'criminal property' is defined, knowledge or suspicion is a required element of this offence. As has been noted (see **Chapter 2**) the definition requires that the alleged offender knows or suspects that property constitutes or represents a benefit from criminal conduct.

A solicitor who holds money in a client account and who transfers such funds or arranges for the removal of such funds from England and Wales could be guilty of an offence where he or she simply suspects that the money constitutes or represents a benefit from criminal conduct. It is therefore important that firms adopt systems to ensure all members of staff act in an appropriate manner when money is paid into client account. Frequently money is paid into a solicitor's client account by BACS or other electronic means. If the solicitor is not expecting this sum, or is initially unaware of the identity of the client or client matter to which the funds are to be applied, it is not appropriate simply to instruct the bank to return the funds to the source without considering the possibility of money laundering offences. If the solicitor has any suspicion concerning the funds, returning the funds to the source could amount to the offence of concealing.

In *Bowman* v. *Fels* the Court of Appeal confirmed that certain activities were excluded from the scope of the s.328 arrangements offence. The excluded activities were described as 'litigation from the issue of proceedings and the securing of injunctive relief or a freezing order up to its final disposal by judgment' (para.83 of the judgment). The exclusion also covered consensual resolution of issues in a litigious context. The Law Society has suggested that the logic of the exclusion in relation to litigation and consensual resolution must apply the exclusion to Alternative Dispute Resolution (ADR) (see paragraph 2.5 of the Law Society Guidance on *Bowman* v. *Fels* – **Appendix B2**).

The guidance further states: '. . . logically solicitors will also not be committing section 327 . . . offences in these circumstances'. They refer to paragraph 95 of the Court of Appeal's judgment where it is stated: 'For the reasons we have already given, the issue or pursuit of ordinary legal proceedings with a view to obtaining the court's adjudication upon the parties' rights and duties is not to be regarded as an arrangement or a prohibited act within ss.327–329.'

An important point to note is that the s.327 offence (unlike the offence in s.338) is not limited to committing the prohibited act for or on behalf of another. Obviously a solicitor could be charged with concealing etc. criminal property on behalf of a client. However, the perpetrator of the original criminal act can also be guilty if the perpetrator conceals etc. his or her own criminal property. This has an important result. The offence of concealing etc., therefore, amounts to money laundering and in certain specified circumstances (notably under PoCA 2002, s.330) a solicitor is required to disclose knowledge or suspicion of any person engaged in money laundering (for details of this requirement, see **Chapter 5**). This might require a solicitor to report a client where the solicitor knows or suspects that a client is removing his own criminal property from the jurisdiction (e.g. where the solicitor is aware that the client has evaded UK taxation and is buying a property abroad). This could be so, even if the solicitor is not involved in any arrangement relating to that criminal property.

3.3   CONCEALING ETC: DEFENCES

Like the offence of arrangements the most important defence in s.327 is one of disclosure. Provided a solicitor makes an authorised disclosure under s.338 (and, if necessary, has appropriate consent to continue acting) no offence will be committed under s.327. Details of this important defence are contained in **Chapter 4**.

Also, in common with the offence of arrangements, four further defences are available.

First it is a defence that the accused intended to make a disclosure under s.338 but had a reasonable excuse for not doing so (s.327(2)(*b*)). As noted above, neither the duty of confidentiality nor legal professional privilege provide a reasonable excuse for these purposes. *Bowman* v. *Fels* has confirmed that common law LPP is not overridden by s.327. However, the Law Society Guidance (para.7.12 – see **Appendix B2**) suggests that where LPP applies this will prevent a solicitor from making a disclosure unless the client provides a waiver of privilege. If the client refuses, the solicitor should withdraw from the transaction and thus not become involved in concealing. The Law Society Guidance does not suggest that it would be proper in these circumstances to become involved in concealing but to use s.328(2)(*b*) as a defence against a failure to disclose.

Secondly it is a defence that the act (i.e. the prohibited act of concealment etc.) 'is done in carrying out a function [the accused] has relating to the enforcement of any provision of [PoCA 2002] or of any other enactment relating to criminal conduct or benefit from criminal conduct'.

Thirdly a new defence has been added by SOCPA 2005. This amendment came into force on 15 May 2006. The new s.327(2A) provides that an offence is not committed under s.327 if the accused:

- knows or believes on reasonable grounds that the relevant criminal conduct occurred outside the UK; and
- the relevant criminal conduct is not unlawful under the criminal law of the place where it occurred and is not of a description prescribed by order made by the Secretary of State.

Commentary on this defence and on the Order made by the Secretary of State can be found in **Chapter 2**.

Fourthly, a defence has been added by SOCPA 2005 for deposit-taking bodies where the body operates and maintains an account and the criminal property is of a value less than the threshold amount. The threshold amount is determined in s.339A and is currently £250 (although the section provides for circumstances where this sum can be increased). This particular amendment came into force on 1 July 2005, but as solicitors are not deposit-taking bodies, this amendment is unlikely to affect them.

3.4   ACQUISITION, USE AND POSSESSION: THE OFFENCE

Section 329(1) makes it an offence to:

- acquire criminal property;
- use criminal property;
- have possession of criminal property.

Clearly this offence could apply to solicitors – particularly in relation to the holding of client money where such money is criminal property. The offence is not, however, limited to money.

As with the offence of concealing (s.327) criminal property for the purposes of s.329 is defined in the same way as for the offence of arrangements (s.328 – see **Chapter 2**). An element of knowledge or suspicion is necessary.

The interpretation of this offence (like the offence of concealing (s.327) and arranging (s.328)) has been changed as a result of *Bowman* v. *Fels*. As noted above, the activities excluded from the scope of the s.328 arrangements offence ('litigation from the issue of proceedings and the securing of injunctive relief or a freezing order up to its final disposal by judgment') would also appear to be excluded from s.329 as a result of para.95 of the Court of Appeal's judgment where it is stated:

> For the reasons we have already given, the issue or pursuit of ordinary legal proceedings with a view to obtaining the court's adjudication upon the parties' rights and duties is not to be regarded as an arrangement or a prohibited act within ss.327–329.

Also, like the offence of concealing (s.327), the offence under s.329 can apply to the perpetrator of a crime. A thief who steals property is guilty under the Theft Act 1968. Having acquired the stolen property and having possession of the stolen property means that the thief can also be charged and convicted under PoCA 2002. For the same reasons as noted above (PoCA 2002, s.330 and see **Chapter 5**) a solicitor may be required to report knowledge or suspicion that a client is engaged in money laundering (the definition of money laundering includes the offence under s.329) simply because the solicitor knows or suspects that the client has committed a crime and is therefore in possession of criminal property.

One problem with this offence arises from the wide definition of criminal property for these purposes (see **Chapter 2**). Since criminal property includes property which represents a benefit from criminal conduct, it is quite possible that property which is legitimately obtained by a person could be treated as criminal property simply because an audit trail is capable of tracing the property back to a crime. Further, a solicitor may be concerned about the payment of costs from a client whom he knows has no legitimate source of income. Potentially the solicitor in these circumstances could be guilty of an offence on the basis of his possession and suspicion that the money is criminal property.

Fortunately, the legislators have foreseen this problem and a defence of 'adequate consideration' is available (see **Paragragh 3.5**).

3.5   ACQUISITION, USE AND POSSESSION: DEFENCES

A defence is available where a person makes an authorised disclosure under PoCA 2002, s.338. This is dealt with in **Chapter 4**.

Also, in common with the offence of concealing (s.327), four further defences are available.

First it is a defence that the accused intended to make a disclosure under s.338 but had a reasonable excuse for not doing so (s.329(2)(*b*)). As noted above, neither the duty of confidentiality nor LPP provide a reasonable excuse for these purposes. Section 338(4) states that 'an authorised disclosure is not to be taken to breach any restriction on the disclosure of information (however imposed).' Note also the comments arising from the Court of Appeal's judgment in *Bowman* v. *Fels* and the Law Society Guidance on the case.

Secondly it is a defence that the act (i.e. the prohibited act of acquisition, use or possession) 'is done in carrying out a function [the accused] has relating to the enforcement of any provision of [PoCA 2002] or of any other enactment relating to criminal conduct or benefit from criminal conduct'.

Thirdly a new defence has been added by SOCPA 2005. This amendment came into force on 15 May 2006. The new s.329(2A) provides that an offence is not committed under s.329 if the accused:

- knows or believes on reasonable grounds that the relevant criminal conduct occurred outside the UK; and
- the relevant criminal conduct is not unlawful under the criminal law of the place where it occurred and is not of a description prescribed by order made by the Secretary of State.

Commentary on this defence and on the Order made by the Secretary of State can be found in **Chapter 2**.

Fourthly, a defence has been added by SOCPA 2005 for deposit-taking bodies where the body operates and maintains an account and the criminal property is of a value less than the threshold amount. The threshold amount is determined in s.339A and is currently £250 (although the section provides for circumstances where this sum can be increased). This particular amendment came into force on 1 July 2005, but as solicitors are not deposit-taking bodies this amendment is unlikely to affect them.

There is, however, the further defence of 'adequate consideration'. Section 329(2)(c) provides that a person does not commit an offence under s.329(1) if 'he acquired or used or had possession of the property for adequate consideration'. Subsection (3) gives further guidance on this defence.

First, consideration is to be taken as inadequate for the purposes of acquisition of property if the value of the consideration is significantly less than the value of the property. Secondly, a person uses or has possession of property for inadequate consideration if the value of the consideration is significantly less that the value of the use or possession. Finally, the provision by a person of goods or services which he knows or suspects may help another to carry out criminal conduct is not consideration.

As a result of these provisions solicitors should treat the defence of adequate consideration with care. Take the following scenario by way of example. A solicitor is acting for a client on a house purchase. The solicitor is aware that the client is on benefits and has no legitimate source of income. When it comes to the payment of the solicitor's fees, the client makes the payment in cash. The solicitor suspects that the cash may be the proceeds of crime but takes the view that the provision by him of the conveyancing services amounts to adequate consideration. This defence is likely to be flawed. First, it is highly probable that the solicitor was suspicious about the house purchase transaction. If that was the case then completing the house purchase is likely to be an offence under s.328 (arrangements). Secondly, the defence of adequate consideration could not apply to the costs if the solicitor suspects that the services have helped the client to carry out criminal conduct.

However, in other circumstances, the defence may be of benefit. The Crown Prosecution Service guidance for prosecutors (referred to in para.2.30 of the Law Society Guidance) states that the defence will apply where professional advisers receive money for or on account of costs provided the charges are reasonable and there is no suspicion that the client is using their services to carry out criminal conduct.

3.6 TERRORISM ACT 2000, SECTION 18

A further money laundering offence appears in the Terrorism Act 2000. Section 18 of that Act provides:

(1) A person commits an offence if he enters into or becomes concerned in an arrangement which facilitates the retention or control by or on behalf of another person of terrorist property –

   (a) by concealment,
   (b) by removal from the jurisdiction,
   (c) by transfer to nominees, or
   (d) in any other way.

(2) It is a defence for a person charged with an offence under subsection (1) to prove that he did not know and had no reasonable cause to suspect that the arrangement related to terrorist property.

The offence is similar to those covered under PoCA 2002. It covers arrangements made to facilitate the retention or control of terrorist property and provides that such facilitation can be by concealment etc. or in any other way. Like the offence under PoCA 2002, s.328 (arrangements) it is not necessary for the accused to have possession of the terrorist property – for example, advising a client in circumstances where the advice assists in the retention of terrorist property will be sufficient.

The crime itself does not specify a requirement for knowledge or suspicion. However, subsection (2) provides for a defence if the person charged can show that he had no knowledge and no reasonable cause to suspect that the arrangement related to terrorist property. Two points are worthy of note regarding this defence. First, the reference to 'no reasonable cause to suspect' suggests that an objective test will be used to determine suspicion. If the individual did not suspect (subjectively) no defence will be available if a reasonable person would have suspected. Secondly, the onus of proving no knowledge or reasonable cause for suspicion rests upon the defence – not the prosecution. Once the prosecution prove that an arrangement exists which falls within subsection (1) a conviction will follow unless the defence can discharge their onus of proof.

It is obviously necessary for the legislation to cover activities relating to terrorist property in addition to those offences involving criminal property. If property used by terrorists is the proceeds of crime, then the offences in PoCA 2002 can obviously be relevant. However, it is also possible that quite legitimate funds are made available for terrorist purposes. It is this possibility which gives rise to the money laundering offence under the Terrorism Act 2000.

The Act defines terrorist property for the purposes of s.18. Section 14 of the Act states:

(1) In this Act 'terrorist property' means:

    (a) money or other property which is likely to be used for the purposes of terrorism (including any resources of a proscribed organisation),

    (b) proceeds of the commission of acts of terrorism, and

    (c) proceeds of acts carried out for the purposes of terrorism.

(2) In subsection (1):

    (a) a reference to proceeds of an act includes a reference to any property which wholly or partly, and directly or indirectly, represents the proceeds of the act (including payments or other rewards in connection with its commission), and

    (b) the reference to an organisation's resources includes a reference to any money or other property which is applied or made available, or is to be applied or made available, for use by the organisation.

The penalty on conviction under the Terrorism Act 2000, s.18 is, on indictment: imprisonment for a term not exceeding 14 years, a fine or both; or on summary conviction: imprisonment for a term not exceeding six months, a fine not exceeding the statutory maximum or both. Further offences under the Terrorism Act 2000 are considered in **Chapter 5**.

CHAPTER 4

Authorised disclosures

4.1 INTRODUCTION

The three money laundering offences created by the Proceeds of Crime Act 2002 (PoCA 2002), (s.327 concealing; s.328 arrangements; and s.329 acquisition, use and possession) all have a common defence available. Each section provides for this defence using the same wording:

> . . . a person does not commit such an offence if:

(a) he makes an authorised disclosure under section 338 and (if the disclosure is made before he does the act mentioned in subsection (1) *[the prohibited act]*) he has the appropriate consent.

For solicitors, the authorised disclosure defence is probably the most important and widely used defence. PoCA 2002 has introduced some complex rules, and failure to comply with these rules will often render the defence ineffective.

In most cases, it will be necessary for solicitors to make an authorised disclosure before undertaking the act prohibited by the relevant section. In these cases, it is important that the concept of appropriate consent is considered carefully.

4.2 AUTHORISED DISCLOSURES (PoCA 2002, s.338)

4.2.1 Definition

Section 338(1)(*a*) of PoCA 2002 defines an authorised disclosure as a disclosure made to:

- a constable;
- a customs officer;
- a nominated officer.

In each case the disclosure, made by the alleged offender, should relate to the knowledge or suspicion that the property is criminal property.

4.2.2 Disclosure to Serious Organised Crime Agency

In practical terms, the reference in s.338(1)(*a*) to a constable or a customs officer means that the disclosure is made to the Serious Organised Crime Agency (SOCA). For practical details associated with disclosures to SOCA, see **Chapter 10**.

4.2.3 Disclosure to a nominated person

Disclosure to a nominated officer is disclosure to a firm's Money Laundering Reporting Officer (MLRO). In practice, many firms' internal money laundering procedures will identify a person (frequently a partner) who has been appointed as MLRO. PoCA 2002 and the Money Laundering Regulations 2003 (see **Chapter 9**) refer to this person as a 'nominated officer'.

Section 338(5) states that a disclosure to a nominated officer is a disclosure which is made to a person nominated by the alleged offender's employer to receive authorised disclosures. Further, the disclosure must be made in the course of the alleged offender's employment. PoCA 2002, as originally drafted, required the disclosure to be made to the nominated officer in accordance with procedures established by the employer for this purpose. This requirement was removed as a result of an amendment to PoCA 2002, contained in SOCPA 2005, s.105(2). Consequently, any disclosure to a nominated officer in the course of employment (whether it is in accordance with internal procedures or not) will serve as a defence.

However, it is still important for all firms to adopt appropriate procedures for internal disclosure of knowledge or suspicion of money laundering and for these procedures to include the appointment of a person to the role of nominated officer. Firms undertaking relevant business (see **Chapter 9** for a full definition) and therefore subject to the Money Laundering Regulations 2003 must appoint a nominated officer. Firms not subject to the Regulations should still consider making such an appointment to enable members of the firm to make internal disclosures and thereby to benefit from the authorised disclosure defence.

It is not strictly necessary for the nominated officer to be a partner or principal in a firm of solicitors. However, in practice, the individual should be a senior member of the firm's management. Severe penalties (including imprisonment for up to five years) can be imposed upon the nominated officer for a failure to comply with his or her obligations under PoCA 2002. Further, under the Money Laundering Regulations 2003 (see **Chapter 9**) a nominated officer must consider, in the light of any relevant information available in the firm, whether a disclosure gives rise to knowledge or suspicion of money laundering. The individual should, therefore, be in a sufficiently senior position to gain access to all relevant information held by the firm concerning clients or others suspected of money laundering.

Although, in the context of a nominated officer, PoCA 2002 refers to a person's employer and a person's employment, s.340(12) provides that:

references to a person's employer include any body, association or organisation (including a voluntary organisation) in connection with whose activities the person exercises a function (whether or not for gain or reward).

The subsection goes on to state that references to employment must be construed accordingly.

Consequently, a sole practitioner or a member of a limited liability partnership (LLP) or partner in a firm of solicitors, will be able to treat the firm or LLP as an employer for these purposes and will be treated as being in employment when making authorised disclosures.

4.2.4 Form of disclosure

Section 339 allows the Secretary of State, by order, to prescribe the form and manner of any disclosure under s.338 and to provide for the form to include a request for further information specified if the information has not been provided in the disclosure. Section 339(1A) (as inserted by SOCPA 2005) makes it an offence to make a disclosure under s.338 otherwise than in the form or manner prescribed unless the accused has a reasonable excuse not to do so.

At the time of writing (December 2006) no order has yet been made regarding the form and content of disclosures under s.338. If a prescribed form is introduced, the Law Society have stated that they will issue further guidance.

In the meantime, a form of disclosure for use by solicitors when making authorised disclosures to SOCA can be found on their website at **www.soca. gov.uk** (see also **Chapter 10** and **Appendix C4**).

For internal disclosure purposes, firms should publish their own precedent for use by members of the firm. A suggested form of an internal disclosure is given in **Appendix C3**.

4.2.5 Time of disclosure

Section 338(2), (2A) and (3) provide for three alternative conditions regarding the timing of the disclosure.

Under subsection (2), the disclosure, to satisfy the requirements of the section, can be made 'before the alleged offender does the prohibited act'. The prohibited act for these purposes would be the act of concealment, etc. under s.327; the act of entering or becoming concerned in an arrangement which facilitates under s.328; or the act of acquisition, use or possession under s.329.

This is, by far, the most practical way to approach the defence. As soon as knowledge or suspicion arises a disclosure should be made to the nominated officer. Most firms of solicitors will not wish to encourage their staff and partners to disclose knowledge or suspicion of money laundering directly to SOCA. Internal disclosure allows the firm to maintain control over what is happening in the firm. It allows for policy decisions to be taken centrally by one person (the nominated officer) or, in bigger firms, a panel of senior members of the firm. It therefore makes sense to have internal procedures requiring this defence to be applied by making an internal disclosure as soon as knowledge or suspicion arises and before any prohibited act is undertaken.

As a result of an amendment brought about by SOCPA 2005, the second way in which the disclosure can satisfy the requirements of the section is where the disclosure is made whilst the alleged offender is doing the prohibited act. This will clearly cover the situation where the prohibited act (the act of concealment, the entering into or becoming concerned with an arrangement or the act of acquisition, use or possession) is a continuing act. If the prohibited act has already occurred and is continuing, the second form of disclosure can afford a defence. However, for this defence to apply, two further conditions must be present:

- at the time the act was begun, the accused did not then know or suspect that the property constituted or represented a person's benefit from criminal conduct (and thus the act was not prohibited); and
- the disclosure must be made on the discloser's own initiative and as soon as is practicable after he or she first knows or suspects that the property constitutes criminal property.

An example of where it might be appropriate to consider this second type of disclosure is where money is held in client account. When originally received by the firm of solicitors, no knowledge or suspicion that the funds were criminal property attached to the possession of the money. However, whilst still in possession of the money, information is received which leads to knowledge or suspicion that the funds are criminal property. The act of holding such funds in client account could amount to being concerned in an arrangement which facilitated the retention or control of criminal property. It might also be an offence under s.329 insofar as the solicitor has possession of criminal property.

Disclosure under the second timing condition is likely to provide the solicitor with a defence. Note, however, that any future dealings with the funds (e.g. by payment to a third party) could amount to a separate money laundering offence for which a further defence would be necessary. Given the existence of knowledge or suspicion, a further disclosure under the first timing condition (i.e. made before the prohibited act of dealing with the funds) would have to be made.

Thirdly, PoCA 2002 provides for a defence where the disclosure is made after the prohibited act.

Section 338(3) provides that a disclosure made after the alleged offender does the prohibited act may provide a defence if two further conditions apply. These are that:

- there was a good reason for the failure to make the disclosure before the prohibited act was undertaken; and
- the disclosure was made on the alleged offender's own initiative and as soon as it was practicable for it to be made.

The second and third 'timing options' are clearly not as satisfactory as the first option. If the disclosure is made before the prohibited act, no further condition relating to the disclosure must be met – the defence is available. In order to obtain the benefit of the defence using the second alternative timing requirement, a solicitor will have to show that he or she was unaware that the property was criminal property when the act commenced: to benefit from the third option, the solicitor will have to show good reason for failing to make the disclosure earlier. Further, in both the second and third options, it must be shown that disclosure was made on the solicitor's own initiative. It is not yet clear how the courts will interpret the phrase 'good reason'.

Firms, in their internal procedures, should treat the second and third options very much as back-stop procedures, available if necessary but not the norm.

4.2.6 Confidentiality

Many solicitors are concerned about their duty in confidentiality when making a disclosure. When a solicitor makes a disclosure to a third person (i.e. in this context, SOCA) which concerns the affairs of a client, the question of confidentiality naturally arises. A solicitor's duty in confidentiality extends to all matters communicated to a solicitor by the client or on behalf of the client, except in certain limited exceptional cases. In addition, any information contained in a disclosure may be privileged information. Communications made between a lawyer and a client are privileged if they are confidential and made for the purpose of seeking legal advice from a lawyer or providing legal advice to a client. Further, where litigation has started or is reasonably in prospect, communications made between a lawyer and client; a lawyer and an agent; or a lawyer and a third party are privileged if they are made for the sole or dominant purpose of the litigation.

The duty of confidentiality does not apply to information acquired by a solicitor where he or she is being used by a client to facilitate the commission of a crime. The Solicitors' Practice Rules 1990, rule 16E covers the topic of confidentiality. The Law Society have issued guidance on rule 16E. Guidance note 17 states that: 'Where you have strong *prima facie* evidence that you have been used by the client to perpetrate a fraud or other crime . . . the duty of confidence does not arise.' (During 2007, the Solicitors' Practice Rules are expected to be replaced by the Solicitors' Code of Conduct. Rule 4 of the new Code of Conduct replicates Practice Rule 16E). Further, section 10(2) of the Police and Criminal Evidence Act 1984 (PACE) states that items are not privileged where they are held 'with the intention of furthering a criminal purpose'. The House of Lords has held that the reference to the word 'intention' in s.10(2) of PACE does not have to be that of the client or the solicitor. It is sufficient that a third party intends the solicitor/client communication to be made with a view to furthering a criminal purpose (see *R.* v. *Central Criminal Court ex parte Francis & Francis* [1989] AC 346).

Clearly, if a solicitor is required to disclose information by way of a defence to SOCA, the solicitor must ensure that such disclosure does not give rise to a breach of the duty in confidentiality or an improper disclosure of privileged information.

Section 338(4) of PoCA 2002 provides: 'An authorised disclosure is not to be taken to breach any restriction on the disclosure of information (however imposed).'

In *Bowman* v. *Fels*, the Court of Appeal considered the effect of PoCA 2002, s.338(4) on LPP. It was argued before the Court that Parliament, by s.338(4), must have intended authorised disclosures to override LPP. However, the Court stated that this provision is used to protect what would otherwise be a breach of a duty of confidence in circumstances which did not amount to the violation of a fundamental human right. The Court stated much stronger language would be required if the legislation was to be interpreted as implying that LPP was to be overridden.

The Law Society Guidance on *Bowman* v. *Fels* (see **Appendix B2**) extends to transactional work and confirms that the authorised disclosure defence does not override LPP. In consequence, where solicitors are required to make a report by way of a defence to the money laundering offences (ss.327–329) they must consider whether the information upon which their knowledge or suspicion is based is subject to LPP. If it is subject to LPP, no disclosure can be made without a waiver by the client of privilege and before the solicitor can seek a waiver, the solicitor would need to consider the tipping off offences (see **Chapter 7**).

If a solicitor has *prima facie* evidence that any communication is made with the intention of furthering a criminal purposes (e.g. by using his or her services to commit a money laundering offence under PoCA 2002, ss.327–329) then any information acquired or communication made in relation to these services will not be confidential nor will it be privileged. Disclosure to SOCA will not be a problem.

However, if a solicitor suspects a client may be using his or her services to commit a money laundering offence, but does not have *prima facie* evidence, the question of confidentiality or privilege depends upon the outcome of any investigation. If the solicitor's suspicions are confirmed, the information or communication is neither confidential nor privileged, and a report can be made to SOCA. If the suspicions turn out to be unfounded, the information or communication will remain confidential and privileged. Before making any disclosure, a waiver of privilege must be obtained. If the client refuses to grant the waiver, or if the solicitor cannot seek a waiver due to tipping off considerations, the only possible course for the solicitor is to stop acting.

4.3 APPROPRIATE CONSENT (PoCA 2002, s.335)

As noted above, ss.327, 328 and 329 provide for a defence where an authorised disclosure is made by the accused and 'if the disclosure is made before he does the [prohibited act] he has the appropriate consent'. Also, as noted above, solicitors are encouraged to make any authorised disclosure before the prohibited act rather than relying upon the disclosure being made after the act and having to show that there was a good reason for a failure to make the disclosure earlier.

For this reason, it is vital to understand the meaning of appropriate consent and the rules attached to the definition in PoCA 2002, s.335.

To illustrate this point, consider the following scenario. A solicitor is acting for the vendor on a property transaction. Contracts have been exchanged and a date for completion has been agreed. The solicitor has no concerns about his client but, in the course of the transaction, becomes suspicious about the funds used by the purchaser (for whom he is not acting). Completing the sale is likely to amount to an arrangement which facilitates the acquisition, use or control of criminal property (if the funds do turn out to be criminal property) – PoCA 2002, s.328. Receiving the funds into client account will potentially be the offence of acquisition, use or possession of criminal property – PoCA 2002, s.329. Receipt of such funds may also amount to the offence of concealing – PoCA 2002, s.327. Note that, in accordance with the Court of Appeal's decision in *Bowman* v. *Fels* (see **Chapter 2**) steps which are no more than steps in preparation for completion or in preparation for the holding of client money will not amount to an arrangement. Consequently, the defence of disclosure only becomes necessary where the solicitor is undertaking a transaction which will, of necessity, lead to an arrangement or to the acquisition, use or possession of criminal property.

In each of the money laundering offences, the defence of an authorised disclosure is available. However, before looking at the defence, the question of confidentiality and privilege must be considered. Where the solicitor has *prima facie* evidence for knowing or believing that the communication (giving rise to the solicitor's knowledge or suspicion that the funds were criminal property) was made with a view to furthering a criminal purpose, such communication will not be privileged nor confidential and disclosure can be made. If the information giving rise to knowledge or suspicion came from the other side (i.e. not from the solicitor's client) it is highly unlikely that the information will be subject to common law LPP – nor will it be confidential and disclosure can be made. However, if the communication came from the solicitor's client it is likely to be subject to common law LPP. The client will not have communicated with a view to furthering a criminal purpose and consequently, before a disclosure can be made to SOCA, the client's waiver must be sought. If the client refuses to waive LPP, the solicitor's only option is to cease to act for the client.

If the solicitor discloses his suspicions after completion (i.e. after the prohibited act) the defence will only be available if there was a good reason for his failure to make the disclosure before completion and the disclosure was made on his own initiative as soon as it was practicable for him to make it. It is unlikely that the simple contractual requirement to complete by a particular date will be a good reason for failing to make the disclosure before that date although, at the time of writing, there is no judicial interpretation of this term. Consequently, the limited circumstances where the defence might apply in this situation include where the solicitor only became suspicious after the completion. If the conditions are not met, the disclosure does not fall within the definition of an authorised disclosure.

The defence of disclosure might be available if the disclosure was made whilst undertaking the prohibited act, provided that at the time when the prohibited act was begun, there was no knowledge or suspicion that the property (i.e. the funds used by the purchaser) constituted the benefit of criminal conduct. In a conveyancing transaction, where the prohibited act will be completion and/or receiving money into client account, this particular defence is likely to have limited practical benefit.

Assuming the solicitor's suspicion arose before the completion date or before suspect funds were received into the solicitor's client account (i.e. the potentially prohibited acts), it would be sensible for the disclosure to be made before any prohibited act was undertaken. In this case, the defence would be available since the disclosure would amount to an authorised disclosure. Having made such disclosure, the solicitor could not then proceed to commit the prohibited act without considering the further requirements of PoCA 2002. The defence of authorised disclosure will only continue to apply if the prohibited act is undertaken with appropriate consent. (Note that in this scenario it may also be necessary to consider the offences of failure to disclose under PoCA 2002, ss.330 *et seq* – see **Chapter 5**.)

Section 335(1) of PoCA 2002 defines appropriate consent as:

- The consent of the nominated officer to do a prohibited act if the authorised disclosure is made to the nominated officer.
- The consent of a constable to do a prohibited act if an authorised disclosure is made to a constable.

- The consent of a customs officer to do a prohibited act if an authorised disclosure is made to a customs officer.

Appropriate consent can therefore be given by a nominated officer (i.e. the firm's MLRO) or by the appropriate authorities (usually SOCA). Since most firms' policies will require members of the firm to report any knowledge or suspicion internally and before the prohibited act, it is sensible for any internal policy to include a requirement that following a disclosure to a firm's MLRO no further work should be undertaken on the file without the MLRO's consent. Given the definition of an 'arrangement' as per *Bowman* v. *Fels* (see **Chapter 2**) it is possible that some work in preparation for the prohibited act could be undertaken without appropriate consent in accordance with PoCA 2002, s.335. However, most firms prefer the decision regarding what is and what is not an 'arrangement' to be taken by those in the firm who have a detailed knowledge of the appropriate law (generally the firm's MLRO) rather than allowing individual fee earners or other members of staff to interpret the complex law. Consequently, a policy which requires no further work on the file without the MLRO's consent allows the MLRO to be involved in any determination as to what might be an 'arrangement' and what might be permissible preparatory activities. Any consent to undertake preparatory activities can be given by the MLRO without considering the rules for consent set out in PoCA 2002. Since preparatory activities do not amount to prohibited acts, no defence is required. However, once the MLRO is satisfied that if the firm were to continue to act, a prohibited act would be committed, appropriate consent can only be given in accordance with the rules set out below.

4.3.1   Appropriate consent by nominated officer

Where disclosure has been made internally to the firm's nominated officer (the MLRO), the officer can only give appropriate consent in accordance with the strict rules set out in PoCA 2002, s.336. This section provides that the nominated officer must not give consent unless the conditions set out in the section are satisfied. There are three conditions, any of which being satisfied will allow the nominated officer to give consent.

Condition 1 (s.336(2))

For this condition to apply the nominated officer must disclose to SOCA (the Act states 'to a person authorised for the purposes of this Part by the Director General of the Serious Organised Crime Agency') that the property is criminal property. Thereafter, before the nominated officer can give appropriate consent, SOCA must consent to the firm continuing to act in such a way that leads to the prohibited act being undertaken.

SOCA operates a fast track scheme where the arrangement is time sensitive. If, for example, completion of a transaction is imminent, disclosure by the nominated officer to SOCA and the consent of SOCA will be necessary before completion can take place. SOCA has indicated that the time sensitive nature of the arrangement should be explicitly stated and highlighted in the written report faxed or sent electronically to the SOCA Consent Desk.

Condition 2 (s.336(3))

As an alternative to condition 1 above, appropriate consent can be given by a nominated officer if condition 2 applies. The nominated officer must make a disclosure to SOCA that property is criminal property and if, before the end of seven working days starting with the first working day after disclosure has been made, no notice of refusal of consent to undertaking the prohibited act is received from SOCA, consent can be given. A working day for these purposes is defined (s.336(9)) as a day other than Saturday, Sunday, Christmas Day, Good Friday or a day which is a bank holiday under the Banking and Financial Dealings Act 1971.

Obviously, in all cases (but particularly where a solicitor is relying upon this second condition) it is important that the solicitor's records show exactly what has happened. The Law Society's *Money Laundering Guidance* (para. 7.7) states:

> Solicitors must ensure that they keep a copy of the report which they have submitted, as well as careful notes of all contacts which they subsequently have with NCIS [now SOCA] or law enforcement agencies. These records should be kept on a separate file by the nominated officer. It would be prudent for these records to be kept by the nominated officer for as long as the transaction and identity records are kept, and probably longer as it can sometimes take many years before an investigation comes to fruition.

Condition 3 (s.336(4))

Where disclosure has been made to SOCA by a nominated officer, SOCA will usually acknowledge receipt and either refuse appropriate consent or provide appropriate consent. If consent is given, then obviously the nominated officer can proceed to give appropriate consent to the fee earner. If consent is refused by SOCA, condition 3 may be relevant in determining whether the nominated officer can give consent to the fee earner.

This condition applies where the nominated officer discloses to SOCA that property is criminal property and before the end of seven working days starting with the first working day after disclosure has been made, notice of refusal of consent to undertaking the prohibited act is received from SOCA. Obviously, where SOCA have refused consent, no further work should be undertaken on the file if such work will amount to a prohibited act. However, s.336(4) allows the nominated officer to give appropriate consent to such work after the moratorium period has expired. For these purposes, s.336(8) defines the moratorium period as 'the period of 31 days starting with the day on which the nominated officer is given notice that consent to the doing of the act is refused'.

Note that, unlike the reference to seven working days in the legislation, the reference to 31 days in the definition of the moratorium period is not a reference to working days.

Take the following example by way of illustration of these points.

A solicitor is acting for a client on the disposal of certain assets. Contracts have been exchanged and the completion is fixed for Friday 10 September. On Wednesday, 8 September, the solicitor receives certain information from his client that leads him to suspect that the funds being used by the purchaser (for whom the solicitor is not acting) derive from criminal conduct. Completion of the transaction on 10 September is likely to amount to an arrangement which facilitates the retention, use or control of these criminal funds (PoCA 2002, s.328). It would also mean that the solicitor would acquire and possess criminal property when the completion money was placed into his client account (PoCA 2002, s.329). Possibly there would also be a breach of PoCA 2002, s.327 (concealing). In all the circumstances, it would be advisable for the solicitor to report his suspicions. The timetable for reporting is as follows:

8 September	Solicitor reports his suspicions to the firm's nominated officer. Although the contractual completion date is only two days away, completion cannot go ahead without the appropriate consent of the nominated officer. If completion did proceed without the consent, the defence of disclosure would not be available.
8 September	The nominated officer cannot give consent to completion unless he has satisfied one of the conditions in PoCA 2002, s.336. Because of the time sensitive nature of this matter, it is likely that he will contact SOCA using the fast track procedure. He makes a disclosure to SOCA, following any necessary waiver of privilege by the client.
9–17 September	Seven working days must be calculated starting with the first working day after the nominated officer makes the disclosure. Consequently, the first working day is Thursday 9 September. Omitting Saturday 11 and Sunday 12 September, the seventh working day is Friday 17 September. If during this period, SOCA consent to the firm undertaking the prohibited act, the nominated officer can give appropriate consent to completion proceeding.

20 September	If before the end of the seven working days (i.e. by midnight on Friday 17 September) the nominated officer has not received consent nor has he received notice of refusal of consent from SOCA, he has received deemed consent and may now give appropriate consent to the matter completing.
17 September – 17 October	If, during the seven working day period, SOCA notifies its refusal to give consent (worst case scenario, the refusal is given on day seven) the moratorium period will apply. This period starts on the day refusal of consent is given and lasts for 31 days. During this period, the prohibited act (i.e. the act of completion) cannot be undertaken since the defence of disclosure will not apply.
18 October	The moratorium period has now expired. Despite the refusal of SOCA, the nominated officer can now give appropriate consent and completion can now take place (assuming the purchaser is still willing or able to complete!)

For the sake of completeness, the following points, dealt with elsewhere in this book, should also be considered:

- Communications with the client (seeking a possible waiver of privilege) and the other side regarding the fact that completion cannot take place on the contractual completion date. It is possible that such communications could amount to the offence of tipping off under PoCA 2002, s.333 – see **Chapter 7**.
- Civil liability. If the client has suffered loss as a result of the delay in completion, there may be civil liability consequences – see **Appendix B1**.
- Disclosure on behalf of the client. In this scenario, if the client is innocent (i.e. the suspicions related to the funds of the purchaser) the client will require a defence against a possible charge under PoCA 2002. The client will be entering into an arrangement (i.e. completion) and in consequence will need the same defence as the solicitor. In this case a joint disclosure by the nominated officer on behalf of the firm and the client should be considered – see **Paragraph 4.4**.

4.3.2 Offence committed by nominated officer if improper consent is given

Where a member of the firm has made disclosure of knowledge or suspicion of criminal property to a nominated officer by way of a defence, the prohibited act cannot be undertaken without the appropriate consent of the nominated officer. As noted above, there are three alternative conditions that the nominated officer must satisfy before giving consent. If a nominated officer gives consent without satisfying any of these conditions, an offence is committed. Section 336(5) provides that:

A person who is a nominated officer commits an offence if:

(a) he gives consent to a prohibited act in circumstances where none of the conditions in subsections (2), (3) and (4) is satisfied, and

(b) he knows or suspects that the act is a prohibited act.

The penalty for such an offence is imprisonment for up to six months and/or a fine not exceeding the statutory maximum for summary conviction; imprisonment for up to five years and/or a fine for conviction on indictment (s.336(6)).

The nominated officer only commits an offence if the two requirements noted in s.336(5) apply. Not only must the nominated officer be shown to have given consent without any of the three conditions being satisfied but also he must be shown to have known or suspected that the act was a prohibited act.

Where a fee earner reports knowledge or suspicion that property is criminal property and the Money Laundering Regulations 2003 apply (see **Chapter 9**), a nominated officer should investigate the circumstance of the report. Regulation 7 of the Regulations states: 'Where a disclosure is made to a nominated officer, he must consider it in the light of any relevant information which is available to [the firm] and determine whether it gives rise to such knowledge or suspicion . . .'

Whether or not the Regulations apply, it would be good practice for the nominated officer to follow this procedure. If, in the light of this internal consideration, the nominated officer comes to the conclusion that there are no grounds for knowledge or suspicion, he may give appropriate consent to the fee earner continuing to work on the file. For example, this might apply where the fee earner is a junior member of staff or a recently joined employee. A particular aspect of a transaction may arouse his suspicion and consequently a report might be made to the nominated officer. On considering the report along with other information held in the firm (including past dealings with the client) the nominated officer may come to the conclusion that there are no grounds for knowledge or suspicion and appropriate consent can be given without the need to satisfy any of the three conditions in PoCA 2002, s.336 and without the risk of committing a criminal offence under PoCA 2002, s.336(5). It goes without saying that particular care must be taken in these circumstances. Nominated officers should err on the side of caution and should only give appropriate consent outside the conditions of s.336 if, having considered all of the information, they have reached a view that no offence is being committed. In these circumstances it is vital for the nominated officer to record full and proper file notes.

4.3.3 Appropriate consent from the authorities

Section 335(1) of PoCA 2002 defines appropriate consent as:

(a) the consent of the nominated officer to do a prohibited act if the authorised disclosure is made to the nominated officer;

(b) the consent of a constable to do a prohibited act if an authorised disclosure is made to a constable; or

(c) the consent of a customs officer to do a prohibited act if an authorised disclosure is made to a customs officer.

As noted above, most firms will encourage all partners and other members of staff to make their disclosure of knowledge or suspicion internally to the firm's nominated officer. In such cases appropriate consent must be obtained from the nominated officer.

However, a valid defence is available if the disclosure is made to a constable or customs officer (although, in practice, this will be a disclosure to SOCA). There are two circumstances where consent from the authorities will allow the prohibited act to be undertaken.

- **Consent from SOCA.** If a disclosure is made to SOCA, their consent to do the prohibited act will amount to appropriate consent under s.335(1)(*b*) or (*c*).
- **Assumed consent from SOCA.** Section 335(2) provides that a person must be treated as having the appropriate consent if he makes an authorised disclosure to a constable or customs officer and either the condition in subsection (3) or subsection (4) is satisfied.

Condition 1: s.335(3)

If, before the end of seven working days starting with the first working day after disclosure has been made, no notice of refusal of consent to undertaking the prohibited act is received from SOCA, consent can be assumed. A working day for these purposes is defined (s.336(9)) as a day other than Saturday, Sunday, Christmas Day, Good Friday or a day which is a bank holiday under the Banking and Financial Dealings Act 1971.

Condition 2: s.335(4)

If, before the end of seven working days starting with the first working day after disclosure has been made, notice of refusal of consent to undertaking the prohibited act is received from SOCA, no further work should be undertaken on the file if such work is likely to amount to a prohibited act. However, consent can be assumed after the moratorium period has expired. For these purposes, s.335(6) defines the moratorium period as the period of

31 days starting with the day on which the person receives notice that consent to the doing of the act is refused.

These two conditions are very similar to the conditions applicable to the nominated officer when giving appropriate consent. Consequently, the timetable noted above could equally be relevant where a fee earner discloses not to the nominated officer but to SOCA direct.

4.4 AUTHORISED DISCLOSURES BY OR ON BEHALF OF OTHERS

In certain circumstances it is not just the solicitor who might need a defence to the money laundering offences contained in PoCA 2002, ss.327–329. In many transactions it will be the client who enters and the solicitor who will be concerned in an arrangement. In some matters a barrister may also be involved in the arrangement. Consequently, solicitors should consider carefully who might need a defence and what steps can be taken in order to provide that defence.

If a client is an innocent party (and particularly if it is the information provided by the client which has given rise to any suspicion) the solicitor should first consider the privileged nature of the communication giving rise to the knowledge or suspicion. If the communication remains privileged, a waiver must be obtained from the client before any disclosure is made to SOCA. Assuming the client is an innocent party, the solicitor should then consider joining in the client when disclosure is made to SOCA. One factor in determining whether the client should be approached to waive privilege and then joined in the disclosure is whether it is possible for the solicitor to disclose details without being in breach of the tipping off offence (PoCA 2002, s.333) or the offence of prejudicing an investigation (PoCA 2002, s.342) – for both sections see **Chapter 7**).

If a client has been joined in a disclosure where the solicitor knows or suspects that another has or is intending to use criminal property, the protection of the defence will only apply from the point of time when disclosure was made. Disclosure made by a client does not operate retrospectively and does not provide a defence against activities undertaken before the disclosure.

Any joint disclosure must be to SOCA in order for the client to benefit from it. Although a solicitor may obtain a defence by disclosing knowledge or suspicion to the firm's nominated officer, such a disclosure will not operate as a defence for the client. The nominated officer is the person nominated by the alleged offender's employer and the disclosure must be made during the course of employment.

CHAPTER 5

Failure to disclose: regulated sector

5.1 INTRODUCTION

The money laundering offences contained in the Proceeds of Crime Act 2002 (PoCA 2002) and the Terrorism Act 2000 (see **Chapters 2** and **3**) all require the alleged offender to take some action in relation to criminal or terrorist property. Section 327 of PoCA 2002 requires an act of concealment etc; PoCA 2002, s.328 requires a person to enter into or become concerned in an arrangement which facilitates; s.329 requires the acquisition, use or control; Terrorism Act 2000, s.18 requires an act of assistance.

Without undertaking any of these acts, a solicitor cannot be convicted under these provisions. A solicitor who, for example, interviews a new potential client and, in the course of the interview becomes suspicious of the funds the client intends to use as part of the transaction, may decline to accept the instructions. Simply having suspicion regarding a client's funds would not be sufficient to justify a charge under PoCA 2002 ss.327–329, or Terrorism Act 2000, s.18. Since no offence under these provisions has been committed (or is about to be committed) no disclosure of the suspicions to SOCA or internally by way of defence is necessary.

However, in certain circumstances, a failure to disclose knowledge or suspicion, or reasonable grounds for knowledge or suspicion, of money laundering is an offence even if no act in relation to the criminal or terrorist property is undertaken.

There are four offences of failure to disclose:

- Failure to disclose: regulated sector (PoCA 2002, s.330)
- Failure to disclose: regulated sector (Terrorism Act 2000, s.21A)
- Failure to disclose: nominated officers in the regulated sector (PoCA 2002, s.331)
- Failure to disclose: other nominated officers (PoCA 2000, s.332)

The first two offences are dealt with in detail in this chapter. The remaining two offences are covered in **Chapter 6**.

5.2   FAILURE TO DISCLOSE: REGULATED SECTOR (PoCA 2002, s.330)

5.2.1   The offence

Section 330 of PoCA 2002, as amended by SOCPA 2005, provides:

(1)   A person commits an offence if the conditions in subsections (2) to (4) are satisfied.

(2)   The first condition is that he –

   (a)   knows or suspects, or
   (b)   has reasonable grounds for knowing or suspecting,

   that another person is engaged in money laundering.

(3)   The second condition is that the information or other matter –

   (a)   on which his knowledge or suspicion is based, or
   (b)   which gives reasonable grounds for such knowledge or suspicion,

   came to him in the course of a business in the regulated sector.

(3A) The third condition is –

   (a)   that he can identify the other person mentioned in subsection (2) or the whereabouts of any laundered property; or
   (b)   that he believes, or it is reasonable to expect him to believe, that the information or other matter mentioned in subsection (3) will or may assist in identifying the other person or the whereabouts of any of the laundered property.

(4)   The fourth condition is that he does not make the required disclosure to –

   (a)   a nominated officer; or
   (b)   a person authorised for the purposes of this Part by the Director General of the Serious Organised Crime Agency, as soon as is practicable after the information or other matter mentioned in subsection (3) comes to him.

There are a number of points that can be made concerning this section and in particular the four conditions that must be satisfied before the offence is committed.

First Condition

> . . . knows or suspects, or has reasonable grounds for knowing or suspecting . . .

Like many of the offences contained in PoCA 2002, this offence can be committed with knowledge or suspicion. However, unlike the other offences, the test of knowledge or suspicion is a subjective and objective test. An alleged offender can be found guilty under s.330 if he or she knows or suspects that another is engaged in money laundering. However, even if subjectively the offender had no actual knowledge or suspicion of matters upon which the charge is based, if the offender has reasonable grounds for knowledge or suspicion of these matters, that will be sufficient for the purposes of this section; the fact that the offender should have known or suspected is all that is required. Consequently, an oversight by a solicitor or incompetence on the part of a solicitor might be sufficient to give rise to liability.

Solicitors must therefore be more proactive in considering whether a particular transaction gives rise to knowledge or suspicion of money laundering. Instead of simply reacting to information which might be suspicious, solicitors should ask themselves: Are there any suspicious circumstances arising from this particular transaction?

... that another person ...

The reference to another person means that, as with the offence under PoCA 2002, s.328 (arrangements), this offence can be committed where the solicitor's knowledge or suspicion relates to the conduct of a client or some third party. It may be that concerns have arisen regarding the other side's client and that the solicitor's own client is above any suspicion – consideration must still be given to the requirements to report that other person.

... is engaged in money laundering.

Section 340(11) of PoCA 2002 provides a definition for the term 'money laundering'. It states:

Money laundering is an act which –

(a) constitutes an offence under section 327, 328 or 329,
(b) constitutes an attempt, conspiracy or incitement to commit an offence specified in paragraph (a),
(c) constitutes aiding, abetting, counselling or procuring the commission of an offence specified in paragraph (a), or
(d) would constitute an offence specified in paragraph (a), (b), or (c) if done in the United Kingdom.

Money laundering is, therefore, widely defined. Since it includes the offences of concealing etc. (PoCA 2002, s.327) and acquisition, use and possession (PoCA 2002, s.329) it follows that the perpetrator of the crime can be 'engaged in money laundering' (see **Chapter 3**).

The offence under PoCA 2002, s.330 obliges a solicitor to report knowledge or suspicion even if the solicitor is not involved in an arrangement which is likely to facilitate the acquisition, retention, use or control of criminal property. Unlike the defence requiring an authorised disclosure, this is a disclosure by way of obligation. It is the failure to disclose which is a criminal offence.

Note that the offence under s.330 can also be committed if a solicitor knows or suspects (or has reasonable grounds for knowing or suspecting) that another is engaged in an attempt, conspiracy or incitement to commit a money laundering offence or where another is engaged in aiding, abetting, counselling or procuring such an offence. However, solicitors must be careful to ensure that they do not report in circumstances where to do so would be inappropriate. A required report (termed a protected disclosure – see below) will not breach a solicitor's duty in confidentiality. However, in the light of the Court of Appeal's decision in *Bowman* v. *Fels* (see **Chapter 4**) LPP will still apply.

Second condition

> . . . the information or other matter –
>
> (a) on which his knowledge or suspicion is based, or
> (b) which gives reasonable grounds for such knowledge or suspicion,
>
> came to him in the course of business . . ..

Information received, other than in the course of business, does not give rise to an obligation to report. If a solicitor overhears a conversation in a public house suggesting that the speaker is engaged in criminal activities, this will not give rise to compulsory reporting, providing the solicitor is drinking in his private capacity. The fact that the information must be received in the course of business does not restrict the operation of this offence to information received on the office premises. However, the circumstances in which the information is received must suggest that the solicitor is operating in a business capacity at the time of receipt.

> . . . in the regulated sector.

The regulated sector is defined in PoCA 2002, Part 1, Sched. 9. The definition was amended by the Proceeds of Crime Act 2002 (Business in the Regulated Sector and Supervisory Authorities) Order 2003, SI 2003/3074. This order (and thus the amended definition of the regulated sector) came into force on 1 March 2004. The following activities are activities which solicitors frequently undertake and will be (as a result of the order) within the regulated sector.

Schedule 9, Part 1 of PoCA 2002 (as amended) provides:

> 1 (1) A business is in the regulated sector to the extent that it engages in any of the following activities in the United Kingdom –
>
> (a) a regulated activity specified in sub-paragraph (2) . . .

Sub-paragraph (2) lists 10 activities, many of which could be relevant to a solicitor's practice. Sub-paragraph (3) states that: 'Paragraph 1(1)(*a*) . . . must be read with section 22 of the Financial Services and Markets Act 2000 and any relevant order under that section . . .'

Section 22 of the Financial Services and Markets Act 2000 provides:

(1) An activity is a regulated activity for the purposes of this Act if it is an activity of a specified kind which is carried on by way of business and –

(a) relates to an investment of a specified kind . . ..

(5) 'Specified' means specified in an order made by the Treasury.

The most relevant order made by the Treasury is the Financial Services and Markets Act 2000 (Regulated Activities) Order 2001, SI 2001/544 (as amended). This order (the RAO) lists both the activities of a specified kind and the investments of a specified kind.

The most common specified investments from a solicitor's point of view are:

- Shares in the share capital of any company (art.76 RAO).
- Instruments creating or acknowledging indebtedness, including debentures, loan stock, bonds and certificates of deposit (art.77 RAO).
- Government securities, including British Government Stocks (gilts) (art.78 RAO).
- Units in collective investment schemes, including unit trusts and shares in open-ended investment companies (art.81 RAO).
- Insurance contracts, including endowment policies, pension policies, annuities, insurance bonds and contracts of general insurance (for example, property insurance, A.T.E. insurance or defective title insurance.
- Regulated mortgage contracts.

Consequently, activities in a solicitor's corporate department (acquisitions, corporate finance) are likely to involve shares, debentures or corporate bonds. Activities in private client work (estate and trust administration) could involve the full range of specified investments. Settlements in matrimonial work could involve some or all of the specified investments. Conveyancing transactions might involve regulated mortgage contracts and associated and other insurance contracts.

Of the 10 activities listed in PoCA 2002, Sched.9, Part 1, para.1(2) the following involving specified investments are likely to be most relevant to solicitors:

- **Dealing in investments as agent**. Dealing is defined as buying, selling, subscribing or underwriting certain specified investments. A solicitor would be dealing where investments were being bought or sold as agent for a client.
- **Arranging deals in investments**. This would catch those circumstances where a solicitor made arrangements for a client to buy, sell, subscribe or underwrite certain specified investments.
- **Managing investments**. Solicitors who are sole trustees or personal representatives or trustees or personal representatives jointly only with others

from their own firm will be managing if the trust fund or estate includes certain specified investments.

- **Safeguarding and administration**. Solicitors who hold documents of title to specified investments in safe custody and who are involved in administration activities relating to those investments will be undertaking this activity. Typically, estate and trust work will give rise to this activity.
- **Advising on investments**. Giving advice on the merits of buying, selling, subscribing for or underwriting certain specified investments will be caught by this activity.

Section 19 of the Financial Services and Markets Act 2000 provides:

(1) No person may carry on a regulated activity in the United Kingdom, or purport to do so, unless he is –

(a) an authorised person; or
(b) an exempt person.

Most solicitors are not authorised persons (i.e. they have not sought nor obtained authorisation from the Financial Services Authority). They are, however, able to undertake many activities which fall within the definition of regulated activities without authorisation as a result of the exemption for professionals provided in Part XX of the Financial Services and Markets Act 2000.

It must be understood that the definition of the regulated sector in PoCA 2002, s.330 (Duty to report: regulated sector), does not require the regulated activity to be undertaken with authorisation from the Financial Services Authority. An exempt regulated activity will fall within the regulated sector.

For further details of the way the Financial Services and Markets Act 2000 applies to solicitors, see *Solicitors and Financial Services: A Compliance Handbook* (3rd Edition, 2002) by Peter Camp, published by Law Society Publishing.

The other relevant activities that will bring a solicitor within the regulated sector as a result of PoCA 2002, Sched. 9, Part 1, para.1(1) (as amended) are as follows:

(f) estate agency work . . ..

Solicitors who provide estate agency services will, in respect of those services, fall within the regulated sector.

(h) the activities of a person appointed to act as an insolvency practitioner within the meaning of section 388 of the Insolvency Act 1986 . . .

Solicitors who are appointed as insolvency practitioners will be within the regulated sector. Solicitors who act for external insolvency practitioners or who act in insolvency matters without an appointment as an insolvency practitioner will not be caught under this head. However, depending upon the type of work, they may be caught under paragraph (l) below.

(i) the provision by way of business of advice about the tax affairs of another person by a body corporate or unincorporate, or in the case of a sole practitioner, by an individual . . .

Solicitors giving tax advice will be within the regulated sector. It appears that any tax advice is capable of triggering the definition of business in the regulated sector. For example, whilst activities relating to will drafting would not bring a solicitor into the regulated sector, if such activities were combined with inheritance tax planning advice this would be considered as business in the regulated sector.

(l) the provision by way of business of legal services by a body corporate or unincorporate or, in the case of a sole practitioner, by an individual and which involves the participation in a financial or real property transaction (whether by assisting in the planning or execution of any transaction or otherwise by acting for, or on behalf of, a client in any transaction) . . ..

This paragraph is clearly aimed at extending the regulated sector to many activities undertaken by solicitors. The reference to financial or real property transactions has the effect of bringing all conveyancing transactions within the scope of the regulated sector.

The *Money Laundering Guidance* issued by the Law Society indicates that the interpretation of 'participation in a financial transaction' is less clear. The *Money Laundering Guidance* seeks clarity from the text of the 2nd European Money Laundering Directive (on which this definition is based). The Directive provides that the following should be included:

Independent legal professionals, when they participate, whether:

(1) by assisting in the planning or execution of transactions for their client concerning the:

• buying and selling of real property or business entities;
• managing of client money, securities or other assets;
• opening or management of bank, savings or securities accounts;
• organisation of contributions necessary for the creation, operation or management of companies; or
• creation, operation or management of trusts, companies or similar structures; or

(2) by acting on behalf of and for their client in any financial or real estate transaction.

The Law Society's *Money Laundering Guidance* indicates that managing client money is narrower than simply handling client money. Simply operating a client account is not intended to be caught within the regulated sector but holding money or receiving money on behalf of clients as part of a transaction, or holding or receiving money as attorney or trustee will be caught.

The Treasury has also confirmed that the following (by themselves) would not generally be viewed as participation in financial transactions:

- A payment on account of costs to a solicitor or payment of a solicitor's bill (because the solicitor is not participating in a financial transaction on behalf of the client).
- Legal advice (assuming such advice does not fall within one or more of the other categories defined as within the regulated sector).
- Participation in litigation (on the basis that litigation is not a transaction).
- Will writing (unless linked with, for example, tax advice).
- Publicly funded work.

    (m) the provision by way of business of services in relation to the formation, operation or management of a company or a trust.

This paragraph clearly covers activities undertaken by solicitors relating to the formation of a company or the administration of a trust fund. There is some doubt over the reference to business services relating to the operation or management of a company. The Treasury has indicated that this phrase should not be interpreted to include any services which assist in the management or operation of a company.

In a letter written to the British Bankers' Association, the Treasury made the following points:

Regulation (m) was intended to cover those who form, operate or manage companies (or trusts) when this activity is provided as a service by way of business. This addresses, among other things, the problem of 'front' or shell companies, which have been recognised as having been used in most complex money laundering operations . . .

It has been argued that regulation (m) covers anyone providing any service by way of business to a company which happens to assist the management or operation of that company e.g. cleaners, advertising agencies or management consultants. Whereas the interpretation of the Regulations is ultimately a matter for the courts, such a wide interpretation of regulation (m) was not our intention and, we believe, is not warranted by the language of regulation (m).

Many services offered by solicitors to companies and trust funds will involve financial transactions. Some will be exempt regulated activities within the meaning of the Financial Services and Markets Act 2000. As such, these activities will be within the regulated sector regardless of regulation (m). Since the Treasury statement indicates that the interpretation is ultimately a matter for the courts, solicitors should, perhaps, err on the side of caution and assume activities relating to company clients and trust clients are likely to be within the regulated sector.

Third Condition

(a) that he can identify the other person mentioned in subsection (2) or the whereabouts of any of the laundered property; or

(b) that he believes, or it is reasonable to expect him to believe, that the information or other matter mentioned in subsection (3) will or may assist in identifying the other person or the whereabouts of any of the laundered property.

This condition was inserted as a result of an amendment contained in SOCPA 2005. It came into force on 1 July 2005. The intention is to avoid the need for disclosure where there is evidence of money laundering which arose in the course of business in the regulated sector but where there is no possibility that the discloser can identify the person engaged in money laundering, the whereabouts of the property or other information which may assist the authorities. For example, in the course of conveyancing (i.e. business in the regulated sector) a solicitor discovers that a client's credit card has been stolen. As a result, the solicitor has reasonable grounds for knowing or suspecting that the thief is engaged in money laundering (the unlawful possession and use of the credit card). However, the solicitor has no information regarding the identity of the thief or of the laundered property. No requirement to disclose will arise in these circumstances.

Fourth Condition

... he does not make the required disclosure ...

The required disclosure is disclosure of the identity of the other person, if he knows it, and the whereabouts of the laundered property, so far as he knows it and the information referred to in paragraph (b) of the third condition. This requirement was added by SOCPA 2005 and came into effect on 1 July 2005. Once a solicitor is satisfied that the first three conditions apply, the disclosure must include the information required by the third condition. The disclosure must be to a nominated officer (i.e. the firm's MLRO) or to a person authorised for the purpose by the Director General of SOCA (PoCA 2002, s.330(5)(a) and (b)). Further, the disclosure must be made to SOCA as soon as it is practicable after the information referred to in the third condition comes to the solicitor. Disclosure to SOCA in the usual way (see **Chapter 10**) will satisfy this requirement. Section 339 allows for the Secretary of State to prescribe the form and manner in which a disclosure under section 330 must be made. At the time of writing no such order has been made.

Any disclosure made will be treated as a protected disclosure under PoCA 2002, s.337. This section provides that such a disclosure is not to be taken to be a breach of any restriction on the disclosure of information (however imposed) if three conditions are satisfied. These three conditions are:

- The information or other matter disclosed came to the person making the disclosure in the course of his trade, profession, business or employment.
- The information caused the discloser to know or suspect or gave him reasonable grounds for knowing or suspecting that another was engaged in money laundering.
- The disclosure was made to a constable, a customs officer or a nominated officer as soon as is practicable after the information or other matter comes to the discloser.

Note that in the light of the Court of Appeal's decision in *Bowman* v. *Fels* this provision would not be sufficient to override common law LPP (for details of the *Bowman* v. *Fels* decision relating to privilege, see **Chapter 3**). Solicitors must carefully consider their position before making a disclosure under s.330 and in particular the question of privilege must be addressed. Section 330(6) (see below) specifically includes a defence to the offence of failure to disclose where the information giving rise to knowledge or suspicion arose in privileged circumstances. Prior to *Bowman* v. *Fels*, a view was taken by some commentators that the disclosure of privileged information could be treated as a 'protected disclosure' even if such disclosure was not strictly required by s.330. Consequently, some solicitors might have been tempted to err on the side of caution and to disclose information even if it might have been privileged. This course of action is no longer open to solicitors. LPP is unaffected by the provisions relating to 'protected disclosures' and if the information is privileged it should not be disclosed to SOCA without an appropriate waiver.

Finally, in relation to disclosures, PoCA 2002, s.330(9A) (added by SOCPA 2005) should be noted. This provides that there will not be a disclosure (as defined) to a nominated officer if the person communicating information to the nominated officer is a professional legal adviser or other relevant professional adviser and such communication (which is not intended to be a formal disclosure) is made for the purpose of obtaining advice about the need to make a formal disclosure. This subsection thus allows a full discussion with the nominated officer in order to obtain advice from the nominated officer without making a formal disclosure. For practical situations where this section might prove useful, see **Chapter 6**.

. . . as soon as is practicable after the information or other matter comes to him.

Both the third condition and the benefit of protected disclosures require the disclosure to be made as soon as practicable after the information comes into the possession of the discloser. Consequently, to avoid committing the crime and to benefit from the protection of s.337 (protected disclosures), solicitors must not delay in making their disclosures. The Law Society's *Money Laundering Guidance* states:

> It is not known how the courts will interpret 'as soon as practicable'. However delays in reporting which arise from taking legal advice or seeking guidance from the Law Society may be acceptable.

5.2.2 Law Society Guidance

Section 330(8) of PoCA 2002 states:

> In deciding whether a person committed an offence under this section the court must consider whether he followed any relevant guidance which was at the time concerned:
> (a) issued by a supervisory authority or any other appropriate body;
> (b) approved by the Treasury; and
> (c) published in a manner it approved as appropriate in its opinion to bring the guidance to the attention of persons likely to be affected by it.

A supervisory body is defined in PoCA 2002, Sched. 9 and the term includes the Law Society.

The Law Society has issued guidance to the solicitors' profession (*Money Laundering Guidance: Professional Ethics*, Pilot, January 2004). The guidance has been amended and now includes specific guidance on the impact of *Bowman* v. *Fels* (see **Appendix B2**). Extracts from the guidance appear in the text of this book and in **Appendix B1**. The Law Society's *Money Laundering Guidance* is described as a pilot and has not been submitted to the Treasury for approval. Consequently, s.330(8) will not apply technically. However, as stated in the *Money Laundering Guidance*, a court 'may still take it into consideration' in deciding whether an offence has been committed under s.330.

5.2.3 Illustrations I

The following scenarios suggest circumstances where a solicitor may be at risk regarding a duty to disclose.

Scenario 1
A solicitor is acting in a corporate transaction, buying shares on behalf of an individual client. In the course of acting, the solicitor becomes suspicious that funds in the possession of the client and to be used on the purchase derive from criminal activities. The solicitor decides that because of the suspicion, she cannot continue to act for the client. She terminates the retainer, avoiding the risk of tipping off or prejudicing an investigation (see **Chapter 7**). Since the retainer has come to

---

an end, the solicitor will not be involved in an arrangement and will not facilitate the acquisition, retention, use or control of criminal property. In order to decide whether a report must nonetheless be made, the solicitor must consider:

- Does she know or suspect that another is engaged in money laundering? On the facts it appears that the client has in his possession criminal property. This would amount to engaging in money laundering as a result of the offence of acquisition, use or possession (PoCA 2002, s.329).
- Has the information on which her suspicion is based come into her possession as a result of business in the regulated sector? The solicitor is acting on the purchase of shares. This is likely to involve advice on the purchase of a specified investment and may consequently be an exempt regulated activity. Further, the transaction is likely to involve participation in a financial transaction. In either case, it would appear that the solicitor is acting within the regulated sector.

The conclusion is, subject to any defence which might be available (see below), that a protected disclosure should be made as soon as practicable.

Scenario 2

A solicitor is approached by a client for tax advice. She is asked to give advice relating to a legal tax avoidance scheme to be implemented in the UK. The advice given will not amount to an arrangement which facilitates the acquisition, retention, use or control of criminal property. However, in the course of taking instructions, the client discloses to the solicitor that he holds funds abroad derived from overseas trading which have not been disclosed to the appropriate tax authorities. The solicitor is not asked to give advice or provide any services relating to this fund. Should she, nonetheless, report her knowledge? She must consider:

- Does she know or suspect the client is engaged in money laundering? The client possibly has in his possession funds which should have been disclosed to an overseas tax authority (and possibly to the UK tax authorities). Money laundering includes the offence of acquisition, use or possession or an act which would have constituted such an offence if done in the UK (PoCA 2002, s.340(11)). Further enquiries need to be made but if, following these enquiries, there appears to be knowledge or reasonable grounds for knowledge that the client is engaged in money laundering PoCA 2002, s.330 would appear to be relevant.
- Has the information on which her suspicion is based come into her possession as a result of business in the regulated sector? It appears that it has come into her possession as a result of tax advice and in consequence is within the regulated sector.

The conclusion is again, subject to any defence which might be available (see below), that a protected disclosure should be made as soon as practicable.

5.2.4 Defences

There are four defences listed in PoCA 2002, s.330:

(a) reasonable excuse for not disclosing;
(b) privilege;
(c) lack of specified training;
(d) money laundering occurred outside the UK.

Reasonable excuse

Section 330(6)(*a*) states:

> But [a person] does not commit an offence under this section if:
>
> (a) he has a reasonable excuse for not making the required disclosure.

Reasonable excuse for these purposes has yet to be defined by the courts. Solicitors should, therefore, treat this defence with care. The Law Society's *Money Laundering Guidance* suggests that solicitors always 'document the reason for not making the disclosure'.

Section 330(6)(*b*) provides a defence if the information came into the possession of the solicitor in privileged circumstances (see below). The Law Society's *Money Laundering Guidance* states:

> Crown Prosecution Service legal guidance for prosecutors indicates that if a solicitor forms a genuine but mistaken belief that legal professional privilege applies (for example the client misleads the solicitor and uses the advice for a criminal purpose) the solicitor would be able to rely on the reasonable excuse defence, **www.cps.gov.uk**.

Privilege

Section 330(6)(*b*) states:

> But [a person does] not commit an offence under this section if . . .
>
> (b) he is a professional legal adviser or other relevant professional adviser; and
>
> > (i) if he knows either of the things mentioned in subsection (5)(a) and (b) [the identity of the person engaged in money laundering and the whereabouts of the laundered property], he knows the thing because of information or other matter that came to him in privileged circumstances, or
> >
> > (ii) the information or other matter mentioned in subsection (3) [the identity of the person engaged in money laundering or the whereabouts of the laundered property or information which may assist in identifying the person or property] came to him in privileged circumstances.

Circumstances will give rise to privilege if communicated or given to the professional legal adviser or other professional adviser in three cases (s.330(10)):

(a) The information is communicated or given to the adviser by a client (or by the client's representative) in connection with the giving by the adviser of legal advice to the client.
(b) The information is communicated or given to the adviser by a person (or by the person's representative) seeking legal advice from the adviser.
(c) The information is communicated or given to the adviser by a person in connection with legal proceedings or contemplated legal proceedings.

However, PoCA 2002, s.330(11) makes it clear that subsection (10) does not apply to information or other matter which is communicated or given with the intention of furthering a criminal purpose.

These provisions can provide a valuable defence. In the Law Society's view (see their guidance on *Bowman* v. *Fels*, **Appendix B2**) it is made clear that there is a distinction to be drawn between common law privilege and the s.330(6) defence. The guidance states:

> When advice is given or received in circumstances where litigation is neither contemplated nor reasonably in prospect, common law LLP will normally only apply to communications between a solicitor and his client for the purpose of obtaining or providing legal advice, or which form part of the chain of correspondence between solicitor and client for the purpose of obtaining legal advice. Therefore, save in limited circumstances, communications between solicitors and third parties will not fall within common law LPP. An exception where common law LPP might apply is where the third party is merely acting as a conduit or post box (see *Jones* v. *Great Central Railway* [1910] AC 4).
>
> In contrast, the [s.]330(6) exemption applies, to any information received by a professional legal adviser from a client or a representative of a client for the purposes of giving or obtaining legal advice. A 'representative' is not defined in POCA but the Law Society takes a wide interpretation. For example, information communicated by a client's tax adviser to the professional legal adviser may fall within the [s.]330(6) exemption when in the professional legal adviser's hands.

Since *Bowman* v. *Fels* preserves common law LPP, the defence in s.330(6) overlaps with a solicitor's obligations arising from LPP. In practice, external disclosures must not be made in circumstances where the information is privileged. Section 330(6) does, however, apply in one situation not covered by LPP, i.e. where the information is received from a 'representative' of a client. In considering whether a disclosure should be made under s.330, solicitors should first consider whether LPP applies to the information. If LPP does not apply because the information was received from a third party, they should then consider whether the third party is a representative of the client, in which case the additional defence in s.330(10) might apply.

A number of further points can be made which should assist solicitors in determining whether privilege applies.

WHAT COMMUNICATIONS ARE PRIVILEGED?

Case law can be helpful in determining what amounts to privilege as a matter of law. The Law Society's *Money Laundering Guidance* in paragraphs 4.6–4.14 (see extract in **Appendix B1**) together with their *Bowman* v. *Fels* guidance (see **Appendix B2**) provide a useful overview of relevant cases.

RELYING UPON THE PRIVILEGE DEFENCE

To rely upon LPP or the defence of privilege in s.330(6) solicitors would have to be satisfied as to two conditions:

- The information must have come to the solicitor in privileged circumstances. Not all communications made by a client are privileged, but only those communicated in connection with the giving or seeking of legal advice or in connection with or contemplation of legal proceedings.
- The information must not have been communicated or given with the intention of furthering a criminal purpose.

If the client or, in the case of the s.330(6) defence, a third party provides information which is unrelated to legal proceedings or the giving or receiving of legal advice, the first condition will not have been satisfied. However, the Law Society's guidance, relying upon the decision of the House of Lords in *Three Rivers District Council and others* v. *Governor and Company of the Bank of England* [2004] UKHL 48, suggests that s.330(10) will cover all communications between a professional legal adviser and his client (or client's representative) relating to a transaction in which the professional legal adviser has been instructed for the purpose of obtaining legal advice, notwithstanding that they do not contain advice on matters of law and construction, provided that they are directly related to the performance by the professional legal adviser of his professional duty as legal adviser of his client.

If the client provides the information with the intention of furthering a criminal purpose, the second condition will not have been satisfied. This leaves the possibility that a solicitor mistakenly believes the information received from a client is privileged but later it turns out that the client had, all along, intended to further a criminal purpose through communicating the information to the solicitor. When the Proceeds of Crime Bill was passing through the House of Lords an attempt was made to amend the privilege defence by including a defence where the information was privileged or there were reasonable grounds for believing it to be privileged. This amendment was not adopted but a statement by Lord Rooker (the Government spokesman in the House of Lords) and quoted in the Law Society's *Money Laundering Guidance* is helpful:

> The criminal law is quite clear: where a criminal offence is silent as to its mental element, the courts must read in the appropriate mental element.

> Therefore, in circumstances where a legal adviser did not know that information was not legally privileged, the courts would read in a requirement that he could not be convicted unless he did know.

The Law Society's *Money Laundering Guidance* goes on to state:

> The effect of this statement is that a solicitor therefore only commits an offence under section 330 for failure to disclose if he receives information in circumstances which he knows are not privileged.

As an alternative, the defence of reasonable excuse may be available in these circumstances (see **Paragraph 5.2.4**, and in particular the guidance from the Crown Prosecution Service). However, the Law Society advises that a solicitor is not absolved from looking at all the circumstances; he should not close his eyes to the obvious and the genuineness of his belief will be judged by the care he exercised in those circumstances.

WHO IS A PROFESSIONAL LEGAL ADVISER?

Communications between lawyers and clients will be privileged at common law if the appropriate conditions apply. The circumstances in which the information is received is what is important, not the status of the person receiving the information. Consequently, at common law communications made to non-qualified members of a solicitor's staff are capable of being privileged and, in litigation, often communications made to and by experts can be protected as privileged.

Section 330(6) of PoCA 2002 applies the defence of privilege to professional legal advisers. As originally drafted, this would appear to rule out the defence where information was passed to a non-solicitor employee or, in litigation, to an expert. This anomaly was identified by the Law Society and brought to the attention of the Government.

A SOCPA 2005 amendment contained in s.330(7B) has improved the position. This subsection (which came into force on 21 February 2006) applies where a person is employed by, or in partnership with, a professional legal adviser or a relevant professional adviser in order to provide the adviser with assistance or support. A defence will exist if the information (giving rise to the requirement to disclose) comes to that person in connection with the provision of such assistance or support and the information came to the adviser in privileged circumstances.

RELEVANT PROFESSIONAL ADVISERS

SOCPA 2005 extended the section 330(6)(*b*) and (7B) defences to 'relevant professional advisers' and this extended defence took effect on 21 February

2006. A 'relevant professional adviser' is defined in a new s.330(14) as an accountant, auditor or tax adviser who is a member of a professional body which is established for accountants, auditors or tax advisers (as the case may be) and which makes provision for testing the competence of those seeking membership and imposes and maintains professional and ethical standards.

Lack of specified training

The third defence appears in PoCA 2002, s.330(7) which provides a defence if a person:

(a) ... does not know or suspect that another is engaged in money laundering, and
(b) ... has not been provided by his employer with such training as is specified by the Secretary of State by order for the purposes of this section.

The offence in PoCA 2002, s.330 imposes a subjective and objective test of knowledge or suspicion (see **Paragraph 5.2**). This defence applies if the accused can show on a subjective or objective basis that he or she did not know or suspect another was engaged in money laundering.

In addition it is necessary to show that specified training had not been provided by the person's employer.

Employer for these purposes means someone who employs others, i.e. the defence will only apply to someone who is an employee, not a partner. Although the definition of employer and employment is extended by PoCA 2002, s.340(12) (see **Chapter 3**), this extended definition only applies to the terms where used for the purposes of a disclosure to a nominated officer.

The specified training requirements are contained in the Money Laundering Regulations 2003, SI 2003/3075. For details of these regulations, see **Chapter 9**. Regulation 3(1)(c) requires those carrying on relevant business to:

take appropriate measures so that relevant employees are –

(i)   made aware of the provisions of these regulations, Part 7 of the Proceeds of Crime Act 2002 (money laundering) and sections 18 and 21A of the Terrorism Act 2000; and
(ii) given training in how to recognise and deal with transactions which may be related to money laundering.

Clearly, it would be embarrassing for a firm (not to say unlawful under the Regulations) not to provide employees with training and for an employee to use the defence in s.330(7). Firms must therefore ensure that employees are unable to use such a defence by providing the necessary level of training. For more details of the training obligations, see **Chapter 9**.

Money laundering occurred outside the UK

A new defence (s.330(7A)) has been added by SOCPA 2005 and applies where the accused knows or believes on reasonable grounds that the money laundering is occurring in a particular country or territory outside the UK and the money laundering:

- is not unlawful under the criminal law applicable in that country or territory; and
- is not of a description prescribed by order made by the Secretary of State.

As noted above, money laundering for these purposes is defined by reference to the money laundering offences in PoCA 2002, ss.327–329. Consequently, the Proceeds of Crime Act 2002 (Money Laundering Exceptions to Overseas Conduct Defence) Order 2006, SI 2006/1070 will be the order referred to in s.330(7A).

Where the apparent money laundering occurred in the UK but involved assets derived from activities committed overseas, it will be necessary to ascertain whether the conduct in the UK was, in fact, money laundering – the defences in ss.327–329 relating to overseas criminal conduct could apply, leading to the conclusion that there was no 'engagement in money laundering' (for details of these defences, see **Chapters 2** and **3**).

However, the definition of money laundering includes the offence of acquisition, use or possession or an act which would have constituted such an offence if done in the UK (PoCA 2002, s.340(11)). Consequently, such activities if undertaken abroad could give rise to an obligation to disclose under s.330. Section 330(7A) provides a defence where the money laundering occurred outside the UK provided the two conditions noted above apply.

5.2.5 Illustrations II

The following illustrations indicate how a defence might apply to a possible charge under PoCA 2002, s.330.

Scenario 1

A solicitor is asked to provide tax advice to a client. The client admits that over the last three years he has not fully disclosed his income and capital gains to the Inland Revenue. The purpose of the solicitor's instructions is to advise on how to legitimise the situation. Does the solicitor have an obligation to disclose under PoCA 2002, s.330? He must consider:

- Does he know or suspect or have reasonable grounds for knowing or suspecting that the client is engaged in money laundering? On the basis that the client is likely to be in possession of criminal property, the answer would appear to be 'yes'.
- Did the information arise in the course of business in the regulated sector? Tax advice is within the regulated sector.

The initial conclusion therefore must be that a disclosure must be made. Do any of the defences apply? The obvious possibility is the defence of privilege under PoCA 2002, s.330(6). The following points can be made.

- The solicitor is a professional legal adviser.
- The information appears to have been provided in privileged circumstances, i.e. it was communicated by a client in connection with the giving by the solicitor of legal advice to the client.
- It does not appear that the information was communicated with the intention of furthering criminal conduct.

The conclusion is likely to be that the defence of privilege will apply and therefore there is no requirement to make the disclosure.

Scenario 2

A solicitor is acting for a client on a matrimonial dispute. In the course of giving advice relating to ancillary relief the solicitor discovers that the funds to be used in connection with a settlement may constitute the proceeds of tax evasion. Does the solicitor have a duty to report his knowledge or suspicion? He must consider:

- Does he know or suspect that another is engaged in money laundering? The answer would appear to be 'yes' since the funds are in the possession of an individual (his client or the other party to the proceedings) and his suspicion is that they are the proceeds of tax evasion.
- Did the information arise in the course of business in the regulated sector? This is more difficult. Advising on ancillary relief is unlikely to be a regulated activity under the Financial Services and Markets Act 2000. If, in the course of giving such advice, the solicitor has given advice about the tax affairs of his client, this will bring the matter within the regulated sector. Do the services involve participation in a financial or real property transaction? If real property is involved in the settlement, again this is likely to bring the matter into the regulated sector. Other financial settlement provisions could bring it within the meaning of a financial transaction. Probably the only safe course would be to assume that this is within the regulated sector.
- Would any defence arise? Since the information came into the possession of the solicitor in the course of giving legal advice or in connection with legal proceedings it would appear that it is privileged. Note, however, that privilege does not attach to a communication received from the other side. Consequently, the defence could only apply if the communication came from the client. Even if it turned out later that the client was intending to further a criminal purpose (by including the criminal proceeds in a financial settlement), the solicitor should either be able to rely upon Lord Rooker's statement in the House of Lords (no mental element – see above) or the reasonable excuse defence as per the Crown Prosecution Service's guidance (see **Paragraph 5.2.4**).

If the solicitor chooses to withdraw from the retainer, the solicitor is unlikely to be involved in a money laundering offence. Further, even if the solicitor chooses to continue to act for the client, his future actions are unlikely to amount to a money laundering offence. The Court of Appeal's decision in *Bowman* v. *Fels* excludes from the definition of 'arrangements' the consensual resolution of issues in a litigious context (see **Chapter 2**). The offences under s.327 (concealing) and s.329 (acquisition, use and possession) also benefit from the Court of Appeal's decision. Although the settlement might facilitate the acquisition, use, retention or control of criminal property no criminal liability will arise. The Law Society's view is that the effect of the judgment extends to dealing with the final division of assets in accordance with the settlement including the actual handling of the assets which are criminal property.

It should be noted, however, that according to the Court of Appeal, litigation (or consensual resolution) does not 'clean' the criminal property. If the client asks the solicitor to use the property in some future transaction (e.g. conveyancing) the *Bowman* v. *Fels* decision will not assist. At this stage a further re-examination of whether a defence (by way of an authorised disclosure) is required to act on the future transaction must be considered.

For the sake of completeness, the earlier two illustrations are set out below with comments upon possible defences:

Scenario 1

A solicitor is acting in a corporate transaction – buying shares on behalf of an individual client. In the course of acting, the solicitor becomes suspicious that funds in the possession of the client and to be used on the purchase derive from criminal activities. The solicitor decides that, because of the suspicion, she cannot continue to act for the client. She terminates the retainer, avoiding the risk of tipping off or prejudicing an investigation (see **Chapter 7**). Since the retainer has come to an end, the solicitor will not be involved in an arrangement and will not facilitate the acquisition, retention, use or control of criminal property. In order to decide whether a report must, nonetheless, be made the solicitor must consider:

- Does she know or suspect that another is engaged in money laundering? On the facts it appears that the client has in his possession criminal property. This would amount to engaging in money laundering as a result of the offence of acquisition, use or possession (PoCA 2002, s.329).
- Has the information on which her suspicion is based come into her possession as a result of business in the regulated sector? The solicitor is acting on the purchase of shares. This is likely to involve advice on the purchase of a specified investment and may consequently be an exempt regulated activity. Further, the transaction is likely to involve participation in a financial transaction. In either case, it would appear that the solicitor is acting within the regulated sector.
- Does the defence of privilege apply? Although the communication appears to be given by a client seeking legal advice, it also appears that the information is given with the intention of furthering a criminal purpose. The solicitor has decided not to act for the client and on that basis the assumption must be made that the solicitor believes that to continue to act would involve a criminal purpose.

The conclusion is that a protected disclosure must be made as soon as practicable. Failure to do so would risk prosecution under PoCA 2002, s.330.

Scenario 2
A solicitor is approached by a client for tax advice. She is asked to give advice relating to a legal tax avoidance scheme to be implemented in the UK. The advice given will not amount to an arrangement which facilitates the acquisition, retention, use or control of criminal property. However, in the course of taking instructions, the client discloses to the solicitor that he holds funds abroad derived from overseas trading which have not been disclosed to the appropriate tax authorities. The solicitor is not asked to give advice or provide any services relating to this fund. Should she, nonetheless, report her knowledge? She must consider:

- Does she know or suspect the client is engaged in money laundering? She possibly has in her possession funds which should have been disclosed to an overseas tax authority (and possibly to the UK tax authorities). Money laundering includes the offence of acquisition, use or possession or an act which would have constituted such an offence if done in the UK (PoCA 2002, s.340(11)). On the facts, there appears to be knowledge or reasonable grounds for knowledge that the client is engaged in money laundering and it does not appear that the defence in s.330(7A) relating to the money laundering occurring outside the UK would apply. Further enquiries need to be made but if, following these enquiries, there appears to be knowledge or reasonable grounds for knowledge that the client is engaged in money laundering then PoCA 2002, s.330 would appear to be a concern.
- Does any defence apply? It would appear that although the communication was made by a client to the solicitor, this communication was not made in connection with the giving of legal advice by the solicitor to the client. The solicitor is not required to give advice nor provide any legal services regarding this fund.

The conclusion is that a protected disclosure must be made as soon as practicable. Failure to do so would risk prosecution under PoCA 2002, s.330.

5.2.6 Penalty

Under section 334(2) a person guilty of an offence under PoCA 2002, s.330 is liable, on summary conviction, to imprisonment for a period of six months or to a fine not exceeding the statutory maximum or to both; on conviction on indictment, to imprisonment for a term not exceeding five years or to a fine or to both.

5.3 FAILURE TO DISCLOSE: REGULATED SECTOR (TERRORISM ACT 2000, s.21A)

5.3.1 The offence

Section 21A was inserted into the Terrorism Act 2000 by the Anti-terrorism, Crime and Security Act 2001. It states:

(1) A person commits an offence if each of the following three conditions is satisfied.

(2) The first condition is that he
   (a) knows or suspects, or
   (b) has reasonable grounds for knowing or suspecting,
   that another has committed an offence under any of sections 15 to 18.

(3) The second condition is that the information or other matter –
   (a) on which the knowledge or suspicion is based, or
   (b) which gives reasonable grounds for such knowledge or suspicion,
   came to him in the course of business in the regulated sector.

(4) The third condition is that he does not disclose the information or other matter to a constable or to a nominated officer as soon as practicable after it comes to him.

There are a number of points that can be made concerning this section and in particular the three conditions that must be satisfied before the offence is committed.

Condition 1

... knows or suspects, or ... has reasonable grounds for knowing or suspecting ...

The offence can be committed where there is an objective or subjective test of knowledge or suspicion.

... that another has committed an offence under any of sections 15 to 18 [Terrorism Act 2000]

Section 15 creates an offence of fund raising for the purpose of terrorism. It is an offence to provide money or property or invite another to provide money or property intending it to be used or having reasonable cause to suspect that it will be used for terrorism. Further, it is an offence to receive money or property intending it to be used or having reasonable cause to suspect that it will be used for terrorism.

Section 16 creates an offence of use or possession for the purpose of terrorism. It is an offence to use or possess money or property for the purpose of terrorism or intending it should be used for terrorism.

Section 17 creates an offence of funding arrangements. It is an offence for a person to enter into or to become concerned in an arrangement as a result of which money or other property is made available or is to be made available to another and there is knowledge or reasonable cause to suspect that it will or may be used for the purpose of terrorism.

Section 18 creates the offence of money laundering. Full details of this offence appear in **Chapter 3**.

Section 21A(11) provides that a person is to be taken to have committed an offence under sections 15–18 of the Terrorism Act 2000 if he has taken an action or has possession of money or property and he would have committed an offence if he had been in the UK at the time. Consequently, activities undertaken overseas can give rise to an obligation to report if such activities would have been an offence under the Terrorism Act 2000 if they had been undertaken in the UK.

Second Condition

> ... the information or other matter on which his knowledge or suspicion is based or which gives reasonable grounds for such knowledge or suspicion came to him in the course of business in the regulated sector.

The offence is limited to disclosing information which came into the possession of the solicitor in the course of business in the regulated sector. This term has been fully defined in **Paragraph 5.2.1**.

Third Condition

> ... he does not disclose the information or other matter to a constable or a nominated officer as soon as is practicable after it comes to him.

The reference to a constable includes a reference to a person authorised for the purposes of this section by the Director General of SOCA (s.21A(14)). For practical purposes this means disclosure to SOCA. A nominated officer is defined in the same way as in PoCA 2002. Consequently, the nominated officer appointed by a firm for PoCA 2002 purposes will be the nominated officer for the purposes of Terrorism Act 2000 disclosures.

5.3.2 Law Society Guidance

Section 21A(6) Terrorism Act 2000 states:

> In deciding whether a person committed an offence under this section the court must consider whether he followed any relevant guidance which was at the time concerned:
>
> (a) issued by a supervisory authority or any other appropriate body;
> (b) approved by the Treasury; and
> (c) published in a manner it approved as appropriate in its opinion to bring the guidance to the attention of persons likely to be affected by it.

A supervisory body is defined in the Terrorism Act 2000, Sched. 3A and the term includes the Law Society.

The Law Society issued guidance to the solicitors' profession (*Money Laundering Guidance: Professional Ethics*, Pilot, January 2004). Extracts from the *Money Laundering Guidance* appear in the text of this book and in **Appendix B1**. The Law Society's *Money Laundering Guidance* is described as a pilot and has not been submitted to the Treasury for approval. Consequently, section 21A(6) will not apply technically. However, as stated in the *Money Laundering Guidance*, a court 'may still take it into consideration' in deciding whether an offence has been committed.

5.3.3 Defences

There are two defences listed in section 21A(5):

(a) Reasonable excuse for not disclosing.
(b) Privilege.

Reasonable excuse

Section 21A(5)(*a*) states:

> But a person does not commit an offence under this section if
>
> (c) he has a reasonable excuse for not disclosing the information or other matter . . ..

Reasonable excuse for these purposes has yet to be defined by the courts. Solicitors should, therefore, treat this defence with care. The Law Society's *Money Laundering Guidance* suggests that solicitors always 'document the reason for not making the disclosure'.

The commentary earlier in **Paragraph 5.2.4** (reasonable excuse defence in PoCA 2002, s.330) would appear to be relevant.

Privilege

Section 21A(5)(*b*) states:

> But a person does not commit an offence under this section if . . .
>
> (b) he is a professional legal adviser and the information or other matter came to him in privileged circumstances . . ..

Circumstances will give rise to privilege if communicated or given to the professional legal adviser in three cases (s.21A(8)).

(a) The information is communicated or given to the legal adviser by a client (or by the client's representative) in connection with the giving by the legal adviser of legal advice to the client.

(b) The information is communicated or given to the legal adviser by a person (or by the person's representative) seeking legal advice from the adviser.

(c) The information is communicated or given to the legal adviser by a person in connection with legal proceedings or contemplated legal proceedings.

However, section 21A(9) makes it clear that subsection (8) does not apply to information or other matter which is communicated or given with the intention of furthering a criminal purpose.

The wording of the privilege defence is the same as the defence to PoCA 2002, s.330. The detailed commentary on that defence earlier in **Paragraph 5.2.4** would appear to apply equally to the defence in the Terrorism Act 2000.

5.3.4 Penalty

Under section 21A(12) a person guilty of an offence under the Terrorism Act 2000, s.21A is liable, on summary conviction, to imprisonment for a period of six months or to a fine not exceeding the statutory maximum or to both; on conviction on indictment, to imprisonment for a term not exceeding five years or to a fine or to both.

CHAPTER 6

Failure to disclose: nominated officers

6.1 INTRODUCTION

As noted in **Chapter 5**, there are two other offences contained in the Proceeds of Crime Act 2002 (PoCA 2002) arising from a failure to disclose knowledge or suspicion of money laundering. Both these offences are aimed at nominated officers. These are:

- Failure to disclose: nominated officers in the regulated sector (PoCA 2002, s.331)
- Failure to disclose: other nominated officers (PoCA 2002, s.332).

Both these offences have been amended by the Serious Organised Crime and Police Act 2005 and are dealt with below.

6.2 FAILURE TO DISCLOSE: NOMINATED OFFICERS IN THE REGULATED SECTOR (PoCA 2002, s.331)

6.2.1 The offence

Section 331 of PoCA 2002 states:

(1) A person nominated to receive disclosures under section 330 commits an offence if the conditions in subsections (2) to (4) are satisfied.

(2) The first condition is that he
   (a) knows or suspects, or
   (b) has reasonable grounds for knowing or suspecting,
   that another person is engaged in money laundering.

(3) The second condition is that the information or other matter
   (a) on which his knowledge or suspicion is based, or
   (b) which gives reasonable grounds for such knowledge or suspicion,
   came to him in consequence of a disclosure made under section 330.

(3A)The third condition is:
   (a) that he knows the identity of the other person mentioned in subsection (2), or the whereabouts of any of the laundered property, in consequence of a disclosure made under section 330,

(b) that that other person, or the whereabouts of any of the laundered property, can be identified from the information or other matter mentioned in subsection (3), or

(c) that he believes, or it is reasonable to expect him to believe, that the information or other matter will or may assist in identifying that other person or the whereabouts of any of the laundered property.

(4) The fourth condition is that he does not make the required disclosure to a person authorised for the purposes of this Part by the Director General of the Serious Organised Crime Agency as soon as is practicable after the information or other matter mentioned in subsection (3) comes to him.

There are a number of points that can be made concerning this section and in particular the four conditions that must be satisfied before the offence is committed.

Subsection (1)

A person nominated to receive disclosures . . .

This offence is aimed at those appointed as a nominated officer of a firm. Section 330(9) states that a disclosure to a nominated officer is a disclosure which is made to a person nominated by the alleged offender's employer to receive authorised disclosures under section 330 and is made in the course of the alleged offender's employment.

Although, in the context of a nominated officer, PoCA 2002 refers to a person's employer and a person's employment, section 340(12) provides that:

references to a person's employer include any body, association or organisation (including a voluntary organisation) in connection with whose activities the person exercises a function (whether or not for gain or reward).

The subsection goes on to state that references to employment must be construed accordingly.

As noted in **Chapter 3** it is not strictly necessary for the nominated officer to be a partner or principal in a firm of solicitors. However, in practice, the individual should be a senior member of the firm's management. Because severe penalties can be imposed upon the nominated officer for a failure to comply with his obligations under PoCA 2002, care should be taken to ensure that the nominated officer is aware of his obligations (this is particularly the case when a non-partner or principal is appointed).

. . . under section 330 . . .

Section 330 requires a disclosure of knowledge or suspicion or reasonable grounds for knowledge or suspicion of money laundering to a nominated officer or to SOCA. Details of this offence can be found in **Chapter 5.**

First Condition

> ... (a) knows or suspects, or
> (b) has reasonable grounds for knowing or suspecting ...

Like the offence contained in PoCA 2002, s.330, this offence can be committed where the nominated officer has knowledge or suspicion or reasonable grounds for knowledge or suspicion. A nominated officer can be found guilty under section 331 even if, subjectively, the nominated officer had no actual knowledge or suspicion of matters upon which the charge is based. If the nominated officer has reasonable grounds for knowledge or suspicion, that will be sufficient for the purposes of this section.

> ... that another is engaged in money laundering ...

The reference to another means that as with the offence under PoCA 2002, s.330, this offence can be committed where the nominated officer's knowledge or suspicion relates to the conduct of a client or some third party.

Further, the definition of money laundering in PoCA 2002, s.340(11) will apply to this offence. It states:

> Money laundering is an act which –
>
> (a) constitutes an offence under section 327, 328 or 329,
> (b) constitutes an attempt, conspiracy or incitement to commit an offence specified in paragraph (a),
> (c) constitutes aiding, abetting, counselling or procuring the commission of an offence specified in paragraph (a), or
> (d) would constitute an offence specified in paragraph (a), (b), or (c) if done in the United Kingdom.

For further commentary on this definition, see **Chapter 5**.

Second Condition

> ... the information or other matter
>
> (a) on which his knowledge or suspicion is based, or
> (b) which gives reasonable grounds for such knowledge or suspicion,
>
> came to him in consequence of a disclosure made under section 330.

This condition is the key to the offence. The nominated officer only commits an offence if he or she fails to act on an internal disclosure made by another member of the firm under PoCA 2002, s.330.

It is vital that all firms adopt appropriate procedures for internal disclosure of knowledge or suspicion of money laundering and that from these procedures it is clear when a formal disclosure has been made to a nominated officer. Many firms will adopt procedures which allow informal discussions to be held between members of staff and more senior members of the management team where there is concern over an individual's responsibilities under PoCA 2002. Sometimes discussions are held with the nominated officer (perhaps on a no-name basis). Where applicable, these procedures must be clearly identified as discussions and not as disclosures. Only by ensuring that procedures identify when a formal disclosure has been made can the nominated officer be sure when potential liability under section 331 arises.

This position has been strengthened by PoCA 2002, s.330(9A) (added by SOCPA 2005) which provides that there will not be a disclosure (as defined) to a nominated officer if the person communicating information to the nominated officer is a professional legal adviser and such communication (which is not intended to be a formal disclosure) is made for the purpose of obtaining advice about the need to make a formal disclosure. This subsection thus allows a full discussion with the nominated officer in order to obtain advice from the nominated officer without triggering the nominated officer's obligations under s.331.

One possibility is for firms to require all internal authorised or protected disclosures to be made formally, in writing and in an approved firm format. Under PoCA 2002, s.339 the Secretary of State may, by order, prescribe the form and manner in which a disclosure under section 330 (failure to report; regulated sector) or section 338 (authorised disclosures) must be made. Although at the time of writing, no order has been made under section 339, it is clear from the wording that the prescribed form could apply to internal disclosures as well as to external disclosures. Until such time as an order is made, it is open to the senior management in the firm to determine the form of internal disclosures. A suggested format for such internal disclosures is contained in **Appendix C3**.

The disclosure by a member of the firm to a nominated officer in accordance with PoCA 2002, s.330 does not automatically require an external disclosure by the nominated officer. It is still necessary for the nominated officer to have knowledge or suspicion or reasonable grounds for knowledge or suspicion that another person is engaged in money laundering, that the necessary information regarding the identity of the person or laundered money is held and for that information to have been received in consequence of a disclosure under section 330. It is possible that a nominated officer, on receiving the disclosure under section 330, considers its contents and comes to the conclusion that there are insufficient grounds to give rise to knowledge or suspicion (either subjectively or objectively).

Where a fee earner makes a disclosure under section 330 the nominated officer should consider the circumstances of the report. As noted previously, Regulation 7 of the Money Laundering Regulations 2003 (see **Chapter 9**) enforces this requirement when the Regulations apply. It states:

> Where a disclosure is made to a nominated officer, he must consider it in the light of any relevant information which is available to [the firm] and determine whether it gives rise to such knowledge or suspicion . . .

If, in the light of any internal consideration, the nominated officer comes to the conclusion, on both a subjective and objective basis, that there are no grounds for knowledge or suspicion, he or she will have no obligation to report to the authorities. This might apply where, for example, the fee earner is a junior member of staff or a recently joined employee. A particular aspect of a transaction may arouse his or her suspicions and consequently a disclosure under section 330 might be made to the nominated officer. On considering the report along with other information held in the firm (including past dealings with the client) the nominated officer may come to the conclusion that there are no grounds for knowledge or suspicion (either subjectively or objectively).

Finally, nominated officers should consider carefully the fact that for their obligations to have arisen under section 331 there must have been a disclosure under section 330. In other words, the disclosure under section 330 must have followed information received in the course of business in the regulated sector. The definition of the regulated sector can be found, together with commentary, in **Chapter 5.**

This is an important point. Section 332 of PoCA 2002 (see below) imposes an obligation on nominated officers to disclose to the authorities any knowledge or suspicion of money laundering received by way of an internal disclosure outside the regulated sector. For such an obligation to arise, the test of knowledge or suspicion is a subjective test. The objective test only applies to disclosures made in the regulated sector.

Third condition

(a) that he knows the identity of the other person mentioned in subsection (2), or the whereabouts of any of the laundered property, in consequence of a disclosure made under section 330,

(b) that that other person, or the whereabouts of any of the laundered property, can be identified from the information or other matter mentioned in subsection (3), or

(c) that he believes, or it is reasonable to expect him to believe, that the information or other matter will or may assist in identifying that other person or the whereabouts of any of the laundered property.

This is a similar condition to that imposed by section 330(3A). Since the required disclosure under section 330 must include the identity of the person engaged in money laundering, the whereabouts of the laundered property and any information giving rise to knowledge or suspicion (or reasonable grounds for such knowledge or suspicion) the information required by the third condition in section 331 is likely to be provided to the nominated officer.

It will still be necessary for the nominated officer to be satisfied that as a result of the disclosure or as a result of enquiries made after the disclosure, he (the nominated officer) knows or believes that he has information which will satisfy the requirements of the third condition. If this is not the case, no requirement to disclose to SOCA will arise.

Fourth Condition

. . . he does not make the required disclosure . . .

The required disclosure is disclosure of:

- the identity of the person engaged in money laundering (if such identity has been disclosed to the nominated officer as a result of a disclosure under section 330);
- the whereabouts of the laundered property (so far as such whereabouts has been disclosed as a result of the section 330 disclosure); and
- the information or other matter on which the knowledge or suspicion is based on or which gives rise to reasonable grounds received as a consequence of the section 330 disclosure.

The disclosure must be to a person authorised for the purpose by the Director General of SOCA (PoCA 2002, s.331(4)). Disclosure to SOCA in the usual way (see **Chapter 10**) will satisfy this requirement.

Any disclosure made will be treated as a protected disclosure under PoCA 2002, s.337. (For the definition of a protected disclosure see **Chapter 5**.) However, in the light of the Court of Appeal's decision in *Bowman* v. *Fels* the wording of section 337 is unlikely to override LPP. Consequently, no disclosure can be made where common law LPP applies.

. . . as soon as is practicable after the information or other matter comes to him.

Both the fourth condition and the benefit of protected disclosures require the disclosure to be made as soon as practicable after the information comes into the possession of the nominated officer. Consequently, to avoid committing the crime and to benefit from the protection of section 337 (protected disclosures), nominated officers must not delay in making their disclosures.

6.2.2 Law Society Guidance

Section 331(7) of PoCA 2002 states:

In deciding whether a person committed an offence under this section the court must consider whether he followed any relevant guidance which was at the time concerned:

(a) issued by a supervisory authority or any other appropriate body;
(b) approved by the Treasury; and
(c) published in a manner it approved as appropriate in its opinion to bring the guidance to the attention of persons likely to be affected by it.

A supervisory body is defined in PoCA 2002, Sched. 9, and the term includes the Law Society.

As noted in **Chapter 5**, the Law Society has issued guidance to the solicitors' profession (*Money Laundering Guidance: Professional Ethics*, Pilot, January 2004, as amended). Extracts from the *Money Laundering Guidance* appear in the text of this book and in **Appendix B1**. The Law Society's *Money Laundering Guidance* is described as a pilot and has not been submitted to the Treasury for approval. Consequently, section 331(7) will not apply technically. However, as stated in the *Money Laundering Guidance*, a court 'may still take it into consideration' in deciding whether an offence has been committed under section 331.

6.2.3 Defences

There are two defences available. The first is contained in section 331(6). This states: '. . . a person does not commit an offence under this section if he has a reasonable excuse for not making the required disclosure'.

As noted in **Chapter 5**, reasonable excuse for these purposes has yet to be defined by the courts. Solicitors should, therefore, treat this defence with care. The Law Society's *Money Laundering Guidance* suggests that solicitors always 'document the reason for not making the disclosure'. Note also, the circumstances where this defence might apply in relation to privileged information.

The second defence is contained in section 331(6A) and applies where the accused knows or believes on reasonable grounds that the money laundering is occurring in a particular country or territory outside the UK and the money laundering:

• is not unlawful under the criminal law applicable in that country or territory, and
• is not of a description prescribed by order made by the Secretary of State.

As noted above, money laundering for these purposes is defined by reference to the money laundering offences in PoCA 2002, ss.327–329. Consequently, the Proceeds of Crime Act 2002 (Money Laundering Exceptions to Overseas Conduct Defence) Order 2006, SI 2006/1070 will be the order referred to in section 330(7A).

The wording is the same as the wording used in the defence in section 330(7A) (see **Chapter 5**) and in many cases a fee-earner may have chosen not to make a section 330 disclosure because of this defence. However, if a section 330 disclosure has been made but the nominated officer is satisfied that the money laundering is occurring outside the UK, section 331(6A) provides a defence provided the two conditions noted above apply and no report to SOCA should be made.

However, in relation to the defence available to a charge under PoCA 2002, s.331 what is notable is the lack of a specific privilege defence. The judgment in *Bowman* v. *Fels* preserves common law LPP and where the nominated officer determines that the information on which the section 330 disclosure was made to him remains subject to LPP no disclosure will be required under section 331. In these circumstances, the privileged nature of the information should be capable of amounting to a 'reasonable excuse' for not making the disclosure (s.331(6)).

Take the following illustration from **Chapter 5**.

A solicitor is asked to provide tax advice to a client. The client admits that over the last three years he has not fully disclosed his income and capital gains to the Inland Revenue. The purpose of the solicitor's instructions is to advise on how to legitimise the situation. Does the solicitor have an obligation to disclose under PoCA 2002, s.330? He must consider:

- Does he know or suspect or have reasonable grounds for knowing or suspecting that the client is engaged in money laundering? On the basis that the client is likely to be in possession of criminal property, the answer would appear to be yes.
- Did the information arise in the course of business in the regulated sector? Tax advice is within the regulated sector.

The initial conclusion therefore must be that a disclosure must be made. Do any of the defences apply? The obvious possibility is the defence of privilege under PoCA 2002, s.330(6). The following points can be made.

- The solicitor is a professional legal adviser.
- The information appears to have been provided in privileged circumstances, i.e. it was communicated by a client in connection with the giving by the solicitor of legal advice to the client.
- It does not appear that the information was communicated with the intention of furthering criminal conduct.

The likely conclusion is that the defence of privilege will apply and therefore there is no requirement to make the disclosure.

However, the firm may have adopted a policy that members of the firm, if in any doubt, should always report any knowledge or suspicion of money laundering to the nominated officer. It is then for the nominated officer to determine whether or not a report should be made to SOCA. This is a sensible policy since it ensures that members of the firm are covered by making such internal reports and allows the nominated officer (who should be more familiar with the detail of the law) to make the final decision.

If the solicitor, in this scenario, reports his knowledge or suspicion to the nominated officer, the information remains subject to LPP and no report to SOCA can be made.

This problem has been somewhat relieved by PoCA 2002, s.330(9A) (added by SOCPA 2005) which provides that there will not be a disclosure (as defined) to a nominated officer if the person communicating information to the nominated officer is a professional legal adviser and such communication (which is not intended to be a formal disclosure) is made for the purpose of obtaining advice about the need to make a formal disclosure. This subsection thus allows a full discussion with the nominated officer concerning the question of privilege without triggering the nominated officer's obligations under section 331. If, following that discussion, the fee-earner and the nominated officer come to the conclusion that the information received by the fee-earner is privileged, then no section 330 disclosure will be made by the fee-earner and no report will need to be made by the nominated officer. If, on the other hand, the discussions lead to the conclusion that privilege does not apply, a formal report will have to be made to the nominated office by the fee-earner and, in turn, the nominated officer will have to consider his or her obligations under section 331.

However, as noted in **Chapter 5**, LPP does not extend to information received from third parties. If, in the scenario above, the information concerning the client's failure to disclose his income came not from the client but from, say, the client's accountant, common law LPP would not attach to the information. In deciding whether to make a section 330 disclosure, the fee-earner (in conjunction with the nominated officer where section 330(9A) is used) could rely upon the section 330(6) defence since this defence extends privilege for these purposes to information received from a client's representative (see **Chapter 5**). However, if despite the availability of the section 330(6) defence a formal report is made to the nominated officer, then the question of the nominated officer's obligation to disclose to SOCA under section 331 arises. The information is not subject to common law LPP and there is no specific 'privilege' defence in section 331 extending privilege to information received from a client's representative. The Law Society's *Money Laundering Guidance* suggests in these circumstances the reasonable excuse defence might apply. The guidance states: 'It is the Law Society's view that in such circumstances a nominated officer has a reasonable excuse under section 331(6) for not disclosing.'

Some firms approach this problem in a different way. Many firms will have experienced litigators as partners or employees who will be well versed in the legal concept of privilege. An alternative approach is for a firm to identify an individual or small group of individuals (the privilege committee) who have the necessary expertise and to require, as part of the firm's money laundering policy, members of the firm initially to disclose details of any knowledge or suspicion of money laundering to the privilege committee. A decision can then be made as to whether the information is or is not privileged (by reference to both common law LPP and the section 330(6) defence). If it is not privileged a formal disclosure can be made to the nominated officer, who in turn will then disclose to SOCA in accordance with PoCA 2002, s.331. If it is decided that the information is privileged, no formal internal disclosure is made and the issue of whether or not the nominated officer can rely upon the privileged circumstances in relation to his duty to disclose under section 331 becomes redundant.

An argument might be made that by disclosing information to the privilege committee, that committee is now in possession of information suggesting someone is engaged in money laundering. However, it is likely that the committee can benefit from the new section 330(7B). This applies where a person is employed by, or in partnership with, a professional legal adviser in order to provide the adviser with assistance or support. A defence will exist if the information (giving rise to the requirement to disclose) comes to that person in connection with the provision of such assistance or support and the information came to the adviser in privileged circumstances. Consequently, the members of the privilege committee should be able to rely upon the 'privilege' defence and as such they will not be required to report to the nominated officer.

Finally, if a firm chooses to rely upon section 330(9A) and/or to use a privilege committee, it should ensure that regardless of what decision is reached in discussions with the nominated officer or by the privilege committee appointed to consider the question of privilege, the fee earner who first brought his or her knowledge or suspicion to the attention of the nominated officer or committee must have the right to make a formal disclosure to the nominated officer. Only in this way will the fee earner be covered in respect of any defence (if an authorised disclosure is required) or obligation (if a duty to disclose under PoCA 2002, s.330 arises).

6.2.4 Penalty

Under section 334(2) a person guilty of an offence under PoCA 2002, s.331 is liable, on summary conviction, to imprisonment for a period of six months or to a fine not exceeding the statutory maximum or to both; on conviction on indictment, to imprisonment for a term not exceeding five years or to a fine or to both.

6.3 FAILURE TO DISCLOSE: OTHER NOMINATED OFFICERS (PoCA, s.332)

6.3.1 The offence

Section 332 of PoCA 2002 states:

(1) A person nominated to receive disclosures under section 337 or section 338 commits an offence if the conditions in subsections (2) to (4) are satisfied.

(2) The first condition is that he knows or suspects that another person is engaged in money laundering.

(3) The second condition is that the information or other matter on which his knowledge or suspicion is based came to him in consequence of a disclosure made under the applicable section.

(3A) The third condition is:

    (a) that he knows the identity of the other person mentioned in subsection (2), or the whereabouts of any of the laundered property, in consequence of a disclosure made under the applicable section,

    (b) that that other person, or the whereabouts of any of the laundered property, can be identified from the information or other matter mentioned in subsection (3), or

    (c) that he believes, or it is reasonable to expect him to believe, that the information or other matter will or may assist in identifying that other person or the whereabouts of any of the laundered property.

(4) The fourth condition is that he does not make the required disclosure to a person authorised for the purposes of this Part by the Director General of the Serious Organised Crime Agency as soon as is practicable after the information or other matter mentioned in subsection (3) comes to him.

The wording of this section is very similar to the wording in PoCA 2002, s.331. It again is a criminal offence aimed at those appointed as nominated officers and the section obliges a nominated officer to make a required disclosure if the circumstances set out in the section apply. Since the wording of this section is similar to section 331, the commentary above on the application of section 331 can be applied with the following two points of contrast.

(1) Section 332 applies where the nominated officer receives disclosure under the applicable section. Section 332(5B) defines the applicable section as PoCA 2002, s.337 or s.338; section 331 applies where there is receipt of a disclosure under PoCA 2002, s.330.

This is an important contrast. Obviously, a disclosure under PoCA 2002, s.330 will only apply if the information on which the disclosure is based has been received in the course of business in the regulated sector. Section 332 will require a nominated officer to make a required disclosure where the original information was received in the regulated or non-regulated sector.

Section 332 refers to the nominated officer receiving a disclosure under the applicable section, i.e. PoCA 2002, s.337 or s.338. Section 337 covers protected disclosures and section 338 covers authorised disclosures. Protected disclosures cover a wide range of disclosures. Section 337 provides that such a disclosure is not to be taken to be a breach of any restriction on the disclosure of information (however imposed) if three conditions are satisfied. These three conditions are:

• The information or other matter disclosed came to the person making the disclosure in the course of his trade, profession, business or employment.

- The information caused the discloser to know or suspect or gave him reasonable grounds for knowing or suspecting that another was engaged in money laundering.
- The disclosure was made to a constable, a customs officer or a nominated officer as soon as is practicable after the information or other matter comes to the discloser.

However, in the light of the Court of Appeal's decision in *Bowman* v. *Fels* the wording of section 337 is unlikely to override LPP.

Two circumstances will give rise to protected disclosures. Only the first in the list below would be relevant for the purposes of section 332. The other would be a disclosure in accordance with section 330 and thus the nominated officer's obligations would arise under section 331. In the circumstances below, the assumption is that the solicitor concerned is not involved in concealing (section 327), arrangements (section 328) or acquisition, use or possession (section 329).

- In the course of business in the non-regulated sector a solicitor knows or suspects that a person is engaged in money laundering and makes a disclosure to a nominated officer (even though there is no legal requirement for him to do so).
- In the course of business in the regulated sector a solicitor knows or suspects or has reasonable grounds for knowing or suspecting that a person is engaged in money laundering and makes a disclosure to a nominated officer.

Section 332 also applies where a disclosure is made to a nominated officer by way of a defence to a possible charge under PoCA 2002, ss.327–329 (the money laundering offences) – otherwise known as an authorised disclosure (see **Chapter 3**). Authorised disclosures will be made by way of defence regardless of whether the knowledge or suspicion of money laundering arose in the course of business in the regulated sector.

> (2) Section 332 applies where the nominated officer knows or suspects that another person is engaged in money laundering; section 331 applies where the nominated officer knows or suspects or has reasonable grounds for knowing or suspecting that another is engaged in money laundering.

The objective test, when assessing whether the nominated officer knew or suspected another was engaged in money laundering only applies to section 331. For section 332, the nominated officer must know or suspect using a subjective test only.

6.3.2 Defences

Again, there are two defences. The first appears in section 332(6). This states '. . . a person does not commit an offence under this section if he has a reasonable excuse for not making the required disclosure'.

The second defence is contained in section 332(7) and applies where the accused knows or believes on reasonable grounds that the money laundering is occurring in a particular country or territory outside the UK and the money laundering:

- is not unlawful under the criminal law applicable in that country or territory; and
- is not of a description prescribed by order made by the Secretary of State.

The commentary on both of these defences as apply to section 331 would appear to be relevant.

As with section 331, there is no specific defence of privilege. However, the judgment in *Bowman* v. *Fels* preserves common law LPP and where the nominated officer determines that the information on which the protected or authorised disclosure was made to him remains subject to LPP no disclosure will be required under section 332. In these circumstances, the privileged nature of the information should be capable of amounting to a 'reasonable excuse' for not making the disclosure (s.332(6)). However, if a protected or authorised disclosure is made to the nominated officer and the information upon which the disclosure was made came not from the client but from the client's representative, no common law LPP would exist. If the disclosure to the nominated officer was made under section 330, the privilege defence in section 330(6) could apply and no obligation under section 331 to disclose to SOCA would arise (see **Paragraph 6.2.3**). Section 332 only applies to protected disclosures which are not made under section 330 and to authorised disclosures. As such, the extended defence of privilege does not apply and unless the information is subject to LPP, where the section 332 conditions apply, the nominated officer must disclose to SOCA.

6.3.3 Penalty

Under section 334(2) a person guilty of an offence under PoCA 2002, s.332 is liable, on summary conviction, to imprisonment for a period of six months or to a fine not exceeding the statutory maximum or to both; on conviction on indictment, to imprisonment for a term not exceeding five years or to a fine or to both.

6.4 CONCLUSION

Given a combination of PoCA 2002, ss.331 and 332, it appears that a nominated officer potentially will be required to disclose to SOCA any disclosure received from other members of the firm where such a disclosure gives rise to knowledge or suspicion on the part of the nominated officer of another engaging in money laundering (reasonable grounds for knowledge or suspicion will be sufficient if the obligation arises under s.331). This will be the case regardless of whether or not the member of the firm making the initial disclosure to the nominated officer is obliged to make the disclosure (as a result of PoCA 2002, s.330) or wishes to make the disclosure by way of a defence (PoCA 2002, s.338).

Consequently, it is vital that firms are able to clearly identify when a member of the firm has made a formal report to the nominated officer. It is, perhaps, safer for firms to encourage fee earners and others with concerns to discuss these concerns informally with more senior members of the firm rather than with the nominated officer (relying on section 330(9A) where appropriate to ensure that such a discussion does not amount to a formal disclosure). This should avoid inadvertently imposing an obligation upon the nominated officer to report to SOCA where there is a defence (e.g. privilege) or where no obligation to report arises (e.g. information arising in the non-regulated sector).

CHAPTER 7

Disclosures which prejudice an investigation

7.1 INTRODUCTION

There are two offences involving disclosures which are likely to prejudice an investigation. The first is contained in PoCA 2002, s.333 and is referred to by the designation tipping off. The second offence is contained in PoCA 2002, s.342 under the heading 'offences of prejudicing investigation'. Both these offences are covered in this chapter.

The main distinction to be drawn between these two offences is the timing of the disclosure. Tipping off applies only where an authorised or protected disclosure has been made and a further disclosure is likely to prejudice an investigation. Section 342 does not require an authorised or protected disclosure to have been made.

7.2 TIPPING OFF (PoCA 2002, s.333)

7.2.1 The offence

Section 333(1) of PoCA 2002 states:

A person commits an offence if:

(a) he knows or suspects that a disclosure falling within section 337 or 338 has been made, and

(b) he makes a disclosure which is likely to prejudice any investigation which might be conducted following the disclosure referred to in paragraph (a).

For this offence to be committed, the solicitor must know or suspect that a disclosure has been made which is an authorised disclosure under PoCA 2002, s.338 or a protected disclosure under PoCA 2002, s.337. (For details of authorised disclosure, see **Chapter 3**; for details of protected disclosures, see **Chapters 5** and **6**.) It is sufficient, in both cases, that the disclosure has been made to a firm's nominated officer. It is not necessary for the initial disclosure to have been made externally to SOCA.

The second disclosure referred to in sub-paragraph (b) can be to the person referred to in the report (i.e. the person suspected of involvement in money laundering) or to any other person. Consequently, if the initial disclosure was made concerning a solicitor's client, the offence of tipping off can potentially be committed if the second disclosure (likely to prejudice an investigation) is made to:

(a) the client;
(b) any other adviser to the client (e.g. accountant, estate agent etc.);
(c) the person on the other side of the transaction;
(d) the other side's solicitor;
(e) the other side's other representative or agent.

If the initial disclosure was made concerning the other side's client, then the second disclosure (likely to prejudice an investigation) could also give rise to a criminal offence if it is made to any of those listed above including the solicitor's own innocent client.

The Law Society's *Money Laundering Guidance* states: 'It is . . . not tipping off to include a paragraph about your obligations under the money laundering legislation in your firm's standard client care letter.' For an indication of possible terms of business, see **Chapter 11**.

It is not necessary that the solicitor knows that an initial disclosure has been made under PoCA 2002, ss.337 or 338. It is sufficient that the solicitor simply suspects that such a disclosure has been made.

Consequently, it is important that the firm's internal procedures include a requirement that once an authorised or protected disclosure has been made to the firm's nominated officer, no communication should be made by any fee earner concerning that transaction matter without the consent of the nominated officer. In this way, firms can protect fee earners from inadvertently committing an offence under section 333 (tipping off).

Before making a protected or authorised disclosure to the firm's nominated officer, fee earners should be permitted to make enquiries concerning a client or other party to the transaction in order to allay any possible causes for concern. Following these enquiries, the firm can then decide whether to act for a client or continue to act for an existing client. Since these enquiries will be made before any protected or authorised disclosure, the communication made to a client or other person cannot give rise to an offence under section 333 (tipping off). However, care must be taken regarding these enquiries since it is still possible that such communications could give rise to an offence under PoCA 2002, s.342 (see **Paragraph 7.3.1**).

For the offence to be committed, it is necessary under subparagraph (2) for the accused to have made a second disclosure 'which is likely to prejudice any investigation conducted following the [protected or authorised] disclosure . . .'. Two points need to be made regarding the wording of sub-paragraph (2).

First, the subparagraph does not require the accused to know or suspect that the second disclosure is likely to prejudice any investigation. This, it would appear, is simply a question of the prosecution showing that, as a matter of fact, the second disclosure was likely to prejudice any investigation. There is a defence (see **Paragraph 7.2.2**) that the accused did not know or suspect that the disclosure was likely to be prejudicial. However, since this appears in the statute as a defence, the onus of proof will rest with the accused. If the prosecution are able to show that, as a matter of fact, the second disclosure was prejudicial, it might be difficult for the accused to adduce evidence that, on a subjective basis, he or she did not know or suspect.

Secondly, what amounts to a likelihood of prejudicing an investigation will, ultimately, be for the courts to decide. However, it is clear from the wording of the paragraph that the investigation prejudiced by the second disclosure must have been conducted following the protected or authorised disclosure. If the second disclosure is prejudicial to some other investigation, section 333 (tipping off) will not apply (but perhaps, in these circumstances, there could be a prosecution under PoCA 2002, s.342 (see **Paragraph 7.3.1**)).

7.2.2 Defences

There are three defences listed in subsection (2). This states:

> (2) But a person does not commit an offence under subsection (1) if –
>
>   (a)   he did not know or suspect that the disclosure was likely to be prejudicial as mentioned in subsection (1);
>
>   (b)   the disclosure is made in carrying out a function he has relating to the enforcement of any provision of this Act or of any other enactment relating to criminal conduct or benefit from criminal conduct;
>
>   (c)   he is a professional legal adviser and the disclosure falls within subsection (3).

The wording of subsection (2) is replicated by way of a defence to a charge under PoCA 2002, s.342 (offences of prejudicing an investigation). Since the same defences can apply to both offences, these defences are dealt with in detail after the commentary on PoCA 2002, s.342 in **Paragraph 7.3.1**.

7.2.3 Penalty

Under section 334(2), a person guilty of an offence under PoCA 2002, s.333 is liable, on summary conviction, to imprisonment for a period of six months or to a fine not exceeding the statutory maximum or to both; on conviction on indictment, to imprisonment for a term not exceeding five years or to a fine or to both.

7.3 OFFENCES OF PREJUDICING INVESTIGATION (PoCA 2002, s.342)

7.3.1 The offence

Section 342 states:

(1) This section applies if a person knows or suspects that an appropriate officer (or in Scotland) a proper person is acting (or proposing to act) in connection with a confiscation investigation, a civil recovery investigation or a money laundering investigation which is being or is about to be conducted.

(2) The person commits an offence if –

    (a) he makes a disclosure which is likely to prejudice the investigation, or

    (b) he falsifies, conceals, destroys or otherwise disposes of, or causes or permits the falsification, concealment, destruction or disposal of, documents which are relevant to the investigation.

For the purposes of money laundering, this offence therefore applies where a solicitor (or member of staff) knows or suspects that an appropriate officer is acting or proposing to act in connection with a money laundering investigation and a disclosure is made which is likely to prejudice the investigation.

The offence can be committed at any stage of a transaction, whether or not a disclosure has been made. However, unlike the tipping off offence, there is no need for a protected or authorised disclosure to have been made. It is just necessary that there is knowledge or suspicion that a money laundering investigation is or is about to be undertaken. It is, however, likely to be relevant to solicitors, for example, where they have knowledge or suspicion of money laundering (either by the client or a third person) and they are considering making a report to SOCA. In this situation, if they choose to disclose to their client, or the other side, that they intend making a report to SOCA, this disclosure could give rise to an offence under PoCA 2002, s.342.

The reference in the section to an appropriate person is a reference to (PoCA 2002, s.378):

(a) an accredited financial investigator;

(b) a constable;

(c) a customs officer.

Further, for the purposes of section 342, in relation to a money laundering investigation, a person authorised for the purposes of money laundering investigations by the Director General of SOCA is also an appropriate officer.

A money laundering investigation is an investigation into whether a person has committed a money laundering offence (PoCA 2002, s.341(4)). A money laundering offence is defined in section 340(11) and is described fully in **Chapter 5**.

Like the offence of tipping off, the prohibited disclosure can be made to:

(a) the client;
(b) any other adviser to the client (e.g. accountant, estate agent etc.);
(c) the person on the other side of the transaction;
(d) the other side's solicitor;
(e) the other side's other representative or agent; or
(f) any other person.

The offence (again like the tipping off offence) does not require knowledge or suspicion that the disclosure is likely to prejudice the investigation. It is sufficient that, as a matter of fact, the disclosure is likely to prejudice the investigation (note the defence that the accused did not know or suspect that the disclosure was likely to prejudice an investigation – for a commentary upon this defence, see **Paragraph 7.4**).

7.3.2 Defences

This topic is dealt with in **Paragraph 7.4**.

7.3.3 Penalty

Under section 342(7) a person guilty of an offence under PoCA 2002, s.342 is liable, on summary conviction, to imprisonment for a period not exceeding six months or to a fine not exceeding the statutory maximum or to both; on conviction on indictment, to imprisonment for a term not exceeding five years or to a fine or to both.

7.4 DEFENCES APPLICABLE TO PoCA 2002, ss.333 AND 342

7.4.1 Introduction

As noted above, the three defences available to a charge under section 333 (tipping off) and section 342 (offences of prejudicing an investigation) are almost identical. The defence in section 333 is to be found in subsection (2); the defence in section 342 in subsection (3). These two subsections state (the wording from section 333(2) in round brackets with the alternative wording of section 342(4) in square brackets):

a person does not commit an offence under subsection (1) [2(*a*)] if-

(a) he (did) [does] not know or suspect that the disclosure was (is) likely to (be prejudicial as mentioned in subsection (1)) [prejudice the investigation];
(b) the disclosure is made in (carrying out a function he has relating to the enforcement of any provision of this Act) [the exercise of a function under this Act] or of any other enactment relating to criminal conduct or benefit

from criminal conduct [or in compliance with a requirement imposed under or by virtue of this Act] ;
(c)   he is a professional legal adviser and the disclosure falls within subsection (3)[4].

Each defence will be dealt with in turn.

7.4.2   Section 333(2)(*a*) and section 342(3)(*a*)

. . . he (did) [does] not know or suspect that the disclosure was (is) likely to (be prejudicial as mentioned in subsection (1)) [prejudice the investigation] . . .

As noted in the commentary on the two offences, there are no requirements in the offences for the accused to know or suspect that their disclosure is likely to prejudice an investigation. The prosecution are likely to have to show that, as a matter of fact, the disclosure was likely to be prejudicial. However, by way of a defence, it is open for the accused to show, on a subjective basis, that he or she did not know or suspect that the disclosure would prejudice an investigation. The onus clearly shifts to the accused to prove the existence of evidence to support the defence. Given that the prosecution will already have adduced evidence that either the accused knew or suspected that a protected or authorised disclosure had been made or that the accused knew or suspected that a money laundering investigation was being or about to be conducted, it might be a difficult onus to discharge.

Undue reliance should not be placed upon this defence.

7.4.3   Section 333(2)(*b*) and section 342(3)(*b*)

. . . the disclosure is made in (carrying out a function he has relating to the enforcement of any provision of this Act) [the exercise of a function under this Act] or of any other enactment relating to criminal conduct or benefit from criminal conduct [or in compliance with a requirement imposed under or by virtue of this Act] . . .

This defence is clearly aimed at law enforcement officers who, in carrying out their law enforcement activities, may make disclosures which technically could be prohibited by these sections. It is unlikely to be of any benefit to solicitors.

7.4.4   Section 333(2)(*c*) and section 342(3)(*c*)

. . . he is a professional legal adviser and the disclosure falls within subsection (3)[4].

This is clearly the most relevant of the defences applicable to solicitors. Sections 333(3) and 342(4) (the wording in both subsections is identical) state:

A disclosure falls within this subsection if it is a disclosure –

(a) to (or to a representative of) a client of the professional legal adviser in connection with the giving by the adviser of legal advice to the client, or

(b) to any person in connection with legal proceedings or contemplated legal proceedings.

However, the disclosure will not fall within the terms of this defence if it is made 'with the intention of furthering a criminal purpose'. (PoCA 2002, ss.333(4) and 342(5).)

The wording of this defence is similar to the defence of privilege contained in PoCA 2002, s.330 (see **Chapter 5**). However, it should be appreciated that the defence of privilege applies to information given *to* a professional legal adviser by a client or other person. This defence applies to information given *by* a professional legal adviser to a client or other person.

Keep in mind that the defence is only necessary if a disclosure has been made in the circumstances envisaged by either section 333 or section 342; in other words, a disclosure has been made which is likely to prejudice an investigation. Despite this fact, it might be possible for a solicitor to make such a disclosure to his or her client or to a third person if the defence applies.

This defence was first considered in detail by Dame Elizabeth Butler-Sloss, P in her judgment in the case of *P* v. *P* [2003] EWHC Fam 2260.

NCIS (the appropriate authority at the time of her judgment) interpreted sections 333(4) and 342(5) very widely, taking the view that if a person intends to use the solicitor for a criminal purpose, even if this was unknown to the solicitor, the benefit of the defence in sections 333(3) and 342(4) would be lost.

In the light of the above, Dame Elizabeth Butler-Sloss had to consider the following issue (among other things): whether and in what circumstances a legal adviser, having made an authorised disclosure, is permitted to tell others of the fact that s/he has done so. In doing so, she had to consider the manner in which the 'legal professional adviser' exemption or defence applies. She quoted from the judgment of Lord Woolf CJ in *Governor and Company of the Bank of Scotland* v. *A Ltd* [2001] EWCA Civ 52; 1 WLR 754. This judgment concerned the exemption to the offence of tipping off contained in section 93D of the Criminal Justice Act 1988 – a provision in almost identical terms to PoCA 2002, s.333(2). Lord Woolf stated:

During argument there was a discussion as to the extent of the defence provided by section 93D(4). Mr Crow helpfully drew our attention to the similarity between the language of section 93D(4) and the scope of legal professional privilege. Based on this assistance, we conclude that the subsection broadly protects a legal adviser when that adviser is engaged in activities which attract legal professional privilege.

Dame Elizabeth Butler-Sloss, in her judgment, stated:

Sections 333 and 342 specifically recognise a legal adviser's duty in ordinary circumstances to make relevant disclosures, even where the result would be to tip off their client, where to do so would fall within the ambit of being in connection with the giving of legal advice or with legal proceedings actual or contemplated. . . . Sections 333(4) and 342(5) must have some purpose and the interpretation suggested by the NCIS cannot in my view be correct. The exemption is lost if a disclosure to a client is made 'with the intention of furthering a criminal purpose'. . .

But unless the requisite improper intention is there, the solicitor should be free to communicate such information to his/her client or opponent as is necessary and appropriate in connection with the giving of legal advice or acting in connection with actual or contemplated legal proceedings.

Following the *P* v. *P* judgment, NCIS issued guidance on disclosures by the legal profession. This guidance, following Dame Elizabeth Butler-Sloss's recommendation as to good practice, suggested that where a disclosure was made to NCIS by a solicitor, no reference should be made to this for a period of seven days following the disclosure.

The Court of Appeal in *Bowman* v. *Fels* considered the question of tipping off and clarified the importance of common law LPP. The judgment strengthened the position of solicitors relying upon the statutory defence and following the judgment the NCIS guidance was withdrawn. The Law Society's own guidance on *P* v. *P* (contained in Annex 3 of their pilot *Money Laundering Guidance* issued in January 2004) has also been withdrawn and replaced by guidance on *Bowman* v. *Fels* (see **Appendix B2**). In relation to the offence of tipping off and the statutory defence, the Law Society's guidance on *Bowman* v. *Fels* states:

Solicitors who are acting in transactions in circumstances where they have knowledge or suspicion of money laundering, and so are going to risk being concerned in an arrangement at some future date, have a legal duty to give legal advice to clients whom they act for, including about the possibility of their client committing money laundering offences if the transaction proceeds without 'appropriate consent' having been obtained.

In considering that legal duty solicitors will need to consider the tipping off offence in section 333, and the similar offence in 342. Both of these offences have exemptions for professional legal advisers. That exemption was explored in *P* v. *P*. The judgment in *Bowman* v. *Fels* further supports the statutory exemption: professional legal advisers have a discretion to give advice to their clients about money laundering reports, although there remains no absolute duty to do so. Depending upon the circumstances, solicitors may prefer to withdraw.

In conclusion, solicitors should be able to rely upon this defence where they are properly advising their client that they have made or will make an authorised or protected disclosure to SOCA because it is necessary and appropriate in connection with the giving of legal advice or acting in connection with actual or contemplated legal proceedings. If, however, the solicitor's intention is to make the disclosure in furtherance of criminal conduct, the defence is lost.

CHAPTER 8

Confiscation and Civil Recovery Orders

8.1 INTRODUCTION

This book has not been written to provide a comprehensive commentary on confiscation and recovery orders that can be made by the courts under their powers contained in the Proceeds of Crime Act 2002 (PoCA 2002), but to give guidance on a solicitor's obligations arising out of PoCA 2002, Part 7 (that part of PoCA 2002 dealing with money laundering). However, as noted in **Chapter 1**, a major stage in the money laundering process is layering – the attempt to hide the proceeds of crime in such a way that it cannot be traced back to the original crime.

Those involved in money laundering may frequently attempt to use the services of solicitors to achieve their aim – the layering stage. This aim is increasingly important in the light of the confiscation and civil recovery procedures set out in PoCA 2002. If a criminal is able to launder successfully his or her criminal proceeds, it is unlikely that any recovery of those proceeds will be possible. If he or she is unsuccessful in the laundering process, those proceeds may be subject to confiscation or civil recovery.

8.2 CONFISCATION ORDERS (PoCA 2002, PART 2)

Under PoCA 2002, s.6 a Crown Court is required to proceed under the section if two conditions are satisfied:

(a) a defendant is convicted of an offence before the Crown Court or is committed to the Crown Court for sentencing or with a view to a confiscation order being considered; and

(b) the prosecutor asks the court to proceed under section 6 or the court believes it is appropriate to do so.

If these two conditions are satisfied, the court must decide whether the defendant has a criminal lifestyle and, if so, whether he has benefited from general criminal conduct. Alternatively, if the court decides that the defendant does not have a criminal lifestyle, it must still consider whether he has benefited from his particular criminal conduct.

A criminal lifestyle for these purposes is defined as arising from a conviction of an offence which constitutes conduct forming part of a course of criminal activity, committed over a period of at least six months and which is listed in PoCA 2002, Sched.2 (serious crimes including specified offences relating to drug trafficking, money laundering, terrorism, people trafficking, arms trafficking, counterfeiting and blackmail). Conduct will form part of a course of criminal activity if in the proceedings in which he was convicted he was convicted of three or more other offences from which he has benefited or in the period of six years ending with the day when the proceedings started, he was convicted on at least two separate occasions of offences from which he has benefited. The defendant must have obtained a benefit of not less than £5,000.

There is a distinction drawn between general criminal conduct arising from a criminal lifestyle and particular criminal conduct arising from the conduct upon which the specific conviction was based. This distinction is relevant to the assumptions the court can make and the amount recoverable under a confiscation order.

Once a court has decided that a defendant has benefited from either general or particular criminal conduct (the decision is taken by the court on a balance of probabilities – PoCA 2002, s.6(7)) it must decide upon the recoverable amount and make a confiscation order requiring the defendant to pay that amount. (There is a discretion where the court believes that any victim of the criminal conduct has started or intends to start proceedings against the defendant to recover in respect of any loss, injury or damage sustained.)

The amount of the recoverable sum is generally the amount equal to the defendant's benefit from the conduct concerned. If the defendant has a criminal lifestyle, the conduct concerned will be his or her general criminal conduct and the recoverable sum will be calculated by reference to all his or her criminal conduct, whether the conduct occurred before or after the passing of PoCA 2002 or whether the property was obtained before or after the passing of PoCA 2002. If the defendant does not have a criminal lifestyle, the conduct concerned will be his or her particular criminal conduct which consists of the conduct constituting the offences for which he or she was convicted (at the same proceedings) and any other offences which the court will be taking into account in sentencing.

If the court decides that a defendant has a criminal lifestyle, it must make four assumptions in deciding whether the defendant has benefited from his or her general criminal conduct and in deciding the benefit from this conduct. The four assumptions are:

- Any property transferred to him at any time after the relevant day (generally the first day of the period of six years ending with the date when proceedings were started against him or her) was as a result of his or her general criminal conduct.

- Any property held by the defendant at any time after the date of conviction was obtained as a result of his or her general criminal conduct.
- Any expenditure incurred by the defendant after the relevant day was from property obtained by him or her as a result of his or her general criminal conduct.
- In any valuation of property obtained (or assumed to be obtained) by the defendant, he obtained it free of any other interests.

The court should only ignore these assumptions if either one or more of the assumptions is shown to be incorrect or there would be a serious risk of injustice if the assumption were made.

SOCPA 2005 s.97 gives the Secretary of State power by order to make provision to allow magistrates' courts to make confiscation orders under PoCA 2002, Part 2. The power for magistrates' courts to make a confiscation order must be restricted to the cases where the amount does not exceed £10,000. Orders above this amount will only be able to be made in the Crown Court.

8.3   CIVIL RECOVERY ORDERS (PoCA 2002, PART 5)

In order to make a confiscation order, the criminal must have been convicted of a criminal offence (either in proceedings before the Crown Court or where there has been a committal to the Crown Court for sentencing or a committal with a view to a confiscation order being considered). In all cases, therefore, the court must have been satisfied that, beyond reasonable doubt, the individual had been involved in criminal conduct.

Civil Recovery Orders are new to the UK, and were introduced as a result of PoCA 2002. They can be distinguished from confiscation orders on the basis that there is no need for a criminal conviction. These orders allow the recovery of property obtained through unlawful conduct and since the application is made in civil proceedings, the test of whether or not conduct is unlawful is on the balance of probabilities.

Section 240 of PoCA 2002 provides that the general purpose of these provisions is to allow the enforcement authority (the Assets Recovery Agency) to recover in civil proceedings before the High Court property which is, or represents, property obtained through unlawful conduct. Further, PoCA 2002, Part 5 allows cash which is, or represents property obtained through unlawful conduct, to be forfeited in civil proceedings before a magistrates' court. In January 2007, the Home Office announced that the Assets Recovery Agency is to be merged into SOCA in 2008.

In both cases it is necessary for there to be unlawful conduct and this is defined in PoCA 2002, s.241 as conduct which is 'unlawful under the criminal law' or conduct which occurs outside the UK and is unlawful under the criminal law of that country and would be unlawful under the criminal law of the UK if it occurred in the UK.

It is for the court to decide on a balance of probabilities whether it is proved that unlawful conduct has occurred (s.241(3)).

8.3.1 Civil recovery in the High Court

Proceedings may be taken by the Assets Recovery Agency (the Agency) (to merge with SOCA in 2008) in the High Court against any person who holds recoverable property (PoCA 2002, s.243(1)). A claim form must be served on the respondent and any other person who holds associated property which the Agency wishes to be subject to a recovery order (PoCA 2002, s.243(2)).

Associated property means (PoCA 2002, s.245) property which is not itself recoverable property but includes:

- Any interest in recoverable property.
- Any other interest in the property in which recoverable property subsists.
- If the recoverable property is a tenancy in common, the tenancy of the other tenant.
- If the recoverable property is part of a larger property, but not a separate part, the remainder of that property.

An interim receiving order can be applied for (either before or after starting the proceedings for a recovery order). This will be an order for the detention, custody or preservation of property and the appointment of an interim receiver (PoCA 2002, s.246). The interim receiver is required to take such steps the court considers necessary to secure the detention, custody or preservation of the property and to establish whether or not the property to which the order applies is recoverable or associated property (PoCA 2002, s.247). Section 98 of SOCPA 2005 amends PoCA 2002, s.246 allowing the Director of the Agency to apply for a property seizing order as an alternative to an order appointing a receiver.

The interim receiving order must prohibit the person to whose property the order applies from dealing with the property, subject to the court making an exclusion to enable the person to meet reasonable living expenses or to carry on any trade, business, profession or occupation (PoCA 2002, s.252). Further, under PoCA 2002, s.253, whilst the order has effect the court may stay any action of legal process in respect of the property. As a result of SOCPA 2005, s.98 defendants who are subject to civil proceedings are able to have access to their frozen assets in order to fund the cost of their legal proceedings.

Where a court is satisfied that property is recoverable, under PoCA 2002, s.266, it must make a recovery order vesting the title to the property in the trustee for civil recovery (a person appointed by the court and nominated by the Agency). The functions of the trustee under PoCA 2002, s.267 are to secure the detention, custody or preservation of the property and, in the case of property which is not money, to realise the value of the property for the benefit of the Agency.

8.3.2 Recovery of cash in summary proceedings

For the purposes of these provisions, cash means:

- notes and coins in any money;
- postal orders;
- cheques of any kind, including travellers' cheques;
- bankers' drafts;
- bearer bonds and bearer shares.

On the application of HM Revenue and Customs (HMRC) or a constable, a magistrates' court may make an order for forfeiture of cash or any part of it if it is satisfied that the cash or part is recoverable property or is intended by any person for use in unlawful conduct (PoCA 2002, s.298) and the cash has been detained under PoCA 2002, s.295 (detention of seized cash – see below). Subject to any appeal, the cash forfeited is paid to the Consolidated Fund (PoCA 2002, s.300).

An officer of HMRC or constable who is lawfully on any premises and who has reasonable grounds for suspecting that there is cash on the premises which is recoverable property or is intended by any person for use in unlawful conduct may search for cash there (PoCA 2002, s.289(1)). Equally, an officer of HMRC or constable who has reasonable grounds for suspecting that a person is carrying cash which is recoverable property or is intended by any person for use in unlawful conduct may require the person to permit a search of any article in his or her possession or permit a search of his or her person and may detain the person for as long as necessary (s.289(2) and (3)). Such searches may only be exercised with the prior approval of a judicial officer (or if that is not practicable) a senior officer (a police officer of at least the rank of inspector or an HMRC officer of equivalent seniority).

Following the search the officer of HMRC or constable may seize the cash (PoCA 2002, s.294) and whilst there are still reasonable grounds for suspicion that the cash is recoverable property or is intended by any person for use in unlawful conduct, may detain the cash for a period of 48 hours (PoCA 2002, s.295). This period may be extended by order made by a magistrates' court, initially for a period of three months and on a second application for extension for a further period of two years. The magistrates must be satisfied that the continued detention of the cash is justified while its derivation is being investigated or consideration is given to bringing proceedings against a person for an offence with which the cash is related or where proceedings have started but have not yet been concluded (PoCA 2002, s.295).

Thereafter, on the application of HMRC or a constable, a magistrates' court may make an order for forfeiture of cash or any part of it if it is satisfied that the cash or part is recoverable property or is intended by any person for use in unlawful conduct (PoCA 2002, s.298).

These provisions are subject to a condition that the cash is not less than the minimum amount. This amount is determined by order of the Secretary of State (PoCA 2002, s.303). The current minimum amount is £5,000 (the Proceeds of Crime Act 2002 (Recovery of Cash in Summary Proceedings: Minimum Amount) Order 2004, SI 2004/420).

8.4 PRODUCTION ORDERS (PoCA 2002, PART 8)

In order to carry out a confiscation, civil recovery or money laundering investigation the authorities may seek a production order requiring the production of material to an appropriate officer or requiring that the appropriate officer be given access to the material. Solicitors' clients might be the subject of an application for such an order and/or solicitors might find themselves the subject of an application.

Confiscation investigations, civil recovery investigations and money laundering investigations are defined in PoCA 2002, s.341. Confiscation investigations are investigations into whether a person has benefited from his or her criminal conduct, or investigations into the extent or whereabouts of his or her benefit from his criminal conduct. Civil recovery investigations are investigations into whether property is recoverable property or associated property; who holds the property; or its extent or whereabouts. A money laundering investigation is an investigation into whether a person has committed a money laundering offence.

An appropriate person must make the application. An appropriate person is defined as a constable or an officer of HMRC, if the warrant is sought for the purposes of a confiscation investigation or a money laundering investigation or a named member of the staff of the Agency, if the warrant is sought for the purposes of a civil recovery investigation. The application is made to a judge entitled to exercise the jurisdiction of the Crown Court (where it is a confiscation or money laundering officer) or a judge of the High Court (if it is a civil recovery investigation).

The production order, if made, will specify the period within which the order must be complied with and this period will be a period of seven days from the date of the order unless the judge is satisfied that a shorter or longer period is appropriate.

Section 346 of PoCA 2002 sets out the requirements for making a production order. The judge must be satisfied:

- That there are reasonable grounds for suspecting a person has benefited from criminal conduct (confiscation investigation) or property is recoverable or associated property (civil recovery investigation) or that a money laundering offence has been committed (money laundering investigation).
- That there are reasonable grounds for believing that the person specified is in possession or control of the specified material.
- That there are reasonable grounds for believing that the specified material is likely to be of substantial value to the investigation.
- That there are reasonable grounds for believing that it is in the public interest for the material to be produced or for access to the material to be granted.

If an order is made requiring an appropriate officer to be given access to material on any premises, an order can also be made granting entry in relation to the premises (PoCA 2002, s.347).

One important restriction on the granting of a production order and of particular relevance to solicitors and their clients is contained in section 348(1). This states: 'A production order does not require a person to produce, or give access, to privileged material.'

Subsection (2) defines privileged material as 'any material which the person would be entitled to refuse to produce on the grounds of legal professional privilege in proceedings in the High Court'.

However, solicitors must bear in mind the decision of the House of Lords in R v. *Central Criminal Court ex p. Francis* v. *Francis* [1989] 1 AC 346. Items are not to be considered as privileged where they are held with the intention of furthering a criminal purpose. The House of Lords held that the intention did not have to be the solicitor's intention. Provided someone had the intention to further a criminal purpose, items held would not be privileged.

CHAPTER 9

Money Laundering Regulations 2003

9.1 INTRODUCTION

The Money Laundering Regulations 2003, SI 2003/3075 came into force on 1 March 2004 and implement the Second European Money Laundering Directive. The full text of the Regulations can be found in **Appendix A3**. When they apply, they impose a requirement that solicitors establish procedures relating to:

(a) training;
(b) client identification;
(c) record keeping; and
(d) reporting procedures;

The Regulations are part of the criminal law. Failure to comply is a criminal offence.

Whilst the Proceeds of Crime Act 2002 (PoCA 2002) and the Terrorism Act 2000 apply to all firms of solicitors (there are few, if any, areas of a solicitor's practice which escape the risk of involvement in money laundering), the Money Laundering Regulations only apply to that part of a solicitor's practice which falls within the definition of 'relevant business'. Consequently, in theory, parts of a solicitor's practice may well fall outside the requirements of the Regulations. However, the Law Society's *Money Laundering Guidance* recommends solicitors to err on the side of caution. It states:

> . . . the scope of the ML Regulations 2003 is as yet untested in the courts, and there is some uncertainty as to their application in some cases. This lack of clarity means it would be wise to comply with the ML Regulations 2003 on a broad, rather than a narrow basis as a form of risk management within your firm. Solicitors may also wish to apply the requirements of the ML Regulations 2003 across the whole scope of their activities in order to protect against committing an offence under the statutory criminal law. This law applies even if the particular activities are not 'relevant business' and, therefore, are not covered by the ML Regulations 2003.

Firms of solicitors which are authorised to conduct mainstream regulated activities by the Financial Services Authority (FSA) are subject to the FSA's

Handbook. Only a small minority of firms are so authorised and this book does not cover details of the FSA's Handbook. Guidance for the UK financial sector has been issued by the Joint Money Laundering Steering Group (March 2006).

9.2 RELEVANT BUSINESS

The Money Laundering Regulations 2003 only apply to that part of a solicitor's practice which falls within the definition of 'relevant business'. Relevant business is defined in regulation 2(2) as meaning:

(a) the regulated activity of –
   (i) accepting deposits;
   (ii) effecting or carrying out contracts of long-term insurance when carried on by a person who has received official authorisation pursuant to Article 4 or 51 of the Life Assurance Consolidation Directive;
   (iii) dealing in investments as principal or as agent;
   (iv) arranging deals in investments;
   (v) managing investments;
   (vi) safeguarding and administering investments;
   (vii) sending dematerialised instructions;
   (viii) establishing (and taking other steps in relation to) collective investment schemes;
   (ix) advising on investments; or
   (x) issuing electronic money;

(b) the activities of the National Savings Bank;

(c) any activity carried on for the purpose of raising money authorised to be raised under the National Loans Act 1968 under the auspices of the Director of Savings;

(d) the business of operating a bureau de change, transmitting money (or any representation of monetary value) by any means or cashing cheques which are made payable to customers;

(e) any of the activities in points 1 to 12 or 14 of Annex 1 to the Banking Consolidation Directive (which activities are, for convenience, set out in Schedule 1 to these Regulations) when carried on by way of business, ignoring an activity falling within any of sub-paragraphs (a) to (d);

(f) estate agency work;

(g) operating a casino by way of business;

(h) the activities of a person appointed to act as an insolvency practitioner within the meaning of section 388 of the Insolvency Act 1986 or Article 3 of the Insolvency (Northern Ireland) Order 1989;

(i) the provision by way of business of advice about the tax affairs of another person by a body corporate or unincorporate or, in the case of a sole practitioner, by an individual;

(j) the provision by way of business of accountancy services by a body corporate or unincorporate or, in the case of a sole practitioner, by an individual;

(k) the provision by way of business of audit services by a person who is eligible for appointment as a company auditor under section 25 of the

Companies Act 1989 or Article 28 of the Companies (Northern Ireland) Order 1990;

(l) the provision by way of business of legal services by a body corporate or unincorporate or, in the case of a sole practitioner, by an individual and which involves participation in a financial or real property transaction (whether by assisting in the planning or execution of any such transaction or otherwise by acting for, or on behalf of, a client in any such transaction);

(m) the provision by way of business of services in relation to the formation, operation or management of a company or a trust; or

(n) the activity of dealing in goods of any description by way of business (including dealing as an auctioneer) whenever a transaction involves accepting a total cash payment of 15,000 euro or more.

The wording of regulation 2(2) is nearly identical to the wording in PoCA 2002, Sched.9 (the definition of the regulated sector) and solicitors should accept that if they are acting within the regulated sector, they will be subject to the Money Laundering Regulations 2003.

The definition of the regulated sector is covered in **Chapter 5.** For the sake of completeness, set out below are the most common activities within a solicitor's practice which will fall within the definition of relevant business.

(a) regulated activities

Section 22 of the Financial Services and Markets Act 2000 provides:

(1) An activity is a regulated activity for the purposes of this Act if it is an activity of a specified kind which is carried on by way of business and –

(a) relates to an investment of a specified kind . . ..

(5) 'Specified' means specified in an order made by the Treasury.

The most relevant order made by the Treasury is the Financial Services and Markets Act 2000 (Regulated Activities) Order 2001, SI 2001/544 (RAO). This Order lists both the activities of a specified kind and the investments of a specified kind.

The most common specified investments from a solicitor's point of view are:

- Shares in the share capital of any company (art.76 RAO).
- Instruments creating or acknowledging indebtedness, including debentures, loan stock, bonds and certificates of deposit (art.77).
- Government securities, including British Government Stocks (gilts) (art.78).
- Units in collective investment schemes, including unit trusts and shares in open-ended investment companies (art.81).
- Insurance contracts, including endowment policies, pension policies, annuities and insurance bonds.

Consequently, activities in a solicitor's corporate department (acquisitions, corporate finance) are likely to involve shares, debentures or corporate bonds. Activities in private client work (estate and trust administration) could involve the full range of specified investments. Settlements in matrimonial work could involve some or all of the specified investments.

Of the 10 activities listed in regulation 2(2)(*a*), the following involving specified investments are likely to be most relevant to solicitors:

- Dealing in investments as agent. Dealing is defined as buying, selling, subscribing or underwriting certain specified investments. A solicitor would be dealing where investments were being bought or sold as agent for a client.
- Arranging deals in investments. This would catch those circumstances where a solicitor made arrangements for a client to buy, sell, subscribe or underwrite certain specified investments.
- Discretionary management of investments. Solicitors who are sole trustees or personal representatives or trustees or personal representatives jointly only with others from their own firm will be managing if the trust fund or estate includes certain specified investments.
- Safeguarding and administration. Solicitors who hold documents of title to specified investments in safe custody and who, at the same time, are involved in administration activities relating to those investments will be undertaking this activity. Typically, estate and trust work will give rise to this activity.
- Advising on investments. Giving advice on the merits of buying, selling, subscribing for or underwriting certain specified investments will be caught by this activity.

Section 19 of the Financial Services and Markets Act 2000 provides:

(1) No person may carry on a regulated activity in the United Kingdom, or purport to do so, unless he is –

(a) an authorised person; or
(b) an exempt person.

Most solicitors are not authorised persons (i.e. they have not sought nor obtained authorisation from the FSA). They are, however, able to undertake many activities which fall within the definition of regulated activities without authorisation as a result of the exemption for professionals provided in Part XX of the Financial Services and Markets Act 2000.

It must be understood that the definition of relevant business in the Money Laundering Regulations 2003 does not require the regulated activity to be undertaken with authorisation from the FSA. An exempt regulated activity will fall within the definition of relevant business.

The other relevant activities that will bring a solicitor within the meaning of relevant business are as follows.

(f)   estate agency work . . ..

Solicitors who provide estate agency services will, in respect of those services, be carrying on relevant business.

(h)   the activities of a person appointed to act as an insolvency practitioner within the meaning of section 388 of the Insolvency Act 1986 . . .

Solicitors who are appointed as insolvency practitioners will be carrying on relevant business. Solicitors who act for external insolvency practitioners or who act in insolvency matters without an appointment as an insolvency practitioner will not be caught under this head. However, depending upon the type of work, they may be caught under paragraph (l) below.

(i)   the provision by way of business of advice about the tax affairs of another person by a body corporate or unincorporate, or in the case of a sole practitioner, by an individual . . .

Solicitors giving tax advice will be undertaking relevant business. It appears that any tax advice will be relevant business. For example, whilst activities relating to will drafting would not be relevant business, if such activities were combined with inheritance tax planning advice, this would be likely to be sufficient for these purposes.

(l)   the provision by way of business of legal services by a body corporate or unincorporate or, in the case of a sole practitioner, by an individual and which involves the participation in a financial or real property transaction (whether by assisting in the planning or execution of any transaction or otherwise by acting for, or on behalf of, a client in any transaction) . . ..

This paragraph is clearly aimed at extending relevant business to many activities undertaken by solicitors. The reference to 'financial or real property transactions' has the effect of bringing all conveyancing transactions within the scope of relevant business.

The *Money Laundering Guidance* issued by the Law Society indicates that the interpretation of participation in a financial transaction is less clear. The *Money Laundering Guidance* seeks clarity from the text of the Second European Money Laundering Directive (on which this definition is based). The Directive provides that the following should be included:

Independent legal professionals, when they participate, whether:

(1)   by assisting in the planning or execution of transactions for their client concerning the:

- buying and selling of real property or business entities;
- managing of client money, securities or other assets;
- opening or management of bank, savings or securities accounts;
- organisation of contributions necessary for the creation, operation or management of companies; or
- creation, operation or management of trusts, companies or similar structures; or

(2) by acting on behalf of and for their client in any financial or real estate transaction.

The Law Society's *Money Laundering Guidance* indicates that managing client money is narrower than simply handling client money. Simply operating a client account is not intended to be caught within the meaning of relevant business but holding money or receiving money on behalf of clients as part of a transaction will be caught.

The Treasury has also confirmed that the following (by themselves) would not generally be viewed as participation in financial transactions:

- A payment on account of costs to a solicitor or payment of a solicitor's bill (because the solicitor is not participating in a financial transaction on behalf of the client).
- Legal advice (assuming such advice does not fall within one or more of the other categories defined as within the regulated sector).
- Participation in litigation (on the basis that litigation is not a transaction).
- Will writing (unless linked with, for example, tax advice).
- Publicly funded work.

(m) the provision by way of business of services in relation to the formation, operation or management of a company or a trust.

This paragraph clearly covers activities undertaken by solicitors relating to the formation of a company or the administration of a trust fund. There is some doubt over the reference to business services relating to the 'operation or management of a company'. The Treasury has indicated that this phrase should not be interpreted to include any services which assist in the management or operation of a company.

In a letter written to the British Bankers' Association, the Treasury made the following points:

Regulation (m) was intended to cover those who form, operate or manage companies (or trusts) when this activity is provided as a service by way of business. This addresses, among other things, the problem of 'front' or shell companies, which have been recognised as having been used in most complex money laundering operations . . .

It has been argued that regulation (m) covers anyone providing any service by way of business to a company which happens to assist the management or operation of that company e.g. cleaners, advertising agencies or management consultants. Whereas the interpretation of the Regulations is ultimately a matter for the courts, such a wide interpretation of regulation (m) was not our intention and, we believe, is not warranted by the language of regulation (m).

Many services offered by solicitors to companies and trust funds will involve financial transactions. Some will be exempt regulated activities within the meaning of the Financial Services and Markets Act 2002. As such, these activities will be relevant business regardless of regulation (m). Since the Treasury statement indicates that the interpretation is ultimately a matter for the courts, solicitors should, perhaps, err on the side of caution and assume activities relating to company clients and trust clients are likely to be relevant business.

9.3 SYSTEMS AND TRAINING ETC. TO PREVENT MONEY LAUNDERING

Regulation 3(1) of the Money Laundering Regulations 2003 states:

Every person must in the course of relevant business carried on by him in the United Kingdom –

(a) comply with the requirements of regulations 4 (identification procedures), 6 (record-keeping procedures) and 7 (internal reporting procedures);

(b) establish such other procedures of internal control and communication as may be appropriate for the purposes of forestalling and preventing money laundering; and

(c) take appropriate measures so that relevant employees are –

    (i) made aware of the provisions of these Regulations, Part 7 of the Proceeds of Crime Act 2002 (money laundering) and sections 18 and 21A of the Terrorism Act 2000; and

    (ii) given training in how to recognise and deal with transactions which may be related to money laundering.

The requirements of regulations 4 (identification procedures), 6 (record-keeping procedures) and 7 (internal reporting procedures) are dealt with in **Paragraph 9.4** et seq.

The other procedures required by regulation 3(1)(*b*) might include those procedures identified earlier in this book, relating to the money laundering substantive law. For example, ensuring that a nominated officer is appointed; the establishment of procedures of internal control and communication; systems for disciplining those who ignore the procedures; and considering whether it is appropriate to appoint a privilege committee to determine whether the defence of privilege might apply in given circumstances. Further information can be found in Chapter 6 of the Law Society's *Money Laundering Guidance*.

Regulation 3(1)(*c*) requires firms to take appropriate measures to ensure relevant employees are trained in relation to the substantive law and in how to recognise and deal with transactions which may be related to money laundering.

There is no specification of what amounts to training for these purposes. Certainly, it does not require firms to provide face-to-face training with a tutor. The training obligations can be complied with by handouts, manuals, video and computer and web-based training. It is, however, important that firms design their training for all relevant staff and that the training is at an appropriate level for individual members of staff.

Fee earners (particularly those involved in higher risk areas of practice) will require full training on the substantive law, the firm's procedures and on recognition of transactions which may be related to money laundering. This training should be updated at frequent intervals.

Members of the accounts staff should also receive training since they will be handling client and other money. Secretaries and receptionists should receive training if they are likely to be in contact with clients. For example, if a fee earner makes an authorised disclosure to the firm's nominated officer as a result of suspicious circumstances and the firm's nominated officer then discloses to SOCA, the seven-working day period will start to run during which limited work only on the relevant file can be undertaken (for details, see **Chapter 4**). During that seven-day period, it might not be possible to explain to the client why nothing is being done on the file subject to the risk of tipping off unless the legal professional adviser defence applies (see **Chapter 7**). Consequently, a fee earner may ask his or her secretary to field calls from the client or other party – the client might even turn up at reception to ascertain what is going on. In both cases the secretary and/or receptionist needs to be aware of the risks in communicating with the client or other side.

New members of staff should receive induction training relating to the firm's procedures. Even if new members of staff have received money laundering training at their previous employers, each firm will have its own internal procedures and it is vital for all members of staff to be aware of these procedures.

The obligation to comply with the procedures laid down in the Money Laundering Regulations 2003 is imposed upon the partners, in a partnership or the sole practitioner in a sole practice or an officer in an incorporated practice. It is, therefore, important that the firm maintains a record of compliance with the training obligations. An attendance sheet should be kept of all face-to-face training. Where other methods of training are used, appropriate records should also be kept.

Although the Regulations came into force on 1 March 2004, the Treasury has made it clear that these obligations should be interpreted with common sense. It recognises that all relevant employees would not be fully trained by 1 March 2004. However, if necessary, firms should be able to demonstrate that they have implemented an on-going training programme satisfying the minimum requirements of regulation 3(1).

9.4   IDENTIFICATION PROCEDURES

9.4.1   The required procedures: regulation 4

Regulation 4 imposes obligations relating to identification of clients and others. It states:

(1) In this regulation and in regulations 5 to 7 –
    (a) 'A' means a person who carries on relevant business in the United Kingdom; and
    (b) 'B' means an applicant for business.

(2) This regulation applies if –
    (a) A and B form, or agree to form, a business relationship;
    (b) in respect of any one-off transaction –
        (i) A knows or suspects that the transaction involves money laundering; or
        (ii) payment of 15,000 euro or more is to be made by or to B; or
    (c) in respect of two or more one-off transactions, it appears to A (whether at the outset or subsequently) that the transactions are linked and involve, in total, the payment of 15,000 euro or more by or to B.

(3) A must maintain identification procedures which –
    (a) require that as soon as is reasonably practicable after contact is first made between A and B –
        (i) B must produce satisfactory evidence of his identity; or
        (ii) such measures specified in the procedures must be taken in order to produce satisfactory evidence of B's identity;
    (b) take into account the greater potential for money laundering which arises when B is not physically present when being identified;
    (c) require that where satisfactory evidence of identity is not obtained, the business relationship or one-off transaction must not proceed any further; and
    (d) require that where B acts or appears to act for another person, reasonable measures must be taken for the purpose of establishing the identity of that person.

This is probably the most onerous of the obligations applicable to solicitors who undertake relevant business. It requires firms to have in place procedures which ensure that satisfactory evidence of client identification is obtained for certain clients where relevant business is undertaken.

A number of points can be made regarding the wording of this regulation.

'A' means a person who carries on relevant business in the United Kingdom; and 'B' means an applicant for business.

Relevant business has been defined above. A will be the firm of solicitors. B will be the client – an applicant for business. This term is defined in regulation 2(1) as 'a person seeking to form a business relationship, or carry out a one-off transaction, with another person acting in the course of relevant business carried on by that other person in the United Kingdom'. Business relationship and one-off transaction are defined below.

> This regulation applies if – (a) A and B form, or agree to form, a business relationship . . .

Identification procedures will be necessary if the solicitor and client form (or agree to form) a business relationship. This term is defined in regulation 2(1) as meaning:

> any arrangement the purpose of which is to facilitate the carrying out of transactions on a frequent, habitual or regular basis where the total amount of any payments to be made by any person to any other in the course of the arrangement is not known or capable of being ascertained at the outset.

This term suggests an on-going relationship between the solicitor and the client where the total amount paid or to be paid cannot be ascertained. Examples might include trust administration or acting on an on-going retainer for a company or individual conducting all legal work as and when it arises.

> This regulation applies if – (b) in respect of any one-off transaction –
>
> (i) A knows or suspects that the transaction involves money laundering; or (ii) payment of 15,000 euro or more is to be made by or to B . . .

If the relationship between the solicitor and client is not a business relationship (e.g. the amount involved in the transaction can be ascertained at the beginning of the transaction) it will be a one-off transaction. This is defined in regulation 2(1) as meaning 'any transaction other than one carried out in the course of an existing business relationship'.

However, where there is a one-off transaction, the requirement to obtain identification only applies if the solicitor knows or suspects the transaction involves money laundering or the amount involved is €15,000 or more. The current rate of exchange (as of December 2006) gives a value in sterling of £10,121. Under the old Regulations (the Money Laundering Regulations 1993) there was a similar definition. However, the rate of exchange for euros was set once a year. Under the 2003 Regulations no such annual exchange rate is provided for. It is likely that the courts will apply the rate applicable when the transaction is entered into.

This regulation applies if – (c) in respect of two or more one-off transactions, it appears to A (whether at the outset or subsequently) that the transactions are linked and involve, in total, the payment of 15,000 euro or more by or to B.

Firms cannot avoid the identification procedures by acting for a client on one or more matters where, individually, the matters involve sums less than €15,000 but collectively the sum involved is €15,000 or more if the matters are linked. The Regulations do not give a definition of 'linked' for these purposes. The Law Society's *Money Laundering Guidance* states:

Identification procedures must be undertaken for linked transactions that together equal or exceed the €15,000 exemption limit. Whether transactions are linked depends upon any obvious connection rather than an arbitrary time limit. However, for lower risk work concerning transactions between which there is no obvious link, a three month period may be a useful yardstick.

A must maintain identification procedures which – (a) require that as soon as is reasonably practicable after contact is first made between A and B . . ..

If the Regulations require identification evidence to be obtained, it must be obtained as soon as is reasonably practicable after the first contact between the solicitor and the client. The Regulations do not define what is reasonably practicable. However, the 1993 Regulations contained a similar requirement – requiring evidence of identity to be obtained as soon as is reasonably practicable after contact is first made. These Regulations provided supplementary provisions relating to this phrase – there is no reason why these supplementary provisions should not be used as guidance in the interpretation of the phrase in the 2003 Regulations. The relevant 1993 regulation provided (reg. 11(2)):

In determining . . . the time span in which satisfactory evidence of a person's identity has to be obtained, in relation to any particular business relationship or one-off transaction, all the circumstances shall be taken into account including, in particular –

(a) the nature of the business relationship or one-off transaction concerned;
(b) the geographical locations of the parties;
(c) whether it is practical to obtain the evidence before commitments are entered into between the parties or before money passes;
(d) in relation to [one-off transactions], the earliest stage at which there are reasonable grounds for believing that the total amount payable by an applicant for business is ecu 15,000 or more.

Many firms will link the identification procedure to their new file opening procedures. In some cases firms will adopt policies which will not allow a file to be formally opened (no file number or reference is allocated to the client) until satisfactory identity procedures have been carried out. In all cases, it makes sense to adopt a policy which requires completion of the identification procedures before significant sums are accepted into client account.

B must produce satisfactory evidence of his identity; or such measures specified in the procedures must be taken in order to produce satisfactory evidence of B's identity;

This is the key to the required procedures. If the identification procedures apply to a client, the client must either produce satisfactory evidence of identity or the firm's procedures should specify what actions can be taken by the firm in order to produce satisfactory evidence of the client's identity.

The Regulations do not specify what amounts to satisfactory evidence for these purposes. However, regulation 2(5) and (6) do give further guidance. They provide:

(5) For the purposes of these Regulations, and subject to paragraph (6), 'satisfactory evidence of identity' is evidence which is reasonably capable of establishing (and does in fact establish to the satisfaction of the person who obtains it) that the applicant for business is the person he claims to be.

(6) Where the person who obtains the evidence mentioned in paragraph (5) knows or has reasonable grounds for believing that the applicant for business is a money service operator, satisfactory evidence of identity must also include the applicant's registered number (if any).

The Law Society's *Money Laundering Guidance* provides a commentary on these two paragraphs. In respect of sub-paragraph (5) it says:

For evidence of identity to be satisfactory, the ML Regulations 2003 require it to pass two tests:

- an objective test in that the evidence must be reasonably capable of establishing that the client is the person he or she claims to be; and
- a subjective test in that the person who obtains the evidence must be satisfied that it does in fact establish that the client is the person he or she claims to be.

In relation to sub-paragraph (6) and the reference to money-service operators the Law Society has this to say:

A money service operator is a person who carries on money service business but does not carry on relevant business falling within sub-paragraphs (a)-(c) of Regulation 2(2). With a few exceptions, a money service business is a business which operates a bureau de change, transmits money, or cashes cheques made payable to customers. Solicitors operating their client or office account would not usually be a money service business. Money service operators are not regulated by the FSA unless they carry on FSA regulated activities but were made subject to a Customs & Excise [now HM Revenue and Customs] registration regime under the 2001 Regulations, and now under the ML Regulations 2003.

Detailed guidance on what amounts to satisfactory evidence of identity should appear in the firm's internal procedures. Partners and principals should not leave it to individual fee earners to decide what is and what is not satisfactory. A firm-wide policy should be adopted and the firm's nominated officer should be consulted where, in an individual case, a client is unable to satisfy the requirements of the policy.

The Law Society has provided detailed and comprehensive guidance in its *Money Laundering Guidance* on what might amount to satisfactory evidence. This guidance helpfully distinguishes between different categories of clients covering:

- Individuals: UK residents.
- Individuals: persons not resident in the UK.
- Individuals: no face-to-face meeting.
- Disadvantaged clients.
- Mentally incapacitated clients.
- Asylum seekers.
- Students and minors.
- Estates.
- Trusts.
- Corporate clients: listed on London Stock Exchange or UK recognised investment exchange.
- Corporate clients: listed on any other recognised, designated or approved exchange.
- Banks, investment firms and insurance companies.
- UK unlisted companies.
- Overseas unlisted companies.
- Subsidiaries.
- Partnerships, limited partnerships and limited liability partnerships.

The full Law Society guidance on evidence of identity appears in **Appendix B1**.

Firms should tailor this guidance to their own requirements, identifying the common categories of clients relevant to the firm's practice and setting out in the firm's money laundering manual details of the firm's policy regarding identification. Most firms will want to adopt a standard form for use by fee earners in the identification process. Examples of a simple money laundering manual and identification forms can be found in **Appendices C1** and **C2**.

Documentary evidence of identity is recommended for most situations, although in some circumstances firms may be prepared to accept evidence from third parties (e.g. credit reference agencies) or to make electronic searches of appropriate databases (e.g. the electoral roll). In each case it will be necessary for the firm to retain a record of the evidence of identity obtained (see below for details of this record). Consequently, the firm's system must ensure that original documentation is photocopied, third party evidence is retained and prints are taken of any electronic evidence relied upon.

Increasingly, firms are being approached by third party businesses offering to provide money laundering verification services for new clients through electronic means. Commercial agencies have access to a wide range of data sources and such information may satisfy the objective test (i.e. that the evidence is reasonably capable of establishing that the client is the person he or she claims to be). However, it is still necessary for the solicitor accepting the information to be satisfied on a subjective basis that it does, in fact, establish that the client is the person he or she claims to be. A useful article by Alison Matthews and Peter Burrell 'E-verifying a client's identity', published in the Law Society's *Gazette*, 12 April 2006, examines the issues surrounding the 'e-verification' of a client identity. The article can be accessed through the *Gazette* website (**www.lawgazette.co.uk**).

> . . . identification procedures . . . must take into account the greater potential for money laundering which arises when B is not physically present when being identified . . .

This requirement did not appear in the 1993 Regulations – it has been prompted by the concern that it is easier for criminals to obtain legal and other services if there is no face-to-face meeting between, for example, the solicitor and a criminal client. It is obviously not appropriate to ask a client to send a copy of his or her passport or driving licence for identification purposes if there is to be no face-to-face meeting.

The Law Society's *Money Laundering Guidance* on this suggests that where it is not possible physically to meet the client, the solicitor should consider requiring that someone else qualified and willing certifies the client's documentation. For example, a local solicitor, accountant, doctor or bank manager may be prepared to examine the original documents and send a certified copy to the firm. If the client is overseas, then original documents can be certified by an embassy or consulate, a qualified lawyer in the jurisdiction, or, in the case of international students, the registrar of a higher education establishment. In each case it is important for the solicitor to check the name and address of the third party by reference to a professional directory or otherwise.

If a third party certification is not available, where a face-to-face meeting is not possible, clients should send the original of the appropriate documents to the solicitor, who should then copy the documents before returning them to the client. Electronic checks might also be relevant in these circumstances.

When a firm is considering its policy on client identification, thought should be given to whether or not the firm is prepared to certify documents for other solicitors and, if so, who should be authorised by the firm to provide such certification.

> . . . identification procedures . . . must require that where satisfactory evidence of identity is not obtained, the business relationship or one-off transaction must not proceed any further . . .

The Regulations do not require a solicitor to take reasonable steps to obtain client identification. Where the Regulations apply, it is an obligation to obtain satisfactory evidence of identity. If such evidence cannot be obtained the firm must not continue to act for the client.

Many firms will not want to commence work on a particular file until satisfactory evidence of identity has been obtained. Firms are advised not to accept money into client account until such evidence has been obtained. Although there is nothing in the Regulations preventing a firm from starting work and accepting money before satisfactory evidence is obtained (the requirement is for such evidence to be obtained as soon as is reasonably practicable after first contact is made) it can be messy if subsequently, when such evidence is not made available, the firm has to withdraw and return the money held in client account.

As noted above, many firms will take the view that all new clients should be subject to identification procedures (regardless of whether or not the firm is undertaking relevant business). Further, most firms will adopt an identification procedure which specifies particular documents or checks. If a client cannot produce evidence strictly in accordance with the firm's procedures, this will not necessarily be fatal to the retainer. The firm's policy should insist that fee earners obtain evidence in accordance with the procedure but if this is not possible reference should be made to the firm's nominated officer.

The officer can decide on the particular facts of the case:

- Whether evidence is strictly necessary. Is the firm undertaking relevant business or is the transaction value of a one-off transaction less than €15,000? or
- If the firm is undertaking relevant business and there is need for identification, can the client supply information which is not strictly within the requirement of the firm's procedures but nevertheless meets the obligation imposed by the Regulations?

One further important matter must be considered at this point. If, for any reason, a client cannot produce satisfactory evidence of identity, this failure might give rise to suspicion that the client or another is involved in money laundering. The requirements of PoCA 2002, ss.327–329 (the money laundering offences), section 330 (failure to disclose), and sections 333 (tipping off) or 342 (prejudicing an investigation) might be relevant. Consider the following scenario.

A client instructs a solicitor on the purchase of an asset (real property, shares etc). The client provides the solicitor with a cheque representing the purchase money or deposit (£20,000 – in excess of the €15,000 limit for one-off transactions). The money is paid into client account. The solicitor is undertaking relevant business and is acting within the regulated sector (the provision of legal services involving participation in a financial or real property transaction). Consequently, it will be necessary for the solicitor to obtain satisfactory evidence of identity. The client prevaricates – initially, there appears to be a good reason why evidence cannot be produced immediately. Eventually, however, it is clear that the client is not going to produce satisfactory evidence within the time scale required by the Regulations. The solicitor must now consider the following points.

(a) Terminating the retainer immediately. Under the Regulations the one-off transaction must not proceed further. However, if the solicitor is likely to report the client (see (b) and (c) below) he must take care in explaining to the client the reason for termination. To explain that he cannot proceed without identification would appear to be acceptable. Any hint that the solicitor suspects the client of money laundering could be tipping off and/or prejudicing an investigation subject to the defence available to professional legal advisers (see **Chapter 7**).

(b) Returning the £20,000 held in client account. However, if the fact that the client has been unable to produce evidence of identity gives rise to a suspicion that the client is benefiting from criminal conduct, then the holding of £20,000 in client account could mean the solicitor is guilty of:

   i.   concealing criminal property (PoCA 2002, s.327);
   ii. being concerned in an arrangement which facilitates the retention, use or control of criminal property (PoCA 2002, s.328); or
   iii. acquisition, use or possession of criminal property (PoCA 2002, s.329).

(c) To avoid committing the offence, but subject to LPP, an authorised disclosure must be made and the £20,000 cannot be returned to the client without appropriate consent (i.e. the consent of SOCA).

(d) Even if no money was held in client account (and therefore the solicitor, by terminating the instructions, could not be guilty of a money laundering offence) any knowledge or suspicion (or reasonable grounds for knowledge or suspicion) of the client's involvement in money laundering would, potentially, have to be reported to prevent a criminal charge under PoCA 2002, s.330 since the solicitor is acting in the regulated sector. Consideration of appropriate defences (e.g. privilege) might be necessary.

... identification procedures ... must require that where B acts or appears to act for another person, reasonable measures must be taken for the purpose of establishing the identity of that person ...

If the client instructing the solicitor acts or appears to be acting on behalf of another person (for example, the client might be an agent or nominee for another), then the Regulations require the solicitor to take 'reasonable measures' to establish the identity of that other person. This is less onerous than the obligation to obtain the client's identity. Whilst it would make sense for firms to adopt the same procedures for obtaining identity as those procedures used for clients, if reasonable steps have been taken and the third party's identity cannot be obtained, this fact does not automatically mean that the retainer cannot proceed. If reasonable steps have been taken and the third party's identity cannot be ascertained, the firm has complied with the Regulations. However, the same points as noted above regarding possible suspicion arising from the inability to obtain identification must be taken into account.

9.4.2 Exceptions: regulation 5

Regulation 5 contains a number of exceptional circumstances where, despite the requirements of regulation 4, no evidence of identity need be obtained. The exceptions will never apply if the circumstances are such that the solicitor knows or suspects that the transaction involved money laundering (regulation 5(1)). The Law Society's *Money Laundering Guidance* states:

> The exceptions are very narrowly drawn and solicitors will in most cases need to obtain satisfactory evidence of identity. Where a solicitor wishes to take advantage of an exception, but is in doubt as to whether or not it applies to the particular facts of a case, then expert legal advice should be taken.

Unless a particular exception applies to a number of clients or to a group of clients, it would appear to be more appropriate for solicitors to ignore the exceptions in individual client matters. It is imposing a burden upon individual fee earners to require them to consider complex exceptions at the outset of each new matter. However, for the sake of completeness, the exceptions are dealt with below.

There is no requirement to obtain evidence of any person's identity in any of the following circumstances.

Regulation 5(2)(a)

> Where A has reasonable grounds for believing that B carries on in the United Kingdom relevant business falling within any of sub-paragraphs (a) to (e) of regulation 2(2), is not a money service operator and, if carrying on an activity falling within regulation 2(2)(a), is an authorised person with permission under the 2000 Act to carry on that activity.

This would cover the situation where the client was a bank or stockbroker or other financial services provider (other than a money service operator).

Regulation 5(2)(b)

> Where A has reasonable grounds for believing that B does not carry on relevant business in the United Kingdom but does carry on comparable activities to those falling within sub-paragraph (a) and is covered by the Money Laundering Directive.

The Money Laundering Directive is defined in regulation 2(1) as meaning the Council Directive 91/308/EEC of 10 June 1991 on prevention of the use of the financial system for the purpose of money laundering as amended by

Directive 2001/97/EC of the European Parliament and of the Council of 4 December 2000.

This exception would cover the situation where the client was a bank or stockbroker or other financial service provider (other than a money service operator) working from an EEA country. EEA countries cover members of the EU together with certain non-EU countries (notably Norway, Iceland and Liechtenstein). Details of non-EU countries which are EEA States can be found at the website: **http://europa.eu.int/comm/external_relations/eea/**.

Regulation 5(2)(c)

Where A has reasonable grounds for believing that B is regulated by an overseas regulatory authority (within the meaning given by section 82 of the Companies Act 1989) and is based or incorporated in a country (other than an EEA State) whose law contains comparable provisions to those contained in the Money Laundering Directive.

This would cover similar institutions and businesses operating outside the EEA but where the country's laws contain comparable provisions to those contained in the directive.

9.4.3   Regulation 5(3)

Where:

(a) A carries out a one-off transaction with or for a third party pursuant to an introduction effected by a person who has provided a written assurance that evidence of the identity of all third parties introduced by him will have been obtained and recorded under procedures maintained by him;
(b) that person identifies the third party; and
(c) A has reasonable grounds for believing that that person falls within any of subparagraphs (a) to (c) of paragraph (2).

This exception only applies to one-off transactions. It allows a firm to ignore the requirement to obtain client identity where the client has been introduced by a person who the solicitor has reasonable grounds for believing falls within one of the three categories noted above. This means that this exception is likely to be limited to introductions from banking and financial service providers in the UK or from EEA countries or countries having equivalent money laundering laws. For the exception to apply, it is necessary for the introducer to have given the solicitor written assurance that all clients introduced will have had their identity obtained and recorded (a general assurance) and that the specific client has been identified by the introducer.

The Joint Money Laundering Steering Group has provided a specimen certificate for use in these circumstances. A copy of this appears in **Appendix B1**.

9.4.4 Regulation 5(4)

In relation to a contract of long-term insurance –

(a) in connection with a pension scheme taken out by virtue of a person's contract of employment or occupation where the contract of long-term insurance –

    (i)   contains no surrender clause; and
    (ii) may not be used as collateral for a loan; or

(b) in respect of which a premium is payable –

    (i)   in one instalment of an amount not exceeding 2,500 euro; or
    (ii) periodically and where the total payable in respect of any calendar year does not exceed 1,000 euro.

Long-term insurance catches such insurance contracts as endowment or pension policies, annuities and single premium bonds issued by insurance companies. It is highly unlikely that a solicitor's retainer would be restricted to the provision of a long-term insurance contract for a client. Although some solicitors undoubtedly make arrangements for clients to purchase such policies, in most cases these arrangements are linked with other services. As such, this particular exception is unlikely to be of assistance to solicitors.

9.4.5 Regulation 5(5)

Where the proceeds of a one-off transaction are payable to B but are instead directly reinvested on his behalf in another transaction –

(a) of which a record is kept; and
(b) which can result only in another reinvestment made on B's behalf or in a payment made directly to B

Again, this exception only applies to a one-off transaction where the firm is acting on a disposal and the proceeds are payable to the client. The second condition appears to rule out a general application of this exception. The Treasury's view is that this exception is intended to apply to pension payments only, not to the sale and purchase of tangible assets. The second tangible asset, which was purchased by way of investment from the proceeds of the first asset, could be disposed of by gift and therefore would not satisfy the requirements of regulation 5(5)(*b*).

9.4.6 Conclusion

If a firm is relying on any of the exceptions, there will be no need for the firm to obtain client identification evidence and therefore no requirement for a record to be kept. However, it must be good practice to record on the client's file (or elsewhere) details of the exception relied upon and (if evidence of identity has been obtained by a third party) details of the evidence and how it was obtained.

9.5 TRANSITIONAL PROVISIONS

Regulation 30 states:

(1) Nothing in these Regulations obliges any person who carries on relevant business falling within any of sub-paragraphs (*a*) to (*e*) of regulation 2(2) to maintain identification procedures which require evidence to be obtained in respect of any business relationship formed by him before 1 April 1994.

(2) Nothing in these Regulations obliges any person who carries on relevant business falling within any of sub-paragraphs (*f*) to (*n*) of regulation 2(2) –

(a) to maintain identification procedures which require evidence to be obtained in respect of any business relationship formed by him before 1 March 2004; . . .

There are two transitional provisions referred to in regulation 30. The first allows firms to avoid the need for identification procedures for clients who formed specified business relationships before 1 April 1994; the second for clients who formed specified business relationships before 1 March 2004.

Before looking at the details of these transitional provisions it must be stressed that they will only apply if the firm has had a business relationship with a client before either 1 April 1994 or 1 March 2004. It is a common mistake to take the view that there is no need to seek client identification where the firm acted for a client prior to 1 April 1994. If the only relationship with a client was a one-off transaction or series of one-off transactions sometime in the past, these transitional provisions will not apply. Further, if the firm has had a business relationship with a client formed, say, before 1 April 1994 and that business relationship has terminated, any new business relationship subsequently formed cannot benefit from these transitional provisions.

9.5.1 Pre-1 April 1994 business relationships

Where a firm has an on-going business relationship formed with the client before 1 April 1994 (the commencement date for the 1993 Money Laundering Regulations) and the retainer related to business falling within regulation 2(2)(*a*)–(*e*), there is no need for any identification procedure to be applied post-1 March 2004 under the terms of the 2003 Regulations. By way of reminder, regulation 2(2)(*a*)–(*e*) covers the following business:

(a) the regulated activity of –

(i) accepting deposits;

(ii) effecting or carrying out contracts of long-term insurance when carried on by a person who has received official authorisation pursuant to Article 4 or 51 of the Life Assurance Consolidation Directive;

(iii) dealing in investments as principal or as agent;

(iv) arranging deals in investments;

    (v)   managing investments;
    (vi) safeguarding and administering investments;
    (vii) sending dematerialised instructions;
    (viii) establishing (and taking other steps in relation to) collective investment schemes;
    (ix) advising on investments; or
    (x)   issuing electronic money;

(b)   the activities of the National Savings Bank;

(c)   any activity carried on for the purpose of raising money authorised to be raised under the National Loans Act 1968 under the auspices of the Director of Savings;

(d)   the business of operating a bureau de change, transmitting money (or any representation of monetary value) by any means or cashing cheques which are made payable to customers;

(e)   any of the activities in points 1 to 12 or 14 of Annex 1 to the Banking Consolidation Directive (which activities are, for convenience, set out in Schedule 1 to these Regulations) when carried on by way of business, ignoring an activity falling within any of sub-paragraphs (a) to (d);

The only relevant business affecting solicitors will be regulation 2(2)(a) regulated activities (although it was always a moot point as to whether the activities referred to in the Banking Consolidation Directive applied to solicitors). The following example is an illustration.

A solicitor was instructed on a particular trust administration in February 1990. The trust fund consists of listed securities. Since February 1990 the firm has arranged the purchase and sale of securities on behalf of the trustees, using the services of stockbrokers. The firm is still currently acting on the administration. On these facts:

(a) it would appear that there is a business relationship – an on-going relationship where the total payment to be made was not known or capable of being ascertained at the outset of the retainer;

(b) it is a relationship which is unbroken since February 1990;

(c) the relevant business undertaken as a result of this relationship would appear to be restricted to:

    i.   dealing as agent or arranging deals in investments;
    ii. safeguarding and administrating investments;
    iii. advising on investments;

(d) these activities all fall within regulation 2(2)(a).

Consequently, the transitional provisions would appear to apply to this case and no steps would have to be taken to obtain client identity as a result of the 2003 Regulations coming into force on 1 March 2004.

9.5.2 Pre-1 March 2004 business relationships

Where a firm has an on-going business relationship formed with the client before 1 March 2004 (the commencement date for the Money Laundering Regulations 2003) and the retainer related to business falling within regulation 2(2)(f)–(n), there is no need for any identification procedure to be applied post-1 March 2004 under the terms of the 2003 Regulations. By way of reminder, regulation 2(2)(f)–(n) cover the following business:

(f) estate agency work;

(g) operating a casino by way of business;

(h) the activities of a person appointed to act as an insolvency practitioner within the meaning of section 388 of the Insolvency Act 1986 or Article 3 of the Insolvency (Northern Ireland) Order 1989;

(i) the provision by way of business of advice about the tax affairs of another person by a body corporate or unincorporate or, in the case of a sole practitioner, by an individual;

(j) the provision by way of business of accountancy services by a body corporate or unincorporate or, in the case of a sole practitioner, by an individual;

(k) the provision by way of business of audit services by a person who is eligible for appointment as a company auditor under section 25 of the Companies Act 1989 or Article 28 of the Companies (Northern Ireland) Order 1990;

(l) the provision by way of business of legal services by a body corporate or unincorporate or, in the case of a sole practitioner, by an individual and which involves participation in a financial or real property transaction (whether by assisting in the planning or execution of any such transaction or otherwise by acting for, or on behalf of, a client in any such transaction);

(m) the provision by way of business of services in relation to the formation, operation or management of a company or a trust; or

(n) the activity of dealing in goods of any description by way of business (including dealing as an auctioneer) whenever a transaction involves accepting a total cash payment of 15,000 euro or more.

The common relevant business affecting solicitors will be regulation 2(2)(i), (l) and (m). The following example is an illustration.

A company client (a property developer) instructed a solicitor in March 2001. The solicitor entered into a general retainer with the client agreeing to act for the client on the sale of all future developments until either party determined the retainer. Since 2001 the solicitor has acted for the client on a number of sales – the retainer is still current. Post-1 March 2004, the client instructs the solicitor to act on the sale of a newly-developed site. On these facts:

- It would appear that there is a business relationship – an on-going relationship where the total payment to be made was not known or capable of being ascertained at the outset of the retainer.
- It is a relationship which is unbroken since March 2001.
- The relevant business undertaken as a result of this relationship would appear to be restricted to the provision by way of business of legal services involving the participation in a real property transaction.
- This activity falls within regulation 2(2)(l).

> Consequently, the transitional provisions would appear to apply to this case and no steps would have to be taken to obtain client identity as a result of instructions relating to the newly-developed site received after the coming into force on 1 March 2004 of the 2003 Regulations.

Because of the complexity of these provisions, firms may prefer to over comply and, post-1 March 2004, seek verification of all new clients' identities and all existing clients' identities on new matters (unless an existing client's evidence of identity is already on file).

9.6 RECORD-KEEPING PROCEDURES

Regulation 5 states:

(1) A must maintain procedures which require the retention of the records prescribed in paragraph (2) for the period prescribed in paragraph (3).

(2) The records are –

    (a) where evidence of identity has been obtained under the procedures stipulated by regulation 4 (identification procedures) . . . –

        i. a copy of that evidence;

        ii. information as to where a copy of that evidence may be obtained; or

        iii. information enabling the evidence of identity to be re-obtained, but only where it is not reasonably practicable for A to comply with paragraph (i) or (ii); and

    (b) a record containing details relating to all transactions carried out by A in the course of relevant business.

(3) In relation to the records mentioned in paragraph (2)(a), the period is –

    (a) where A and B have formed a business relationship, at least five years commencing with the date on which the relationship ends; or

    (b) in the case of a one-off transaction (or a series of such transactions), at least five years commencing with the date of the completion of all activities taking place in the course of that transaction (or, as the case may be, the last of the transactions).

(4) In relation to the records mentioned in paragraph (2)(b), the period is at least five years commencing with the date on which all activities taking place in the course of the transaction in question were completed.

As a result of regulation 5, firms must maintain two records as part of their money laundering procedures. A record must be kept of the evidence of the client identity and a record must be kept of details of the transaction which amounts to relevant business.

9.6.1 Evidence of client identity

The regulation permits two types of record to be kept, with a third type available where neither of the first two types are reasonably practicable. In most cases, firms will keep a copy of the evidence obtained. This can be by way of a photocopy, or the original document can be scanned and a digital copy maintained.

Since the Regulations require the evidence to be reasonably capable of establishing (and does, in fact, establish to the satisfaction of the person who obtains it) that the client is the person he claims to be, the onus is very much upon the individual fee earner who accepts the evidence to be satisfied. Consequently, to bring this point to the attention of all members of staff who are responsible for accepting evidence of identity, firms will frequently require members of staff personally to sign a statement confirming that they have seen the original of any document relied upon and that they are satisfied from the evidence that it is reasonably capable of establishing that the client is the person he claims to be. In the case of photographic evidence, the member of staff should certify the copy by way of confirming that the client appears to be the person shown in the photograph.

Where a passport is used for identification purposes, reference should be made to guidance from HMSO (Note 20) dated 5 December 2002. The Law Society's *Money Laundering Guidance* refers to this and it is reproduced below:

3.79 The HMSO guidance note no. 20 dated 5 December 2002 confirms that copies of the personal details page of a UK passport may be made for the purposes of record keeping by the following persons only:

(a) the holder of the passport
(b) notaries, solicitors, UK government departments and British consulates;
(c) financial institutions and other persons and firms who are subject to the ML Regulations 2003; and
(d) any person or firm for the purpose of certifying that identification checks have been made in accordance with the ML Regulations 2003.

3.80 The Guidance says that copies must be in black and white only so that they cannot be mistaken for a real passport page. Copying for these purposes includes photocopying, scanning, filming, reproduction in any other medium, including placing material on the Internet. The original document is the evidence of identity. The photocopy of the original is used to record and certify that identification checks have been made. There is no need to apply for a licence or pay a fee to take such copies.

If evidence is obtained from an electronic database, a print out of the evidence should be made and kept by way of evidence.

Since the Regulations do not specify what can and cannot be used as evidence of identity, firms may agree to accept personal knowledge of an individual partner or established member of staff as sufficient evidence of identity of clients introduced by them. It would appear to be over zealous to demand a passport or other formal evidence of identity from a partner's long-established friend or family member. However, in these circumstances, a record must still be retained in accordance with regulation 5: an appropriate written confirmation of the partner's knowledge of the client's identity should be retained.

If the firm does not hold the copy of the evidence, an alternative record that satisfies regulation 5 will be information as to where a copy of that evidence may be obtained. Only if it is not reasonably practicable to keep records in this form can a firm satisfy the requirements of regulation 5 by retaining information enabling the evidence of identity to be reobtained.

9.6.2 Evidence of transaction

The Law Society's *Money Laundering Guidance* indicates that, in most cases, keeping a copy of the client file and the accounting records for each client for whom the firm undertakes relevant business should satisfy this requirement of regulation 5.

In earlier guidance applicable to the Money Laundering Regulations 1993 (which imposed similar record-keeping requirements) the Law Society recommended that firms should keep a record of the origin of funds paid by the client to the firm (and, where appropriate, details of cheques should be noted). Whilst the client file is likely to contain general details of the origin of any funds, specific details such as the bank address and sort code, account name and number from which funds have been drawn may not necessarily have been recorded on the file. Consideration should be given to photocopying cheques before paying them into client account (if the volume of cheques makes this practicable). Alternatively, adjustments can be made to a firm's internal paying-in slip, used by fee earners to send cheques to the accounts department, requiring the paying bank's sort code and account number to be recorded.

9.6.3 Retention periods

The evidence of client identity must be retained for a period of at least five years from the date on which a business relationship ends or a period of at least five years from the date of completion of all activities carried out in the course of a one-off transaction. If there is a series of linked one-off transactions, the five-year period commences on completion of the activities carried out in the course of the last of the linked transactions.

The evidence of the transaction must be retained for the period of at least five years commencing with the date on which all activities taking place in the course of the transaction in question were completed.

Given that the five-year period commences in all cases at the end of the relationship or transaction, firms must recognise that in some cases the period might extend beyond the normal file retention period or accounting record retention. It is important for procedures to be maintained to ensure the money laundering records are not destroyed before the end of the retention period.

Further, given that most firms will use the client files for regulation 5 purposes, care must be taken at the end of a transaction not to simply hand over the client's file to the client or to a client's new solicitors without first creating a separate record of the transaction for regulation 5 purposes.

Although the Regulations do not specify where the records must be kept, there are compelling reasons for considering a central record of client identification evidence. If client identification records are kept on a client file, at the end of the transaction the file may be sent to storage (this will still satisfy the retention requirements, provided the firm is able to recover the file from storage). However, if after say, three years, the client returns to the firm, it is useful to have access to a central record of client identities to avoid the embarrassment of asking the client to provide verification details again, rather than to have to access a file in storage.

9.7   INTERNAL REPORTING PROCEDURES

Regulation 7 states:

(1)   A must maintain internal reporting procedures which require that –

   (a)   a person in A's organisation is nominated to receive disclosures under this regulation ('the nominated officer');

   (b)   anyone in A's organisation to whom information or other matter comes in the course of relevant business as a result of which he knows or suspects or has reasonable grounds for knowing or suspecting that a person is engaged in money laundering must, as soon as is practicable after the information or other matter comes to him, disclose it to the nominated officer or a person authorised for the purposes of these Regulations by the Director General of the Serious Organised Crime Agency;

   (c)   where a disclosure is made to the nominated officer, he must consider it in the light of any relevant information which is available to A and determine whether it gives rise to such knowledge or suspicion or such reasonable grounds for knowledge or suspicion; and

   (d)   where the nominated officer does so determine, the information or other matter must be disclosed to a person authorised for the purposes of these Regulations by the Director General of the Serious Organised Crime Agency.

In this context, A means a person who carries on relevant business in the United Kingdom (reg. 4(1)).

A number of procedures are required as a result of this regulation.

127

9.7.1 Appointment of nominated officer: regulation 7(1)(*a*)

The firm must appoint someone as a nominated officer. His or her role is to receive disclosures from members of the firm. The nominated officer does not have to be a partner (or, in an incorporated practice, an officer) but should be of sufficient seniority to have access to the firm's clients' files and other internal business records.

A sole practitioner who does not employ staff or acts in association with anyone else is not subject to regulation 7 and therefore does not have to appoint a nominated officer. Regulation 7(2) provides: 'Paragraph (1) does not apply where A is an individual who neither employs nor acts in association with any other person.'

Larger firms may wish to appoint deputy nominated officers who may undertake some of the functions of the nominated officer, subject to the nominated officer's overall supervision. All firms, whatever their size, should make arrangements covering the absence of the nominated officer as a result of holidays, sick leave or other reason.

Firms authorised under the Financial Services and Markets Act 2000 will have to seek approval of the Financial Services Authority to the appointment of the nominated officer.

9.7.2 Disclosure of knowledge or suspicion of money laundering: regulation 7(1)(*b*)

The Regulations impose an obligation on anyone in a firm to make a disclosure to the firm's nominated officer where they know or suspect (or have reasonable grounds for knowing or suspecting) that another is engaged in money laundering and where the information came into their possession as a result of relevant business. Alternatively, the disclosure can be made to SOCA, although most firms will require members to disclose internally.

This provision effectively replicates PoCA 2002, s.330 (see **Chapter 5**), since the definition of relevant business in the Money Laundering Regulations mirrors the definition of the regulated sector in section 330. Like PoCA 2002, s.330, regulation 7(1)(*b*) applies an objective test of knowledge or suspicion.

The Regulations provide for a defence of privilege (similar to the defence available in PoCA 2002, s.330). Regulation 7(3)–(7) (amended by PoCA 2002 and Money Laundering Regulations 2003) provides:

(3) Paragraph (1)(b) does not apply in relation to a professional legal adviser or other relevant professional adviser where the information or other matter comes to him in privileged circumstances.

(4) Information or other matter comes to a professional legal adviser or other relevant professional adviser in privileged circumstances if it is communicated or given to him –

    (a) by (or by a representative of) a client of his in connection with the giving by the adviser of legal advice to the client;

    (b) by (or by a representative of) a person seeking legal advice from the adviser; or

    (c) by a person in connection with legal proceedings or contemplated legal proceedings.

(5) But paragraph (4) does not apply to information or other matter which is communicated or given with the intention of furthering a criminal purpose.

(6) A relevant professional adviser is an accountant, auditor or tax adviser who is a member of a professional body which is established for accountants, auditors or tax advisers (as the case may be) and which makes provision for –

    (a) testing the competence of those seeking admission to membership of such a body as a condition for such admission; and

    (b) imposing and maintaining professional and ethical standards for its members, as well as imposing sanctions for non-compliance with those standards.

(7) Paragraph (1)(b) also does not apply to a person if–

    (a) he is employed by, or is in partnership with, a professional legal adviser or a relevant professional adviser to provide the adviser with assistance or support,

    (b) the information or other matter mentioned in paragraph (1)(b) comes to the person in connection with the provision of such assistance or support, and

    (c) the information or other matter came to the adviser in privileged circumstances.

The wording of these subparagraphs is almost identical to the wording in PoCA 2002, s.330 as noted in **Chapter 5**. The 'privilege' defence has been extended to relevant professional advisers (e.g. accountants) and the paragraph preserves privilege where the individual who receives the information is neither a professional legal adviser nor a relevant professional adviser, but is employed with such a person and provides them with help or support. For a full commentary on the defence of privilege, see **Chapter 5**.

9.7.3 Consideration and determination by the nominated officer: regulation 7(1)(*c*)

The Regulations require a nominated officer to consider any disclosures made by members of the firm in the light of all relevant information available in the firm. Hence, there is a requirement for the nominated officer to be of sufficient seniority to gain access to this information. The Regulations do not specifically require the nominated officer to keep a record of this consideration but it would be good practice to do so. The information recorded can include:

(a) The name of the member of staff making the disclosure.
(b) The details of, and reasons for, the disclosure.
(c) The other relevant information taken into account by the nominated officer in making his determination.
(d) The decision whether or not to report to SOCA and the reason for the decision.

If the firm requires internal reports to be submitted to the nominated officer on specified forms, retention of these forms would satisfy the record-keeping requirements of (a) and (b) above although additional records would have to be kept to satisfy (c) and (d).

9.7.4 Disclosure to SOCA: regulation 7(1)(d)

If a nominated officer determines that the information gives rise to knowledge or suspicion (or reasonable grounds for knowledge or suspicion) that another is engaged in money laundering, the information must be disclosed to SOCA. This replicates the provisions of PoCA 2002, s.331 (see **Chapter 5**). Consequently, a nominated officer who does not comply with regulation 7(1)(d), in addition to any penalties for breaching the money laundering regulations, risks committing an offence under PoCA 2002, s.331.

9.7.5 Transitional provisions

Regulation 30(2) provides:

> (2) Nothing in these Regulations obliges any person who carries on relevant business falling within any of sub-paragraphs (f) to (n) of regulation 2(2) –
> ... (b) to maintain internal reporting procedures which require any action to be taken in respect of any knowledge, suspicion or reasonable grounds for knowledge or suspicion which came to that person before 1st March 2004.

Reference to subparagraphs (f) to (n) of regulation 2(2) can be found in **Paragraph 9.5.2**. This provision ensures that if, for example, information giving rise to knowledge or suspicion of another's engagement in money laundering came into the possession of a solicitor as a result of a property transaction (reg. 2(2)(l)) in February 2004 no action under the internal reporting procedures would be required. (No action under PoCA 2002, ss.330 or 331 would be required since the amendment to the definition of the regulated sector only came into force on 1 March 2004. Real property transactions were not within the regulated sector before that date.) However, if the property transaction continued into March 2004 and beyond, any information received after 1 March 2004 and giving rise to knowledge or suspicion of money laundering would be subject to regulation 7 (and to PoCA 2002, ss.330 and 331).

Note, however, that this transitional provision only applies to the requirements contained in the Money Laundering Regulations 2003. There may be obligations under the substantive law that would require disclosure by way of a defence to the money laundering offences.

9.8 PENALTIES

Regulation 3(2) states:

> (2) A person who contravenes this regulation is guilty of an offence and liable –
>
> (a) on conviction on indictment, to imprisonment for a term not exceeding 2 years, to a fine or to both;
> (b) on summary conviction, to a fine not exceeding the statutory maximum.

Further, regulation 27 provides that where it is shown that an offence under regulation 3 has been committed by a body corporate or partnership with the consent of or the connivance of an officer (in the case of an incorporated practice) or a partner (in the case of a partnership) or to be attributable to any neglect on their part, the officer as well as the body corporate or the partner as well as the partnership is guilty of an offence and liable to be proceeded against and punished accordingly. Partners and principals should note that personal liability can therefore arise where there is a failure to comply with the Regulations.

Regulation 3(3) states:

> (3) In deciding whether a person has committed an offence under this regulation, the court must consider whether he followed any relevant guidance which was at the time concerned –
>
> (a) issued by a supervisory authority or any other appropriate body;
> (b) approved by the Treasury; and
> (c) published in a manner approved by the Treasury as appropriate in their opinion to bring the guidance to the attention of persons likely to be affected by it.

A supervisory body is defined in regulation 2(8) and the term includes the Law Society.

As noted in previous chapters, The Law Society has issued Guidance to the solicitors' profession (*Money Laundering Guidance: Professional Ethics*, Pilot, January 2004). Extracts from the *Money Laundering Guidance* appear in the text of this book and in **Appendix B1**. The Law Society's *Money Laundering Guidance* is described as a pilot and has not been submitted to the

Treasury for approval. Consequently, regulation 3(3) will not apply techni-cally. However, as stated in the *Money Laundering Guidance*, a court 'may still take it into consideration' in deciding whether an offence has been committed under regulation 3.

9.9 FUTURE DEVELOPMENTS

On 7 June 2005 the Directive of the European Parliament and of the Council on the prevention of the use of the financial system for the purpose of money laundering and terrorist financing (the Third EC Money Laundering Directive) reached political agreement. The Directive entered into force on 15 December 2005 meaning that it will need to be implemented by 15 December 2007. New Money Laundering Regulations were published for consultation purposes in January 2007.

The Directive extends customer due diligence measure to the identifica-tion (where applicable) of the beneficial owner (e.g. in the case of companies and trusts). The Directive also states that the due diligence requirements may be determined on a risk-sensitive basis depending on the type of customer, business relationship, product or transaction.

Clearly, until the new Money Laundering Regulations are published in their final form, it is not possible to say exactly how this provision will be implemented by the UK Government. However, the possibility is that the identification requirements currently applicable will move from the existing prescriptive obligations to a more risk-based procedure.

PART 2

Practical Guidance

CHAPTER 10

Reporting suspicions

10.1 INTRODUCTION

The substantive law and the Money Laundering Regulations 2003 require disclosure of knowledge or suspicion of money laundering by way of defence and/or by way of obligation. In both cases, the disclosure can be internal (to the firm's nominated officer) or external. External authorised and protected disclosures need to be made to a constable, or an officer of HMRC. Other external disclosures are made to a person authorised by the Director General of the Serious Organised Crime Agency (SOCA). In practice this means that all external disclosures are made to SOCA.

10.2 INTERNAL DISCLOSURES

Firms can decide themselves on the manner of internal disclosures. Although the Proceeds of Crime Act 2002 (PoCA 2002), s.339 provides that the form of disclosures (both internal and external) can be prescribed by order of the Secretary of State (see **Chapter 4**), at the time of writing no such order has been made. For internal disclosures, it is recommended that firms use an appropriate written form of disclosure. The consequences of making a disclosure are such that it is vital for firms to be able to recognise when a formal disclosure has been made internally – distinguishing this from an informal discussion with a more senior member of the firm. A precedent (which may be adapted depending upon the size and nature of the firm) can be found in **Appendix C3**.

As noted in **Chapter 9**, it is also recommended that nominated officers keep a record of internal disclosures and the steps taken by them in the light of such disclosures. This is particularly important where the decision is made not to report to SOCA.

If firms use an internal reporting form, it is vital that a copy of this form is not kept on the client's file. At the end of a transaction (or during a transaction, if a client chooses to change solicitors) and on the payment of a solicitor's costs, the client may require the firm to hand over the file (either to himself or to his new solicitors). If details of the internal disclosure remain, inadvertently, on the file, this could lead to a conviction for tipping off in extreme circumstances. (For details of the offence of tipping off, see **Chapter 7**.)

10.3   EXTERNAL DISCLOSURES

External disclosures by members of staff to SOCA should not be encouraged by way of a defence or compliance with an obligation. Members of staff will obtain the necessary defence or fulfil any obligation by making an internal disclosure to the firm's nominated officer. Complex questions of confidentiality and LPP can more easily be dealt with where the disclosure is internal. External reporting should be limited to the firm's nominated officer and will arise where the officer's obligations under PoCA 2002, ss.331 or 332 or regulation 7 of the Money Laundering Regulations 2003 apply. (For details of PoCA 2002, ss.331 and 332, see **Chapter 5**; for details of reg. 7, see **Chapter 9**.)

Disclosures by a nominated officer can be to SOCA using the form, available for downloading from the SOCA website (**www.soca.gov.uk**). There are two forms available: one for standard disclosures (the standard report form) and one for limited intelligence disclosure reports. Full guidance notes on how to complete the forms are provided on the website. The forms for disclosure are reproduced in **Appendix C4** together with the guidance for their completion. SOCA's preferred method for reporting is for these forms to be submitted electronically but hard copy versions can be printed using the templates found on their website. A new web-based reporting mechanism was introduced in April 2006 and can be used by anyone with access to the internet at **www.ukciu.gov.uk/saronline.aspx**.

10.3.1   Standard report form

The standard report form should be used where firms are making protected or authorised disclosures under PoCA 2003, ss.337 and 338. The form can also be used where it is necessary to make a disclosure as a result of the Terrorism Act 2000 ss.18 or 21A.

SOCA guidance states that although these forms are not mandatory, they are the preferred format and have been designed to facilitate the efficient and effective handling of disclosures by SOCA. The downloaded version of the report can be completed on the firm's own computer. SOCA have advised that the downloaded version must not be used for hand written reports. Hand written reports should only be completed on a special version of the form available by telephoning 020 7238 8282.

Where firms are using a computer-completed form (downloaded from the SOCA website) it will be necessary for the form to be printed and submitted by post or fax. The form cannot be submitted through the Internet. Forms should be faxed to 020 7238 8286 or sent by post to UK FIU, PO Box 8000, London SE11 5EN.

The downloaded version is available in PDF format. Unless firms have the commercial version of the Acrobat Reader, the completed form cannot be saved to firms' computer files as a PDF document. It can, however, be printed and a hard copy retained. If firms wish to retain an electronic version, the completed PDF format document can be copied into a Word document and saved.

The standard form consists of six sheets and these can be submitted in different combinations depending upon the information disclosed. Since the form has been designed to be read by Image Character Recognition technology, amendments or additions outside the structure of the form will hamper the capability of SOCA to process the form efficiently. The six sheets consist of:

- **Sheet 1: Report details**. SOCA state that it is necessary for this sheet to be clearly completed enabling SOCA to check that it has received the correct number of sheets.
- **Sheet 2: Subject details**. This sets out the details of the subject of the report (victim or suspect).
- **Sheet 3: Additional details**. This sets out addresses of the subject.
- **Sheet 4: Transaction details**. This sets out the type of transaction and the amounts involved.
- **Sheet 5: Reasons for suspicion**. These must be set out in full.
- **Sheet 6: Reason for suspicion continuation**.

In addition, the first time a firm submits a disclosure to SOCA or when the firm's contact details have changed, it will be necessary to submit the Source Registration Document.

10.3.2 Limited intelligence value reports

Dame Elizabeth Butler-Sloss in her judgment in *P* v. *P* stated:

> It is important for the legal profession to take into account . . . that the Act [PoCA 2002] makes no distinction between degrees of criminal property. An illegally obtained sum of £10 is no less susceptible to the definition of 'criminal property' than a sum of £1 million. Parliament clearly intended this to be the case. Whatever may be the resource implications, the legal profession would appear to be bound by the provisions of the Act in all cases, however big or small. If this approach is scrupulously followed by the legal advisers, the result is likely to have a considerable and adverse impact upon NCIS [now SOCA] . . .

Acknowledging the problem, SOCA has provided a limited intelligence value report for use in certain specified circumstances. As with the standard report, the form of this report can be downloaded from the SOCA website and completed on the solicitor's own computer (see above for further details). Special versions of the form are available where the solicitor wishes to complete the form by hand. The form must be submitted by fax or post, and the contact fax number and address is the same as used to submit the standard form (see **Paragraph 10.3.1**).

The form itself is a single sheet. A copy, together with the guidance notes for completion, can be found in **Appendix C4**.

SOCA has issued guidance on the types of circumstances that are appropriate for abbreviated information to be provided in this form. It accepts that the provisions of PoCA 2002 mean that solicitors may be required to make disclosures but the information is likely to be of limited intelligence value to law enforcement agencies. However, SOCA reserves the right to ask solicitors to submit details on a standard form if it believes this is necessary.

The circumstances where a limited intelligence value report is appropriate can be found in the table included in the guidance notes at **Appendix C4**. Limited intelligence reports can only be used for reports made under PoCA 2002 – all reports made under the Terrorism Act 2000 must be in the standard form format.

10.3.3   Consent report

As noted in **Chapter 4**, on occasions solicitors may be under time constraints (e.g. completion of the transaction may be set for two or three days' time). In these circumstances, if an authorised disclosure is made, no further action which might facilitate the acquisition, retention, use or control of criminal property can be undertaken without appropriate consent. If the disclosure has been made internally, the firm's nominated officer cannot give appropriate consent unless SOCA has been notified and it has either consented to the action proposed or seven working days have elapsed during which SOCA has not given notice of refusal to act. (For details of these provisions, see **Chapter 3**.)

Where time is important the nominated officer should make the disclosure electronically or by fax (020 7238 8286) indicating that the matter is urgent and giving details of the time critical issues so that consent can be given quickly. In most cases there is no need to telephone the duty desk at SOCA first to explain the urgency (telephone 020 7238 8282). The 'consent required' box should be marked on the standard form. Details of the timescale and the impact of a delayed response should be included in the report.

Where a consent request is submitted the Consent Team will contact the person making the report by telephone with a decision. Written confirmation will subsequently be posted to the firm.

10.3.4 After the report

The Law Society has given guidance in relation to a solicitor's duty and obligations after making a report to SOCA. This guidance also deals with the tension between an obligation not to tip off and an individual's right to access to all of his personal data under the terms of the Data Protection Act 1998. The guidance, which still refers to SOCA's predecessor NCIS, is set out below.

> Even after a report has been made, firms should continue to be vigilant for any related transactions or instructions that cause the solicitor concern/suspicion and which may need to be reported. Follow up reports may need to be made because circumstances change or develop.
>
> If appropriate consent is withheld during the moratorium period, NCIS [now SOCA] and/or law enforcement agencies will usually advise the organisation which made the report why this decision has been taken. Solicitors should not communicate these reasons to their clients or other parties.
>
> The submission of a report and/or the receipt of appropriate consent is not intended to override commercial judgement. It will be for solicitors to decide whether to continue to act. Terminating a retainer will not in itself amount to tipping off but the manner in which the retainer is terminated will be important. NCIS and/or law enforcement agencies may be able to provide some assistance to solicitors in explaining why they no longer wish to act for a client.
>
> There are concerns that reports may be revealed by the authorities to the suspected person or organisation, often a solicitor's own client. NCIS would prefer all information which they provide to law enforcement agencies to remain confidential, and for the reports to be included in the sensitive material bundle of any eventual prosecution papers. This means that the information will not automatically be disclosed by the prosecution to the defence lawyers. However, this is at the discretion of the prosecuting body. If the prosecuting body is sympathetic to the discloser's desire to remain anonymous they can mount Public Interest Immunity arguments. On occasion prosecuting bodies have discontinued cases rather than risk the identity of sources being revealed. The Law Society remains concerned that there should be official assurances about how this issue will be approached.
>
> Both NCIS and solicitors' firms are subject to the Data Protection Act 1998 which means that clients or others can make subject access requests under section 7. Such a request raises the question of whether a report to NCIS should be disclosed to the person making the subject access request. The tension between the obligation not to tip off, and the individual's right of access to all of his personal data is addressed in guidance issued by HM Treasury in consultation with the Information Commissioner. Section 29 of the Data Protection Act provides an exemption from the need to provide personal data where disclosure would be likely to prejudice the prevention or detection of crime or the apprehension or prosecution of offenders. The guidance says that where disclosure would constitute a tipping off offence, the section 29 exemption would be likely to apply. The guidance applies even if a suspicion has been made internally within a solicitor's firm and not reported externally. Note that the Treasury guidance may be reviewed in the light of recent case law on the definition of personal data.
>
> If solicitors receive a subject access request but are in doubt as to whether the provision of information, e.g. a copy report made to NCIS, would be likely to prejudice an investigation or potential investigation they should approach NCIS and

the relevant law enforcement agency for guidance. Solicitors should keep records of any steps they take in determining whether disclosure would involve tipping off and/or the availability of a section 29 exemption. These records may be useful if the solicitor is asked to respond to enquiries made subsequently by the Information Commissioner or courts.

It is important to note that where a piece of information is not disclosed because of the section 29 exemption there is no obligation to tell the individual that the information has been withheld.

CHAPTER 11

Management of money laundering procedures

11.1 INTRODUCTION

This chapter provides guidance on how firms can organise their management and administration of money laundering procedures to promote compliance with the Money Laundering Regulations 2003 and to avoid risking inadvertent involvement in money laundering offences. The dangers from the legislation of undertaking any legal services on behalf of clients are such that it is vital for even the smallest of firms to adopt anti-money laundering systems and policies.

11.2 POLICY DECISIONS

Firms should make a number of policy decisions in respect of their anti-money laundering procedures. It is vital to undertake all areas of practice within a framework of positive policy decisions rather than allowing the organisation to develop procedures in an unstructured way. Clear policy decisions allow all those involved in relevant business within the firm and those involved in other risk areas of the practice to understand their responsibilities and obligations. A senior partner (or officer) should be responsible for ensuring business decisions on anti-money laundering procedures. This partner (or officer) will frequently be the firm's nominated officer although where the nominated officer is not a partner (or officer) overall responsibility for the firm's policies should rest with a partner or officer.

The policy decisions required to be taken by the firm are listed below. This may not be an exhaustive list. Further details are provided on each heading in the paragraphs which follow. The policies include:

- Appointment of a nominated officer.
- Type of work at risk from money laundering activities.
- Amendments to the firm's Terms of Business.
- Internal reporting procedures.
- Client identification procedures.

- Record-keeping procedures.
- Branch or overseas offices.
- Staff training.

11.2.1 Appointment of a nominated officer

Regulation 7 of the Money Laundering Regulations 2003 requires firms to nominate a person to receive disclosures of knowledge or suspicion of money laundering. If the firm is undertaking relevant business, it is mandatory for such an officer to be appointed in accordance with regulation 7. A failure to do so will amount to a criminal offence under the terms of regulation 3.

However, even if the firm is not undertaking relevant business (in the light of the current definition of relevant business, this is likely to apply to a very small number of firms) the appointment of a nominated officer is still good practice. The substantive law contained in the Proceeds of Crime Act 2002 (PoCA 2002) and the Terrorism Act 2000 does not oblige firms to appoint a nominated officer, however, without the appointment authorised or protected disclosures could only be made to SOCA. The appointment of a nominated officer ensures that internal disclosures can be made. (The fact that a firm does not undertake relevant business under the Money Laundering Regulations 2003 does not avoid the risk that members of the firm may commit offences under PoCA 2002 or the Terrorism Act 2000.)

Most firms will appoint a partner to the role and this partner can then be made responsible for the overall anti-money laundering policies of the firm. However, there is no requirement that the nominated officer be a partner. The requirement in regulation 7 that the nominated officer should consider reports from members of staff 'in the light of any relevant information' which is available in the firm means the nominated officer should be of sufficient seniority to have access to this information.

The role is an important and onerous one. A nominated officer will be subject to PoCA 2002, ss. 331 and 332 (see **Chapter 6**) which give rise to criminal offences if the nominated officer fails to follow the requirements of the sections. Further criminal offences can arise under regulation 7 of the Money Laundering Regulations 2003. Consequently, individuals should be prepared to accept the role only if they are able to take on the responsibilities, which in many cases will be time consuming. Thought might be given to the role rotating between specified partners, with each individual partner undertaking the role for a period of, say, six months, providing those undertaking the role have sufficient knowledge.

One important part of the role is the ability to provide detailed advice to members of the firm on their responsibilities and compliance with the firm's procedures. Nominated officers will need to keep up to date with developments in this area making the necessary amendments to the firm's procedures.

Larger firms will frequently appoint deputy officers to whom certain duties can be delegated. The nominated officer should, however, remain in overall control and will be the person ultimately responsible for complying with the legal obligations of an officer.

All firms must ensure that temporary cover is provided when the nominated officer is absent from the firm, for whatever reason.

11.2.2 Type of work at risk from money laundering activities

There is probably no area of practice which is not at risk, to some extent, from involvement in money laundering activities. However, some areas of practice are undoubtedly at more risk than others and firms need to identify the high-risk areas to ensure proper risk management procedures are put in place for the fee earners and others operating in these areas. Details of individual practice areas and the common risks are contained in **Chapter 12**.

11.2.3 Terms of business

The firm's terms of business should be reconsidered in the light of the substantive law and money laundering regulations. It will not be tipping off or the offence of prejudicing an investigation for firms to amend their standard terms of business, thereby explaining to clients the basis on which the money laundering requirements apply to all retainers. Clauses to consider might include some or all of the following:

- **Client identification**
  This term can be to the effect that Government regulations now require firms to obtain details of clients' identity before acting for them and in the absence of satisfactory evidence of identity, the firm will not be able to act or continue to act for the client.
- **Reporting obligations**
  This term can indicate that the firm has an obligation to report knowledge or suspicion of certain criminal activities to the authorities and that in many cases this must be done without reference to, or the consent of, the client.
- **Terminating the retainer**
  This term can indicate that, in extreme cases, the firm might have to terminate the client's instructions in circumstances where the firm may not be able to communicate the reason for the termination to the client. (This could be relevant where an authorised disclosure is made to SOCA and the firm receives notice of refusal of consent to the firm continuing to act. The fee earner could be tipping off if the reason for the termination was communicated to the client.)

- **Limitation of liability**

  Theoretically, solicitors could be liable in civil law to clients (and others who might be victims of criminal activities). The Law Society's *Money Laundering Guidance* provides an excellent and comprehensive statement of the law on civil liability arising in the context of money laundering and offers practical guidance on how to reduce the risk of liability. Its guidance on this topic is printed in full in **Appendix B1**.

  Although an exclusion clause will not assist a solicitor where a victim who is not a client makes a civil claim, such a clause may assist in relation to claims by clients. If a completion is delayed as a result of an authorised disclosure and the client is consequently in breach of contract, the client may seek to obtain damages from the solicitor, particularly if it turns out that the suspected criminal conduct did not exist. A clause which seeks to limit liability from civil claims arising from a decision by a solicitor relating to his or her money laundering obligations may be helpful. Any such clause is likely to be subject to the reasonableness test in section 2(2) Unfair Contract Terms Act 1977. The Law Society's guidance on limitation of liability by contract is contained in paragraph 12.11 of *The Guide to The Professional Conduct of Solicitors* (8th edition 1999). This provides that solicitors may, by contract, seek to limit their liability provided such limitation is not below the minimum level of compulsory insurance cover (currently £2 million for unincorporated practices, £3 million for most incorporated practices). The *Guide to Professional Conduct of Solicitors* is likely to be replaced by the new solicitors' Code of Conduct sometime in 2007. At the time of writing the new code contains similar provisions relating to the limiting of liability. Rule 2.07 states:

  If you are a principal in a firm you must not exclude or attempt to exclude by contract all liability to your clients. However, you may limit civil liability, provided that such limitation is not below the minimum level of cover required by the Solicitors' Indemnity Insurance Rules for a policy of qualifying insurance, and the agreement is in writing.

- **Source of funds**

  This term may specify that, as a result of Government regulations, the firm must have regard to the source of any funds to be used by the client in any transaction and that, consequently, the firm will require clients to fully disclose details of the source of funds. Failure to do may lead to the firm terminating the retainer.

  Where funds are sourced from abroad, consideration might be given to a requirement that such funds are brought into the UK through a UK clearing bank rather that directly into the solicitor's client account. In this way some comfort can be obtained from the bank's anti-money laundering procedures. However, it must be acknowledged that the use of a UK bank in these circumstances will not completely avoid any risks on the part of the solicitor. The solicitor may have information obtained in the course of acting which the bank does not have and which gives rise to suspicion or knowledge of criminal intent.

11.2.4　Internal reporting procedures

A key decision to be taken by firms is how members of staff should report their knowledge or suspicion of money laundering matters. For most firms, the decision will be that all members of staff should use the internal reporting procedures rather than external reporting. The name of the nominated officer together with the name of the deputy and/or alternative should be made known to all members of staff. Firms should consider using a standard form for internal reporting purposes, allowing for a clear distinction to be made between informal discussions with the nominated officer and formal disclosures.

A clear policy for post-disclosure requirements must be adopted and communicated. This policy should be that once an internal disclosure has been made:

- No further work should be undertaken on the file without the consent of the nominated officer. Failure to abide by this requirement could lead to the loss of any defence afforded by an authorised disclosure (see **Chapter 4**). Whilst in practice it may be possible for a limited amount of preparatory work to be undertaken on the file (i.e. that work which does not facilitate the acquisition, retention, use or control of criminal property) it is dangerous to allow individual fee earners to make a decision as to what might be possible and what activities might negate any defence. The nominated officer should take this decision centrally, after careful consideration of the facts.
- No communication should be made to anyone concerning the disclosure, without the consent of the nominated officer. Failure to comply with this requirement may lead to tipping off and/or the offence of prejudicing an investigation (see **Chapter 7**). Again, it makes sense to keep control of any subsequent communications centrally rather than to allow individual members of staff to make their own decisions. This restriction on communicating should be absolute. In other words, those making the disclosure should not communicate details to anyone, including other members of staff.

One problem arising from these policies (particularly the policy of restricting communications regarding the disclosure) is that if a fee earner leaves the firm or otherwise ceases to act on a file, any new fee earner may not be aware that concerns have been expressed regarding money laundering and that an authorised disclosure may have been made internally. To overcome this problem some firms operate a black book system. The nominated officer enters all reports (formal or otherwise) in a black book which he/she keeps confidential.

New fee earners can make a black book search by approaching the nominated officer who can simply confirm if any entry regarding that file has been made. Files which have given rise to a report could be tagged (extra number/letter on file reference) which would then indicate to any fee earner coming to the file that a black book search should be made. Tagging using a discreet indication should not give rise to any risk of tipping off where the client requires access to the file.

This system may be of particular relevance where a litigation matter is conducted with knowledge or suspicion that the funds or property involved might be criminal property. Although *Bowman* v. *Fels* excludes litigation from the effects of the money laundering offences (PoCA 2002, ss.327–329), the litigation process does not 'clean' the criminal property. Recording knowledge or suspicion in these circumstances allows fee earners to consider whether any future transaction matter undertaken on behalf of the client might have to be reported to the authorities.

11.2.5   Client identification procedures

In addition to deciding exactly what evidence of identity is acceptable for different categories of client (for details see **Chapter 9** and, in particular, **Appendix B1**) a policy decision must be taken specifying which clients are subject to verification of their identity.

If firms wish to apply the Money Laundering Regulations 2003 strictly a complex new file opening procedure will have to be adopted which will have to be capable of ascertaining:

* Whether relevant business will be undertaken.
* If so, whether it is a business relationship or one-off transaction.
* If it is a one-off transaction, whether the amount involved is €15,000 or more or whether there is knowledge or suspicion of money laundering.
* Whether any of the exceptions apply.
* Whether the transitional provisions apply.

Even if, in the light of this complex checklist, a decision is taken that no identification procedures are necessary, the firm's procedures must be able to identify when a one-off transaction (which initially did not require identification) becomes a business relationship or when a transaction which starts as non-relevant business becomes relevant business (as a result perhaps of tax advice being sought and given).

There is a lot to be said for applying verification procedures to all clients regardless of the type of business.

The firm should also adopt a clear policy on what can and cannot be undertaken on behalf of clients before satisfactory evidence of identity is received. This should include reference to the holding of client money (see **Chapter 9** for further detail).

11.2.6 Record-keeping requirements

Details of the formal records required under the Money Laundering Regulations 2003 are contained in **Chapter 9**. However, the firm should consider keeping records (possibly using internally agreed forms) covering the following areas:

- Record of the evidence of the client's identity (as required by the Regulations).
- Record of the transaction (as required by the Regulations). In many cases this record can be satisfied by reference to the contents of the client file and accounting records.
- Copy of the client verification form (for an example, see **Appendix C1**).
- Details of the client's source of funds.
- Record of internal disclosures.
- Record of the nominated officer's consideration and determination regarding internal disclosures.
- Record of external disclosures.
- Record of staff training.

11.2.7 Branch or overseas offices

Where a firm has a branch and/or an overseas office, firms should consider how best to ensure compliance by those offices with their anti-money laundering procedures. If the firm has a branch office in England and Wales, staff at the branch office will be subject to the same obligations as those working in the main office. Effective control procedures must be devised in accordance with the firm's general procedures. Deputy nominated officers may be appointed in each branch office.

Overseas offices will not, strictly, be subject to UK law or to the Money Laundering Regulations 2003. However, many overseas jurisdictions impose similar anti-money laundering requirements on local practitioners. EU countries will be subject to the Second EU Money Laundering Directive and, as such, should have introduced similar provisions to the UK Regulations. As a general rule, however, it appears that the UK's legislation and money laundering regulations impose a greater obligation upon practitioners compared with overseas jurisdictions (with the possible exception of the Netherlands). Consequently, many English and Welsh firms with overseas offices have adopted a policy that their overseas offices should comply with the UK requirements to enable a common set of procedures throughout the firm's offices. Local nominated officers can be appointed in each office with similar roles to the nominated officer in the UK.

11.2.8   Staff training

The training requirements are contained in regulation 3 of the Money Laundering Regulations 2003 and are dealt with in **Chapter 9**.

Firms should determine their training policies so as to ensure that all relevant members of staff receive training in the substantive law, the Regulations, the firm's own procedures and in the recognition and dealing with transactions which may involve money laundering.

The firm's money laundering manual (see **Paragraph 11.3**) should be distributed to all relevant members of staff and, if appropriate, members of staff should be asked to sign a declaration that they have read and understood its contents.

Training should be a rolling programme, with regular updating sessions and sessions for newly joined members of staff. It should cover all members of staff, fee earning as well as support staff, but should be tailored to individual group requirements.

11.3   THE COMPLIANCE MANUAL

PoCA 2002, the Terrorism Act 2000 and the Money Laundering Regulations 2003 require firms to comply with a fairly complex framework of rules. Full compliance with these requirements is essential.

Poor compliance in some circumstances can lead to a criminal conviction and the possibility of disciplinary action being taken against members of the firm. The firm's procedures for compliance with the requirements must therefore be given attention by high-level management within the firm. Once determined, the firm's policies and procedures must be communicated to all personnel who at any time may be involved in financial transactions.

The most satisfactory method of recording and communicating the firm's procedures is by the use of a compliance manual. The manual should be in an easily readable form and should not attempt to reiterate all the provisions of PoCA 2002, the Terrorism Act 2000 or the Money Laundering Regulations 2003. Instead, it should seek to provide explanations and instructions in a practical way in respect of the anti-money laundering procedures adopted by the firm. The manual should be arranged in suitable sections. It is essential that the manual is kept up to date.

The contents of the manual will vary from firm to firm. It is suggested that the following should be included in the manual:

- **Policy decisions**
  The policies which have been determined by the firm should be clearly stated. The names of the nominated officer, deputies and alternative officer should be stated.
- **Brief explanation and illustration of the Acts and the Regulations as they apply to the firm**
  The manual should not seek to reiterate all the provisions of PoCA 2002 or the Terrorism Act 2002 and other material. However, the emphasis should be on explanation and illustration of how the Acts and Regulations apply to the firm's business.
- **The firm's procedures for compliance**
  The firm's procedures should be recorded to ensure that all personnel understand how clients must be identified, how internal reports should be made and which records need to be maintained and where they are held.
- **Specimen forms**
  All forms relating to the firm's anti-money laundering procedures should be included with instructions for their use.
- **Instructions to departments of the firm on procedures which relate specifically to work undertaken in those departments**
  Procedures to be followed when dealing with clients of the various departments should be recorded where possible using one subsection per department. The procedures should, of course, be consistent with the policy decisions made on the type and extent of any risk and the possibility of the work involving activities in the regulated sector.
- **A list of warnings**
  A simple list of warnings could be included to inform staff when they are stepping outside the firm's policies or their individual authority.
- **Help**
  No matter how well written the manual is, the Acts and the Regulations can present a considerable compliance problem. The manual should give clear instructions on how to obtain assistance and advice from within the firm. A call for help at a crucial point by a fee earner could prevent a breach of the firm's internal policies and prevent the inadvertent commission of a crime.

CHAPTER 12

How to spot money laundering activities in a solicitor's practice

12.1 INTRODUCTION

It should be clear from the previous chapters in this book that almost all areas of a solicitor's practice are at risk from possible involvement in money laundering transactions. This chapter identifies specific practice areas and highlights the activities within those areas that could give rise to the risk.

It is impossible to define what amounts to a suspicion of involvement in criminal activities. Some parts of PoCA 2002 (e.g. the money laundering offences in ss.327–329) require the test of whether the accused had knowledge or suspicion to be satisfied on a subjective basis. In other parts of PoCA 2002 (notably failure to report, s.330) the test is a subjective and objective test. Some individuals are more suspicious than others, so in applying a subjective test, different results can be obtained using the same facts. Firms must encourage their staff to err on the side of caution; staff must be encouraged to consult with more senior members of the firm and, if necessary, with the firm's nominated officer. The Law Society's *Money Laundering Guidance* suggests that the thought processes which need to be undertaken after an initial cause for concern has been raised might include:

What is the cause for concern?

- Does your cause for concern relate to money, assets, or property which are the subject of a transaction?
- Is the cause for concern a lack of knowledge or understanding? If so, make enquiries, e.g. client does not appear wealthy but is buying a second home.
- Is your cause for concern based on fact, or rumour and gossip? For example, you may be aware that your client has a previous conviction for an acquisitive crime, which might lead you to question whether the money the client is using is profit from that crime. Alternatively, if the source of the information is more dubious, perhaps an obscure internet site, it may be necessary to verify the information through a better source.

Knowledge is likely to mean actual knowledge. In its *Money Laundering Guidance* the Law Society refers to *Archbold* (2004) at paragraphs 17–49 and reproduces the following quote:

There is some authority for the view that in the criminal law 'knowledge' includes 'wilfully shutting one's eyes to the truth': see, e.g. per Lord Reid in *Warner* v. *Metropolitan Police Commr* [1969] 2 AC 256 at 279, HL; *Atwal* v. *Massey*, 56 Cr.App.R. 6, DC. However such a proposition must be treated with great caution. The clear view of the courts at present is that this is a matter of evidence, and that nothing short of actual knowledge (or, in the case of dishonest handling, belief) will suffice.

12.2 CORPORATE DEPARTMENT

Activities in a firm's corporate department can give rise to a high risk of involvement in possible money laundering. Company formation services and financial transactions involving corporate clients will be within both the regulated sector for the purposes of the offence of failure to report (PoCA 2002, s.330) and within the definition of relevant business for the purposes of the Money Laundering Regulations 2003.

Consequently, corporate clients should be subject to identification procedures at the outset of new instructions (unless identification evidence is already held by the firm as a result of an earlier retainer). Further, members of staff will be required to report their knowledge or suspicion of criminal activities even if the retainer does not involve an arrangement which facilitates the acquisition, retention, use or control of criminal property or involve the holding in client account of possible criminal funds.

The following are specific areas of concern.

12.2.1 Formation of companies without any apparent commercial or other purpose

HM Treasury have identified front or shell companies as being a factor in many complex money laundering operations. Solicitors must be satisfied as to the commercial reason for a company formation transaction. They must understand why the client has come to the solicitor for assistance. In most cases, solicitors will be used because there will be an underlying legal service being provided along with the actual company formation: advising on the structure of the shareholding, the rights of shareholders, the constitution of the company etc. Instructions where a client (particularly one unknown to the firm) simply asks the firm to form a company should be treated with a degree of suspicion.

12.2.2 Formation of subsidiaries in circumstances where there appears to be no commercial or other purpose (particularly overseas subsidiaries)

For the same reason, formation of subsidiary companies should be treated with care where there appears to be no commercial or other proper purpose.

Any corporate transaction in an overseas jurisdiction should be considered carefully, particularly if the overseas jurisdiction is a country on the FATF's (Financial Action Task Force on Money Laundering) list of Non-Cooperative Countries and Territories (NCCTs). The FATF seeks to identify non-cooperative countries in the worldwide fight against money laundering. An up-to-date list of NCCTs can be found on the FATF's website (**www. fatf-gafi.org**).

12.2.3 Appointment of solicitors as directors with little or no commercial involvement

It might be flattering for a solicitor to be asked to serve as a director of a client company and in many cases there may be compelling commercial reasons for such an appointment. However, those involved in money laundering will wish to project any company they use as a legitimate concern and having a reputable solicitor on the board of directors will assist in this aim. Solicitors must consider the possibility of involvement in money laundering before accepting any board appointment.

12.2.4 Purchase of private company using suspect funds

The purchase (or sale) of any asset can involve a money laundering transaction. The funds used to purchase the asset may fall within the definition of criminal property (see **Chapter 2**). Because of the wide definition, company shares may have been purchased in the past using criminal funds meaning that the shares could represent a person's benefit from criminal conduct and thus be criminal property. As with the purchase of any asset, solicitors should be concerned about the source of funds and/or the legitimacy of any asset.

12.2.5 Large payments for unspecified services to consultants, related parties, employees, etc

In the course of acting for a corporate client, solicitors are likely to become aware of many facts relating to the running of the company. Some of these facts (such as large payments for unspecified services or suspected tax evasion) may give rise to knowledge or suspicion of money laundering. Other examples might include the discovery of unauthorised transactions or improperly recorded transactions (particularly where the company has poor/inadequate accounting systems).

Even if the solicitor is not involved in a transaction relating to these payments, the fact that corporate work is likely to be within the regulated sector means that knowledge or suspicion of these matters could give rise to an obligation to report.

12.2.6 Unusual transactions (including purchase/sale transactions significantly above/below market price)

Transactions may be unusual in themselves or because they are unusual by reference to the normal type of work done by the firm or for the particular client.

Fee earners should not act outside their normal range of expertise. Undoubtedly, money launderers play on the fact that firms might be persuaded to accept instructions (frequently at an attractive fee) in circumstances where the firm or fee earner has no in-depth knowledge of the type of transaction involved. In this way the money launderers will avoid detailed questions from the firm concerning the transaction.

Firms should be aware of the normal transactions their clients have been involved in over recent years. The most difficult transaction to identify involving money laundering is where the client has been a good client providing the firm with legitimate business over a number of years. Such clients who suddenly go rogue can be very difficult to identify as money launderers. Enquiries should be made where established clients instruct the firm in unusual circumstances.

Transactions which are unusual in themselves obviously give rise to concern and these will include any transaction which appears to be significantly over- or under-valued.

12.2.7 Long delays over the production of company accounts

Those using companies for unlawful purposes are unlikely to want to make public financial disclosures by filing accounts for the company. The penalties for late filing of company accounts are unlikely to concern the individuals behind the company – they will hope to have achieved their object and be well away before steps are taken to enforce the filing requirements.

12.2.8 Dubious businesses often use more than one set of professional advisers. Ask 'why me?'

Solicitors should be particularly concerned where they discover that a particular corporate client has instructed another firm of solicitors in similar circumstances, where, for example, there appears to be a parallel deal involving different advisers. One common approach used by money launderers is to split up a complex transaction into a number of smaller transactions, using different professional advisers in each of the smaller transactions. In this way, no one firm sees the overall picture. However, firms should be suspicious if the facts of a case suggest that this is what is going on. (An illustration of this method, where a corporate client uses a number of solicitors in a conveyancing transaction, is given in **Paragraph 12.3**.)

12.3 PROPERTY DEPARTMENT

Activities in a firm's property department also give rise to a high risk of involvement in possible money laundering. Real property transactions will be within both the regulated sector for the purposes of the offence of failure to report (PoCA 2002, s.330) and within the definition of relevant business for the purposes of the Money Laundering Regulations 2003.

In December 2005 the Law Society issued *Anti-money laundering guidance for solicitors undertaking property work*. This is reproduced in **Appendix B3**.

Property clients should be subject to identification procedures at the outset of new instructions (unless identification evidence is already held by the firm as a result of an earlier retainer). Further, members of staff will be required to report their knowledge or suspicion of criminal activities even if the retainer does not involve an arrangement which facilitates the acquisition, retention, use or control of criminal property or involve the holding in client account of possible criminal funds.

The following are specific areas of concern.

12.3.1 Fictitious buyers (introduced by third party) and not known to the solicitor

Criminals commonly used the fictitious buyer scam to obtain mortgage advances by deception. Frequently, this involves individuals who claim to represent a large numbers of clients all of whom have suddenly decided to purchase houses and most of whom can never find time to meet the solicitor.

Mortgage applications would be made in fictitious names to many financial institutions (often using the same properties) using a number of innocent solicitors. The mortgage advance would clearly amount to criminal property (having been obtained by deception) and solicitors would clearly be at risk of involvement in money laundering activities. Any arrangement in which the solicitor was concerned (typically, the completion of the mortgage) would facilitate the acquisition, retention, use or control of criminal property. This could apply where the client was involved in the criminal activity or where the solicitor was acting for the financial institution and another firm represented the perpetrator of the crime. Holding and/or dealing with the mortgage advance money in these circumstances could also give rise to the offence of acquisition, use or possession (PoCA 2002, s.329) or possibly the offence of concealing (PoCA 2002, s.327).

Whilst it is fair to say that the requirements for obtaining verification of the client's identity have undoubtedly reduced the number of frauds using this particular scam, solicitors must nonetheless be vigilant – this illustrates the importance of adopting proper and effective client identification procedures.

12.3.2 Payment of deposit directly to vendor (particularly where the deposit paid is excessive)

Another typical method of defrauding mortgage providers is to misrepresent the purchase price – using a price which appears to suggest that the value of the security is greater than it is in reality. Often this scam is achieved by a direct payment to the vendor by the purchaser, rather than making the payment through the solicitors.

By way of illustration, a client is purchasing property at an agreed price of £400,000. The client's building society agrees a maximum mortgage advance of 80 per cent of the purchase price, i.e. £320,000. Because of a poor survey report, the vendor agrees with the purchaser to reduce the price to £350,000. This would have the effect of reducing the mortgage advance if it came to the knowledge of the building society. The vendor and purchaser decide not to notify their own solicitors or the building society of the reduction. On exchange of contracts, the purchaser informs his solicitor that he has paid a deposit direct to the purchaser of £50,000, leaving only £350,000 to be paid on completion. Of course, no deposit has been paid and the property is purchased at a price of £350,000 albeit the paperwork shows a price of £400,000. The payment of a direct deposit (greater than the normal 10 per cent of the purchase price) should put the purchaser's solicitor on notice that the transaction needs to be considered with care.

12.3.3 Purchase of property using suspect funds

The purchase (or sale) of property can involve a money laundering transaction. The funds used to purchase the property may fall within the definition of criminal property (see **Chapter 2**). Further, because of the wide definition, property may have been purchased in the past using criminal funds meaning that the property could represent a person's benefit from criminal conduct and thus be criminal property. As with the purchase of any asset, solicitors should be concerned at the source of funds and/or the legitimacy of any asset.

12.3.4 Purchase of property using a corporate vehicle where there is no good commercial or other reason

As noted above, corporate vehicles are frequently used in money laundering transactions. It is sometimes easier to split complex transactions into smaller matters where companies are used. Firms must be satisfied that there are good commercial or legal reasons for using a company.

A group of criminal individuals intend purchasing a chain of 12 hotels. The total purchase price amounts to, say, £15 million. However, the individuals (perhaps using a crooked surveyor) intend applying for finance of £20 million using the hotels as security. To do this they will represent the value of the hotels as being in the region of £25 million.

The original purchase will go through at the legitimate price: £15 million. Rather than purchasing the group in the names of the individuals (or by way of a share purchase), the transaction will be an asset purchase, transferring the title to the 12 hotels into the name of a company (possibly an overseas company created using nominees for the individuals). This transaction will appear to be legitimate (although the purchase in the name of an off-shore company held by nominees might give rise to suspicion on the part of the purchaser's solicitor). Indeed, at this stage, it appears that no criminal activity has been undertaken. To avoid any further suspicion at the next stage (which will amount to criminal activity) the individuals are likely to instruct 12 different firms of solicitors, each of whom will be asked to act for the off-shore company on the sale of a single hotel to individuals (or other companies connected with them). The purchasers will also instruct 12 different firms of solicitors to act on their behalf. The total purchase price for these 12 transactions will be shown at £25 million, financed by loans of, in total, £20 million.

All solicitors acting in this scenario could be involved in an arrangement contrary to PoCA 2002, s.328 and guilty of a criminal offence if they knew or suspected that the arrangement facilitated the acquisition, retention, use or control of criminal property. The use of a company in the original transaction (solicitors acting on the second stage will be made aware that the individual hotels had been recently purchased by the off-shore company) and the possible knowledge that other professionals were involved in similar transactions could be sufficient to put the firms involved on notice that the circumstances were suspicious.

12.4 PRIVATE CLIENT DEPARTMENT

Activities in a firm's trust department can give rise to a high risk of involvement in possible money laundering. Probate work is less likely to give rise to a high risk of involvement but, nonetheless, since assets of various categories are involved, money laundering cannot be ruled out completely. Both trust administration and probate transactions are likely to be within both the regulated sector for the purposes of the offence of failure to report (PoCA 2002, s.330) and within the definition of relevant business for the purposes of the Money Laundering Regulations 2003.

In February 2006 the Law Society issued *Anti-money laundering guidance for solicitors conducting private client work*. This is reproduced in **Appendix B4**.

In trust administration, the client will be the trustee(s). Unless the firm is acting for beneficiaries there is no need to establish the identity of beneficiaries for the purposes of the Money Laundering Regulations 2003. Trustees should be subject to identification procedures at the outset of new instructions (unless identification evidence is already held by the firm as a result of an earlier retainer) using the procedures for individual clients (or, if the trustee is a trust corporation, for companies). In probate matters, the client is the executor(s) or administrator(s) and again their identity should be established using the procedures for individuals or companies.

If the trust or estate administration work involves financial or real property transactions, tax advice, advice and arrangements relating to the purchase or sale of specified investments or acting on the formation, operation or management of a trust, the work will be in the regulated sector. This means that members of staff will be required to report their knowledge or suspicion of criminal activities even if the retainer does not involve an arrangement which facilitates the acquisition, retention, use or control of criminal property or involve the holding in client account of possible criminal funds.

The following are specific areas of concern.

12.4.1   The formation of trusts with no apparent commercial or other purpose

HM Treasury have identified trust funds as being a factor in many complex money laundering operations. Solicitors must be satisfied as to the commercial reason for a trust formation. They must understand why the client has come to the solicitor for assistance. In most cases, solicitors will be used because there will be an underlying legal service being provided along with the actual trust formation: administering the trust, or giving tax advice on the use of the trust. Instructions where a client (particularly one unknown to the firm) simply asks the firm to form a trust should be treated with a degree of suspicion. This is particularly so where the trust is intended to be an off-shore trust. Sometimes, the identity of off-shore trustees may be difficult to ascertain. Fee earners must be reminded that, where the firm is undertaking relevant business in the UK and satisfactory evidence of identification cannot be obtained, the business retainer must not proceed further.

If the intended trust fund is to be established in an NCCT (see **Paragraph 12.2.2**) particular care must be taken to ensure the identity of the trustees and the legitimacy of the trust fund.

12.4.2   The appointment of solicitors as trustees with little or no commercial involvement

As with the appointment of a solicitor as a director of a corporate client, it can be flattering for a solicitor to be asked by a settlor to act as a trustee of a trust. In many cases there may be compelling commercial or legal reasons for such an appointment. However, those involved in money laundering will wish to project any trust fund they use as a legitimate fund and having a reputable solicitor as a trustee will assist in this aim. Solicitors must consider the possibility of involvement in money laundering before accepting any trust appointment.

157

12.4.3   The receipt of suspect funds into the trust fund

The purchase (or sale) of any asset held in a trust fund can involve a money laundering transaction. The funds used to purchase the asset may fall within the definition of criminal property (see **Chapter 2**). Further, because of the wide definition, assets or investments held in the fund may have been purchased in the past using criminal funds meaning that those assets could represent a person's benefit from criminal conduct and thus be criminal property. As with the purchase of any asset, solicitors should be concerned at the source of funds and/or the legitimacy of any asset.

12.5   TAXATION ADVICE

The provision by way of business advice about the tax affairs of another will fall within the definition of relevant business (for the purposes of the Money Laundering Regulations 2003) and the regulated sector for the purposes of the offence of failure to report (PoCA 2002, s.330). Consequently, in any practice area where tax advice is given, clients should be subject to identification procedures at the outset of new instructions (unless identification evidence is already held by the firm as a result of an earlier retainer) even if the practice area itself would not involve relevant business. For example, drafting a will, or giving employment advice, will not be within the definition of relevant business. However, if in the course of will drafting, advice is given on inheritance tax planning, this advice will be sufficient to bring the matter within the definition of relevant business. Similarly, if in the course of employment advice, tax advice is given, this matter will then amount to relevant business.

Because tax advice will amount to business in the regulated sector, members of staff will be required to report their knowledge or suspicion of criminal activities even if the retainer does not involve an arrangement which facilitates the acquisition, retention, use or control of criminal property or involve the holding in client account of possible criminal funds.

Where a client admits tax evasion to a solicitor, that client is likely to be engaged in money laundering, that is, the client is in possession of criminal property, money or assets that represent money that should have been paid to HM Revenue and Customs authorities. If the solicitor's transaction will involve any part of these funds or assets, the solicitor is in danger of being involved in an arrangement that will facilitate the retention, use or control of criminal property. It is likely that an authorised disclosure must be made. Even if the particular funds are not going to be used as part of a transaction, a report under PoCA 2002, s.330 will have to be made unless one of the appropriate defences applies (in particular, the information may have been passed on to the solicitor in privileged circumstances). Careful consideration must be given to the facts of the transaction.

There is a narrow dividing line between the concepts of tax evasion (which is a criminal offence) and tax avoidance (which is legitimate). Solicitors giving tax advice must take care not to cross that line so that the advice leads to tax evasion. The advice in these circumstances could amount to an arrangement which facilitates the acquisition of criminal property.

12.6 TRANSACTIONAL MATTERS – GENERAL

The Law Society has issued a flowchart as part of its guidance following *Bowman* v. *Fels* (see **Appendix B2**). This provides a helpful step-by-step guide to the approach to take in transactional matters where there is knowledge or suspicion of money laundering. It covers the necessary steps to take where the knowledge or suspicion is based on common law LPP as well as where the privilege defence applies in respect of PoCA 2002, s.330 (failure to report).

12.7 LITIGATION DEPARTMENT

The Court of Appeal's decision in *Bowman* v. *Fels* (see **Chapter 2**) means that litigation activities are unlikely to involve solicitors in any of the money laundering offences (PoCA 2002, ss.327–329). Further, litigation, in itself, is not in the regulated sector and thus will not give rise to an obligation to disclose under section 330 (see **Chapter 5**). However, as noted in **Chapter 2**, care must be taken if any criminal property comes into the possession of a solicitor following litigation. The litigation has not 'cleaned' the criminal property and subsequent transactions involving the property may well give rise to money laundering implications.

12.8 CONCLUSION

In whatever practice area a solicitor works, there will be some element of risk from involvement in money laundering. The Law Society's Warning Card to Solicitors about money laundering highlights the following causes for concern.

Unusual settlement requests
Anything that is unusual or unpredictable or otherwise gives cause for concern should lead you to ask more questions about the source of the funds. Remember, proceeds of crime can arrive through the banking system as well.
Think carefully if any of the following are proposed or occur:

- Settlements by cash
- Surprise payments by way of third party cheque
- Money transfers where there is a variation between account holder or the signatory

- Requests to make regular payments out of client account
- Settlements which are reached too easily.

Unusual transactions

- Why has the client chosen your firm? Could the client find the same services nearer their home?
- Are you being asked to do something that does not fit in with the normal pattern of your business?
- Be cautious if instructions change without a reasonable explanation
- Be cautious about transactions which take an unusual turn

Use of your client account

- Using solicitors' client accounts to transmit money is useful to money launderers
- Do not provide a banking facility if you do not undertake any related legal work
- Be cautious if you are instructed to do legal work, receive funds into your client account, but then the instructions are cancelled and you are asked to return the money either to your client or a third party.

Remember you may still be assisting a money launderer even though money does not pass through your firm's bank accounts.

Suspect territory

- If you are instructed in transactions with an international element you can refer to the FATF who produce up to date information about different countries.

Finally, take heed of the contents of the following paragraph taken from the Law Society's *Money Laundering Guidance*:

Where appropriate, anti-money laundering procedures should place barriers between prospective clients and the services you provide. To cross those barriers successfully clients will need to provide sufficient information about themselves and their instructions to give you the confidence you need to act for them. The extent of the barriers you put in place will depend upon the assessed level of money laundering risk. If the initial information which clients provide is insufficient, more information will be needed. In some cases the information provided at the outset may lead to a suspicion of money laundering, in which case consideration will need to be given to whether a report should be made under POCA. In other cases the developments which happen in the client's matter might give rise to the solicitor asking more questions, or to form a suspicion. When sufficient information is known it is for the solicitor's own professional judgement whether he is suspicious.

PART 3

Appendices

A1

Extracts from the Proceeds of Crime Act 2002 (as amended at May 2006)

[...]

PART 7
MONEY LAUNDERING

Offences

327 Concealing etc

(1) A person commits an offence if he–

(a) conceals criminal property;
(b) disguises criminal property;
(c) converts criminal property;
(d) transfers criminal property;
(e) removes criminal property from England and Wales or from Scotland or from Northern Ireland.

(2) But a person does not commit such an offence if–

(a) he makes an authorised disclosure under section 338 and (if the disclosure is made before he does the act mentioned in subsection (1)) he has the appropriate consent;
(b) he intended to make such a disclosure but had a reasonable excuse for not doing so;
(c) the act he does is done in carrying out a function he has relating to the enforcement of any provision of this Act or of any other enactment relating to criminal conduct or benefit from criminal conduct.

(2A) Nor does a person commit an offence under subsection (1) if–

(a) he knows, or believes on reasonable grounds, that the relevant criminal conduct occurred in a particular country or territory outside the United Kingdom; and
(b) the relevant criminal conduct–
    (i)   was not, at the time it occurred, unlawful under the criminal law then applying in that country or territory; and
    (ii) is not of a description prescribed by an order made by the Secretary of State.

(2B) In subsection (2A) 'the relevant criminal conduct' is the criminal conduct by reference to which the property concerned is criminal property.

(2C) A deposit-taking body that does an act mentioned in paragraph (c) or (d) of subsection (1) does not commit an offence under that subsection if–

    (a) it does the act in operating an account maintained with it; and

    (b) the value of the criminal property concerned is less than the threshold amount determined under section 339A for the act.

(3) Concealing or disguising criminal property includes concealing or disguising its nature, source, location, disposition, movement or ownership or any rights with respect to it.

328 Arrangements

(1) A person commits an offence if he enters into or becomes concerned in an arrangement which he knows or suspects facilitates (by whatever means) the acquisition, retention, use or control of criminal property by or on behalf of another person.

(2) But a person does not commit such an offence if–

    (a) he makes an authorised disclosure under section 338 and (if the disclosure is made before he does the act mentioned in subsection (1)) he has the appropriate consent;

    (b) he intended to make such a disclosure but had a reasonable excuse for not doing so;

    (c) the act he does is done in carrying out a function he has relating to the enforcement of any provision of this Act or of any other enactment relating to criminal conduct or benefit from criminal conduct.

(3) Nor does a person commit an offence under subsection (1) if–

    (a) he knows, or believes on reasonable grounds, that the relevant criminal conduct occurred in a particular country or territory outside the United Kingdom; and

    (b) the relevant criminal conduct–

        (i) was not, at the time it occurred, unlawful under the criminal law then applying in that country or territory; and

        (ii) is not of a description prescribed by an order made by the Secretary of State.

(4) In subsection (3) 'the relevant criminal conduct' is the criminal conduct by reference to which the property concerned is criminal property.

(5) A deposit-taking body that does an act mentioned in subsection (1) does not commit an offence under that subsection if –

    (a) it does the act in operating an account maintained with it; and

    (b) the arrangement facilitates the acquisition, retention, use or control of criminal property of a value that is less than the threshold amount determined under section 339A for the act.

329 Acquisition, use and possession

(1) A person commits an offence if he–

(a) acquires criminal property;
(b) uses criminal property;
(c) has possession of criminal property.

(2) But a person does not commit such an offence if–

(a) he makes an authorised disclosure under section 338 and (if the disclosure is made before he does the act mentioned in subsection (1)) he has the appropriate consent;
(b) he intended to make such a disclosure but had a reasonable excuse for not doing so;
(c) he acquired or used or had possession of the property for adequate consideration;
(d) the act he does is done in carrying out a function he has relating to the enforcement of any provision of this Act or of any other enactment relating to criminal conduct or benefit from criminal conduct.

(2A) Nor does a person commit an offence under subsection (1) if–

(a) he knows, or believes on reasonable grounds, that the relevant criminal conduct occurred in a particular country or territory outside the United Kingdom; and
(b) the relevant criminal conduct –
  (i) was not, at the time it occurred, unlawful under the criminal law then applying in that country or territory; and
  (ii) is not of a description prescribed by an order made by the Secretary of State.

(2B) In subsection (2A) 'the relevant criminal conduct' is the criminal conduct by reference to which the property concerned is criminal property.

(2C) A deposit-taking body that does an act mentioned in subsection (1) does not commit an offence under that subsection if–

(a) it does the act in operating an account maintained with it; and
(b) the value of the criminal property concerned is less than the threshold amount determined under section 339A for the act.

(3) For the purposes of this section–

(a) a person acquires property for inadequate consideration if the value of the consideration is significantly less than the value of the property;
(b) a person uses or has possession of property for inadequate consideration if the value of the consideration is significantly less than the value of the use or possession;
(c) the provision by a person of goods or services which he knows or suspects may help another to carry out criminal conduct is not consideration.

330 Failure to disclose: regulated sector

(1) A person commits an offence if the conditions in subsections (2) to (4) are satisfied.

(2) The first condition is that he–

(a) knows or suspects, or
(b) has reasonable grounds for knowing or suspecting,
that another person is engaged in money laundering.

(3) The second condition is that the information or other matter–

(a) on which his knowledge or suspicion is based, or
(b) which gives reasonable grounds for such knowledge or suspicion,
came to him in the course of a business in the regulated sector.

(3A) The third condition is–

(a) that he can identify the other person mentioned in subsection (2) or the whereabouts of any of the laundered property; or
(b) that he believes, or it is reasonable to expect him to believe, that the information or other matter mentioned in subsection (3) will or may assist in identifying the other person or the whereabouts of any of the laundered property.

(4) The fourth condition is that he does not make the required disclosure to–

(a) a nominated officer; or
(b) a person authorised for the purposes of this Part by the Director General of the Serious Organised Crime Agency, as soon as is practicable after the information or other matter mentioned in subsection (3) comes to him.

(5) The required disclosure is a disclosure of–

(a) the identity of the other person mentioned in subsection (2), if he knows it;
(b) the whereabouts of the laundered property, so far as he knows it; and
(c) the information or other matter mentioned in subsection (3).

(5A) The laundered property is the property forming the subject-matter of the money laundering that he knows or suspects, or has reasonable grounds for knowing or suspecting, that other person to be engaged in.

(6) But he does not commit an offence under this section if–

(a) he has a reasonable excuse for not making the required disclosure;
(b) he is a professional legal adviser or other relevant professional adviser; and
(i) if he knows either of the things mentioned in subsection (5)(a) and (b), he knows the thing because of information or other matter that came to him in privileged circumstances, or
(ii) the information or other matter mentioned in subsection (3) came to him in privileged circumstances, or
(c) subsection (7) or (7B) applies to him.

(7) This subsection applies to a person if–

    (a) he does not know or suspect that another person is engaged in money laundering, and

    (b) he has not been provided by his employer with such training as is specified by the Secretary of State by order for the purposes of this section.

(7A) Nor does a person commit an offence under this section if–

    (a) he knows, or believes on reasonable grounds, that the money laundering is occurring in a particular country or territory outside the United Kingdom; and

    (b) the money laundering–
        (i) is not unlawful under the criminal law applying in that country or territory; and
        (ii) is not of a description prescribed in an order made by the Secretary of State.

(7B) This subsection applies to a person if–

    (a) he is employed by, or is in partnership with, a professional legal adviser or a relevant professional adviser to provide the adviser with assistance or support;

    (b) the information or other matter mentioned in subsection (3) comes to the person in connection with the provision of such assistance or support; and

    (c) the information or other matter came to the adviser in privileged circumstances.

(8) In deciding whether a person committed an offence under this section the court must consider whether he followed any relevant guidance which was at the time concerned–

    (a) issued by a supervisory authority or any other appropriate body,

    (b) approved by the Treasury, and

    (c) published in a manner it approved as appropriate in its opinion to bring the guidance to the attention of persons likely to be affected by it.

(9) A disclosure to a nominated officer is a disclosure which–

    (a) is made to a person nominated by the alleged offender's employer to receive disclosures under this section, and

    (b) is made in the course of the alleged offender's employment.

(9A) But a disclosure which satisfies paragraphs (a) and (b) of subsection (9) is not to be taken as a disclosure to a nominated officer if the person making the disclosure–

    (a) is a professional legal adviser or other relevant professional adviser;

    (b) makes it for the purpose of obtaining advice about making a disclosure under this section; and

    (c) does not intend it to be a disclosure under this section.

(10) Information or other matter comes to a professional legal adviser or other relevant professional adviser in privileged circumstances if it is communicated or given to him–

    (a) by (or by a representative of) a client of his in connection with the giving by the adviser of legal advice to the client,

    (b) by (or by a representative of) a person seeking legal advice from the adviser, or

    (c) by a person in connection with legal proceedings or contemplated legal proceedings.

(11) But subsection (10) does not apply to information or other matter which is communicated or given with the intention of furthering a criminal purpose.

(12) Schedule 9 has effect for the purpose of determining what is–

    (a) a business in the regulated sector;

    (b) a supervisory authority.

(13) An appropriate body is any body which regulates or is representative of any trade, profession, business or employment carried on by the alleged offender.

(14) A relevant professional adviser is an accountant, auditor or tax adviser who is a member of a professional body which is established for accountants, auditors or tax advisers (as the case may be) and which makes provision for–

    (a) testing the competence of those seeking admission to membership of such a body as a condition for such admission; and

    (b) imposing and maintaining professional and ethical standards for its members, as well as imposing sanctions for non-compliance with those standards.

331   Failure to disclose: nominated officers in the regulated sector

(1) A person nominated to receive disclosures under section 330 commits an offence if the conditions in subsections (2) to (4) are satisfied.

(2) The first condition is that he–

    (a) knows or suspects, or

    (b) has reasonable grounds for knowing or suspecting,

    that another person is engaged in money laundering.

(3) The second condition is that the information or other matter–

    (a) on which his knowledge or suspicion is based, or

    (b) which gives reasonable grounds for such knowledge or suspicion,

    came to him in consequence of a disclosure made under section 330.

(3A) The third condition is–

    (a) that he knows the identity of the other person mentioned in subsection (2), or the whereabouts of any of the laundered property, in consequence of a disclosure made under section 330;

    (b) that that other person, or the whereabouts of any of the laundered property, can be identified from the information or other matter mentioned in subsection (3); or

(c) that he believes, or it is reasonable to expect him to believe, that the information or other matter will or may assist in identifying that other person or the whereabouts of any of the laundered property.

(4) The fourth condition is that he does not make the required disclosure to a person authorised for the purposes of this Part by the Director General of the Serious Organised Crime Agency as soon as is practicable after the information or other matter mentioned in subsection (3) comes to him.

(5) The required disclosure is a disclosure of–

    (a) the identity of the other person mentioned in subsection (2), if disclosed to him under section 330;
    (b) the whereabouts of the laundered property, so far as disclosed to him under section 330; and
    (c) the information or other matter mentioned in subsection (3).

(5A) The laundered property is the property forming the subject-matter of the money laundering that he knows or suspects, or has reasonable grounds for knowing or suspecting, that other person to be engaged in.

(6) But he does not commit an offence under this section if he has a reasonable excuse for not making the required disclosure.

(6A) Nor does a person commit an offence under this section if–

    (a) he knows, or believes on reasonable grounds, that the money laundering is occurring in a particular country or territory outside the United Kingdom, and
    (b) the money laundering–
        (i) is not unlawful under the criminal law applying in that country or territory, and
        (ii) is not of a description prescribed in an order made by the Secretary of State.

(7) In deciding whether a person committed an offence under this section the court must consider whether he followed any relevant guidance which was at the time concerned–

    (a) issued by a supervisory authority or any other appropriate body,
    (b) approved by the Treasury, and
    (c) published in a manner it approved as appropriate in its opinion to bring the guidance to the attention of persons likely to be affected by it.

(8) Schedule 9 has effect for the purpose of determining what is a supervisory authority.

(9) An appropriate body is a body which regulates or is representative of a trade, profession, business or employment.

332   Failure to disclose: other nominated officers

(1) A person nominated to receive disclosures under section 337 or 338 commits an offence if the conditions in subsections (2) to (4) are satisfied.

(2) The first condition is that he knows or suspects that another person is engaged in money laundering.

(3) The second condition is that the information or other matter on which his knowledge or suspicion is based came to him in consequence of a disclosure made under the applicable section.

(3A) The third condition is–

- (a) that he knows the identity of the other person mentioned in subsection (2), or the whereabouts of any of the laundered property, in consequence of a disclosure made under the applicable section;
- (b) that that other person, or the whereabouts of any of the laundered property, can be identified from the information or other matter mentioned in subsection (3); or
- (c) that he believes, or it is reasonable to expect him to believe, that the information or other matter will or may assist in identifying that other person or the whereabouts of any of the laundered property.

(4) The fourth condition is that he does not make the required disclosure to a person authorised for the purposes of this Part by the Director General of the Serious Organised Crime Agency as soon as is practicable after the information or other matter mentioned in subsection (3) comes to him.

(5) The required disclosure is a disclosure of–

- (a) the identity of the other person mentioned in subsection (2), if disclosed to him under the applicable section;
- (b) the whereabouts of the laundered property, so far as disclosed to him under the applicable section; and
- (c) the information or other matter mentioned in subsection (3).

(5A) The laundered property is the property forming the subject-matter of the money laundering that he knows or suspects that other person to be engaged in.

(5B) The applicable section in section 337 or, as the case may be, section 338.

(6) But he does not commit an offence under this section if he has a reasonable excuse for not making the required disclosure.

(7) Nor does a person commit an offence under this section if–

- (a) he knows, or believes on reasonable grounds, that the money laundering is occurring in a particular country or territory outside the United Kingdom; and
- (b) the money laundering–
    - (i) is not unlawful under the criminal law applying in that country or territory; and
    - (ii) is not of a description prescribed in an order made by the Secretary of State.

333   Tipping off

(1) A person commits an offence if–

(a) he knows or suspects that a disclosure falling within section 337 or 338 has been made, and

(b) he makes a disclosure which is likely to prejudice any investigation which might be conducted following the disclosure referred to in paragraph (a).

(2) But a person does not commit an offence under subsection (1) if–

(a) he did not know or suspect that the disclosure was likely to be prejudicial as mentioned in subsection (1);

(b) the disclosure is made in carrying out a function he has relating to the enforcement of any provision of this Act or of any other enactment relating to criminal conduct or benefit from criminal conduct;

(c) he is a professional legal adviser and the disclosure falls within subsection (3).

(3) A disclosure falls within this subsection if it is a disclosure–

(a) to (or to a representative of) a client of the professional legal adviser in connection with the giving by the adviser of legal advice to the client, or

(b) to any person in connection with legal proceedings or contemplated legal proceedings.

(4) But a disclosure does not fall within subsection (3) if it is made with the intention of furthering a criminal purpose.

334 Penalties

(1) A person guilty of an offence under section 327, 328 or 329 is liable–

(a) on summary conviction, to imprisonment for a term not exceeding six months or to a fine not exceeding the statutory maximum or to both, or

(b) on conviction on indictment, to imprisonment for a term not exceeding 14 years or to a fine or to both.

(2) A person guilty of an offence under section 330, 331, 332 or 333 is liable–

(a) on summary conviction, to imprisonment for a term not exceeding six months or to a fine not exceeding the statutory maximum or to both, or

(b) on conviction on indictment, to imprisonment for a term not exceeding five years or to a fine or to both.

(3) A person guilty of an offence under section 339(1A) is liable on summary conviction to a fine not exceeding level 5 on the standard scale.

Consent

335 Appropriate consent

(1) The appropriate consent is–

(a) the consent of a nominated officer to do a prohibited act if an authorised disclosure is made to the nominated officer;

(b) the consent of a constable to do a prohibited act if an authorised disclosure is made to a constable;

(c) the consent of a customs officer to do a prohibited act if an authorised disclosure is made to a customs officer.

(2) A person must be treated as having the appropriate consent if–

(a) he makes an authorised disclosure to a constable or a customs officer, and

(b) the condition in subsection (3) or the condition in subsection (4) is satisfied.

(3) The condition is that before the end of the notice period he does not receive notice from a constable or customs officer that consent to the doing of the act is refused.

(4) The condition is that–

(a) before the end of the notice period he receives notice from a constable or customs officer that consent to the doing of the act is refused, and

(b) the moratorium period has expired.

(5) The notice period is the period of seven working days starting with the first working day after the person makes the disclosure.

(6) The moratorium period is the period of 31 days starting with the day on which the person receives notice that consent to the doing of the act is refused.

(7) A working day is a day other than a Saturday, a Sunday, Christmas Day, Good Friday or a day which is a bank holiday under the Banking and Financial Dealings Act 1971 (c. 80) in the part of the United Kingdom in which the person is when he makes the disclosure.

(8) References to a prohibited act are to an act mentioned in section 327(1), 328(1) or 329(1) (as the case may be).

(9) A nominated officer is a person nominated to receive disclosures under section 338.

(10) Subsections (1) to (4) apply for the purposes of this Part.

336 Nominated officer: consent

(1) A nominated officer must not give the appropriate consent to the doing of a prohibited act unless the condition in subsection (2), the condition in subsection (3) or the condition in subsection (4) is satisfied.

(2) The condition is that–

(a) he makes a disclosure that property is criminal property to a person authorised for the purposes of this Part by the Director General of the Serious Organised Crime Agency, and

(b) such a person gives consent to the doing of the act.

(3) The condition is that–

(a) he makes a disclosure that property is criminal property to a person authorised for the purposes of this Part by the Director General of the Serious Organised Crime Agency, and

(b) before the end of the notice period he does not receive notice from such a person that consent to the doing of the act is refused.

(4) The condition is that–

(a) he makes a disclosure that property is criminal property to a person authorised for the purposes of this Part by the Director General of the Serious Organised Crime Agency,

(b) before the end of the notice period he receives notice from such a person that consent to the doing of the act is refused, and

(c) the moratorium period has expired.

(5) A person who is a nominated officer commits an offence if–

(a) he gives consent to a prohibited act in circumstances where none of the conditions in subsections (2), (3) and (4) is satisfied, and

(b) he knows or suspects that the act is a prohibited act.

(6) A person guilty of such an offence is liable–

(a) on summary conviction, to imprisonment for a term not exceeding six months or to a fine not exceeding the statutory maximum or to both, or

(b) on conviction on indictment, to imprisonment for a term not exceeding five years or to a fine or to both.

(7) The notice period is the period of seven working days starting with the first working day after the nominated officer makes the disclosure.

(8) The moratorium period is the period of 31 days starting with the day on which the nominated officer is given notice that consent to the doing of the act is refused.

(9) A working day is a day other than a Saturday, a Sunday, Christmas Day, Good Friday or a day which is a bank holiday under the Banking and Financial Dealings Act 1971 (c. 80) in the part of the United Kingdom in which the nominated officer is when he gives the appropriate consent.

(10) References to a prohibited act are to an act mentioned in section 327(1), 328(1) or 329(1) (as the case may be).

(11) A nominated officer is a person nominated to receive disclosures under section 338.

Disclosures

337   Protected disclosures

(1) A disclosure which satisfies the following three conditions is not to be taken to breach any restriction on the disclosure of information (however imposed).

(2) The first condition is that the information or other matter disclosed came to the person making the disclosure (the discloser) in the course of his trade, profession, business or employment.

(3) The second condition is that the information or other matter–

(a) causes the discloser to know or suspect, or
(b) gives him reasonable grounds for knowing or suspecting,
that another person is engaged in money laundering.

(4) The third condition is that the disclosure is made to a constable, a customs officer or a nominated officer as soon as is practicable after the information or other matter comes to the discloser.

(4A) Where a disclosure consists of a disclosure protected under subsection (1) and a disclosure of either or both of–

(a) the identity of the other person mentioned in subsection (3); and
(b) the whereabouts of property forming the subject-matter of the money laundering that the discloser knows or suspects, or has reasonable grounds for knowing or suspecting, that other person to be engaged in the disclosure of the thing mentioned in paragraph (a) and (b) (as well as the disclosure protected under subsection (1)) is not to be taken to breach any restriction on the disclosure of information (however imposed).

(5) A disclosure to a nominated officer is a disclosure which–

(a) is made to a person nominated by the discloser's employer to receive disclosures under section 330 or this section, and
(b) is made in the course of the discloser's employment.

338 Authorised disclosures

(1) For the purposes of this Part a disclosure is authorised if–

(a) it is a disclosure to a constable, a customs officer or a nominated officer by the alleged offender that property is criminal property, and
(b) the first, second or third condition set out below is satisfied.

(2) The first condition is that the disclosure is made before the alleged offender does the prohibited act.

(2A) The second condition is that–

(a) the disclosure is made while the alleged offender is doing the prohibited act;
(b) he began to do the act at a time when, because he did not then know or suspect that the property constituted or represented a person's benefit from criminal conduct, the act was not a prohibited act; and
(c) the disclosure is made on his own initiative and as soon as is practicable after he first knows or suspects that the property constitutes or represents a person's benefit from criminal conduct.

(3) The third condition is that–

(a) the disclosure is made after the alleged offender does the prohibited act,
(b) there is a good reason for his failure to make the disclosure before he did the act, and
(c) the disclosure is made on his own initiative and as soon as it is practicable for him to make it.

(4) An authorised disclosure is not to be taken to breach any restriction on the disclosure of information (however imposed).

(5) A disclosure to a nominated officer is a disclosure which–

(a) is made to a person nominated by the alleged offender's employer to receive authorised disclosures, and
(b) is made in the course of the alleged offender's employment.

(6) References to the prohibited act are to an act mentioned in section 327(1), 328(1) or 329(1) (as the case may be).

339 Form and manner of disclosures

(1) The Secretary of State may by order prescribe the form and manner in which a disclosure under section 330, 331, 332 or 338 must be made.

(1A) A person commits an offence if he makes a disclosure under section 330, 331, 332 or 338 otherwise that in the form prescribed under subsection (1) or otherwise than in the manner so prescribed.

(1B) But a person does not commit an offence under subsection (1A) if he has a reasonable excuse for making the disclosure otherwise than in the form prescribed under subsection (1) or (as the case may be) otherwise than in the manner so prescribed.

(2) The power under subsection (1) to prescribe the form in which a disclosure must be made includes power to provide for the form to include a request to a person making a disclosure that the person provide information specified or described in the form if he has not provided it in making the disclosure.

(3) Where under subsection (2) a request is included in a form prescribed under subsection (1), the form must–

(a) state that there is no obligation to comply with the request; and
(b) explain the protection conferred by subsection (4) on a person who complies with the request.

(4) A disclosure made in pursuance of a request under subsection (2) is not to be taken to breach any restriction on the disclosure of information (however imposed).

(5) The discloser is the person making a disclosure mentioned in subsection (1).

(6) Money laundering investigation must be construed in accordance with section 341(4).

(7) Subsection (2) does not apply to a disclosure made to a nominated officer.

339A Threshold amounts

(1) This section applies for the purposes of sections 327(2C), 328(5) and 329(2C).

(2) The threshold amount for acts done by a deposit-taking body in operating an account is £250 unless a higher amount is specified under the following provisions of this section (in which event it is that higher amount).

(3) An officer of Revenue and Customs, or a constable, may specify the threshold amount for acts done by a deposit-taking body in operating an account–

    (a) when he gives consent, or gives notice refusing consent, to the deposit-taking body's doing of an act mentioned in section 327(1), 328(1) or 329(1) in opening, or operating, the account or a related account; or

    (b) on a request from the deposit-taking body.

(4) Where the threshold amount for acts done in operating an account is specified under subsection (3) or this subsection, an officer of Revenue and Customs, or a constable, may vary the amount (whether on a request from the deposit-taking body or otherwise) by specifying a different amount.

(5) Different threshold amounts may be specified under subsections (3) and (4) for different acts done in operating the same account.

(6) The amount specified under subsection (3) and (4) as the threshold amount for acts done in operating an account must, when specified, not be less than the amount specified in subsection (2).

(7) The Secretary of State may by order vary the amount for the time being specified in subsection (2).

(8) For the purposes of this section, an account is related to another if each is maintained with the same deposit-taking body and there is a person who, in relation to each account, is the person or one of the persons entitled to instruct the body as respects the operation of the account.

Interpretation

340 Interpretation

(1) This section applies for the purposes of this Part.

(2) Criminal conduct is conduct which–

    (a) constitutes an offence in any part of the United Kingdom, or

    (b) would constitute an offence in any part of the United Kingdom if it occurred there.

(3) Property is criminal property if–

(a) it constitutes a person's benefit from criminal conduct or it represents such a benefit (in whole or part and whether directly or indirectly), and

(b) the alleged offender knows or suspects that it constitutes or represents such a benefit.

(4) It is immaterial–

(a) who carried out the conduct;

(b) who benefited from it;

(c) whether the conduct occurred before or after the passing of this Act.

(5) A person benefits from conduct if he obtains property as a result of or in connection with the conduct.

(6) If a person obtains a pecuniary advantage as a result of or in connection with conduct, he is to be taken to obtain as a result of or in connection with the conduct a sum of money equal to the value of the pecuniary advantage.

(7) References to property or a pecuniary advantage obtained in connection with conduct include references to property or a pecuniary advantage obtained in both that connection and some other.

(8) If a person benefits from conduct his benefit is the property obtained as a result of or in connection with the conduct.

(9) Property is all property wherever situated and includes–

(a) money;

(b) all forms of property, real or personal, heritable or moveable;

(c) things in action and other intangible or incorporeal property.

(10) The following rules apply in relation to property–

(a) property is obtained by a person if he obtains an interest in it;

(b) references to an interest, in relation to land in England and Wales or Northern Ireland, are to any legal estate or equitable interest or power;

(c) references to an interest, in relation to land in Scotland, are to any estate, interest, servitude or other heritable right in or over land, including a heritable security;

(d) references to an interest, in relation to property other than land, include references to a right (including a right to possession).

(11) Money laundering is an act which–

(a) constitutes an offence under section 327, 328 or 329,

(b) constitutes an attempt, conspiracy or incitement to commit an offence specified in paragraph (a),

(c) constitutes aiding, abetting, counselling or procuring the commission of an offence specified in paragraph (a), or

(d) would constitute an offence specified in paragraph (a), (b) or (c) if done in the United Kingdom.

(12) For the purposes of a disclosure to a nominated officer–

    (a) references to a person's employer include any body, association or organisation (including a voluntary organisation) in connection with whose activities the person exercises a function (whether or not for gain or reward), and

    (b) references to employment must be construed accordingly.

(13) References to a constable include references to a person authorised for the purposes of this Part by the Director General of the Serious Organised Crime Agency.

(14) 'Deposit-taking body' means:

    (a) a business which engages in the activity of accepting deposits; or

    (b) the National Savings Bank.

PART 8
INVESTIGATIONS
CHAPTER 1
INTRODUCTION

341 Investigations

(1) For the purposes of this Part a confiscation investigation is an investigation into–

    (a) whether a person has benefited from his criminal conduct, or

    (b) the extent or whereabouts of his benefit from his criminal conduct.

(2) For the purposes of this Part a civil recovery investigation is an investigation into–

    (a) whether property is recoverable property or associated property,

    (b) who holds the property, or

    (c) its extent or whereabouts.

(3) But an investigation is not a civil recovery investigation if–

    (a) proceedings for a recovery order have been started in respect of the property in question,

    (b) an interim receiving order applies to the property in question,

    (c) an interim administration order applies to the property in question, or

    (d) the property in question is detained under section 295.

(4) For the purposes of this Part a money laundering investigation is an investigation into whether a person has committed a money laundering offence.

342 Offences of prejudicing investigation

(1) This section applies if a person knows or suspects that an appropriate officer or (in Scotland) a proper person is acting (or proposing to act) in connection with a confiscation investigation, a civil recovery investigation or a money laundering investigation which is being or is about to be conducted.

(2) The person commits an offence if–

   (a) he makes a disclosure which is likely to prejudice the investigation, or

   (b) he falsifies, conceals, destroys or otherwise disposes of, or causes or permits the falsification, concealment, destruction or disposal of, documents which are relevant to the investigation.

(3) A person does not commit an offence under subsection (2)(a) if–

   (a) he does not know or suspect that the disclosure is likely to prejudice the investigation,

   (b) the disclosure is made in the exercise of a function under this Act or any other enactment relating to criminal conduct or benefit from criminal conduct or in compliance with a requirement imposed under or by virtue of this Act, or

   (c) he is a professional legal adviser and the disclosure falls within subsection (4).

(4) A disclosure falls within this subsection if it is a disclosure–

   (a) to (or to a representative of) a client of the professional legal adviser in connection with the giving by the adviser of legal advice to the client, or

   (b) to any person in connection with legal proceedings or contemplated legal proceedings.

(5) But a disclosure does not fall within subsection (4) if it is made with the intention of furthering a criminal purpose.

(6) A person does not commit an offence under subsection (2)(b) if–

   (a) he does not know or suspect that the documents are relevant to the investigation, or

   (b) he does not intend to conceal any facts disclosed by the documents from any appropriate officer or (in Scotland) proper person carrying out the investigation.

(7) A person guilty of an offence under subsection (2) is liable–

   (a) on summary conviction, to imprisonment for a term not exceeding six months or to a fine not exceeding the statutory maximum or to both, or

   (b) on conviction on indictment, to imprisonment for a term not exceeding five years or to a fine or to both.

(8) For the purposes of this section–

   (a) 'appropriate officer' must be construed in accordance with section 378;

   (b) 'proper person' must be construed in accordance with section 412.

A2

Extracts from the Terrorism Act 2000 (as amended)

[. . .]

Offences

15 Fund-raising

(1) A person commits an offence if he–

- (a) invites another to provide money or other property, and
- (b) intends that it should be used, or has reasonable cause to suspect that it may be used, for the purposes of terrorism.

(2) A person commits an offence if he–

- (a) receives money or other property, and
- (b) intends that it should be used, or has reasonable cause to suspect that it may be used, for the purposes of terrorism.

(3) A person commits an offence if he–

- (a) provides money or other property, and
- (b) knows or has reasonable cause to suspect that it will or may be used for the purposes of terrorism.

(4) In this section a reference to the provision of money or other property is a reference to its being given, lent or otherwise made available, whether or not for consideration.

16 Use and possession

(1) A person commits an offence if he uses money or other property for the purposes of terrorism.

(2) A person commits an offence if he–

- (a) possesses money or other property, and
- (b) intends that it should be used, or has reasonable cause to suspect that it may be used, for the purposes of terrorism.

17 Funding arrangements

A person commits an offence if–

(a) he enters into or becomes concerned in an arrangement as a result of which money or other property is made available or is to be made available to another, and
(b) he knows or has reasonable cause to suspect that it will or may be used for the purposes of terrorism.

18 Money laundering

(1) A person commits an offence if he enters into or becomes concerned in an arrangement which facilitates the retention or control by or on behalf of another person of terrorist property–

(a) by concealment,
(b) by removal from the jurisdiction,
(c) by transfer to nominees, or
(d) in any other way.

(2) It is a defence for a person charged with an offence under subsection (1) to prove that he did not know and had no reasonable cause to suspect that the arrangement related to terrorist property.

[. . .]

(As inserted by the Anti-Terrorism, Crime and Security Act 2001, s.3, Sched.2, Part 3, para. 5(1), (2))

21A Failure to disclose: regulated sector

(1) A person commits an offence if each of the following three conditions is satisfied.

(2) The first condition is that he–

(a) knows or suspects, or
(b) has reasonable grounds for knowing or suspecting,
that another person has committed an offence under any of sections 15 to 18.

(3) The second condition is that the information or other matter–

(a) on which his knowledge or suspicion is based, or
(b) which gives reasonable grounds for such knowledge or suspicion,
came to him in the course of a business in the regulated sector.

(4) The third condition is that he does not disclose the information or other matter to a constable or a nominated officer as soon as is practicable after it comes to him.

(5) But a person does not commit an offence under this section if–

(a) he has a reasonable excuse for not disclosing the information or other matter;
(b) he is a professional legal adviser and the information or other matter came to him in privileged circumstances.

(6) In deciding whether a person committed an offence under this section the court must consider whether he followed any relevant guidance which was at the time concerned–

(a) issued by a supervisory authority or any other appropriate body,
(b) approved by the Treasury, and
(c) published in a manner it approved as appropriate in its opinion to bring the guidance to the attention of persons likely to be affected by it.

(7) A disclosure to a nominated officer is a disclosure which–

(a) is made to a person nominated by the alleged offender's employer to receive disclosures under this section, and
(b) is made in the course of the alleged offender's employment and in accordance with the procedure established by the employer for the purpose.

(8) Information or other matter comes to a professional legal adviser in privileged circumstances if it is communicated or given to him–

(a) by (or by a representative of) a client of his in connection with the giving by the adviser of legal advice to the client,
(b) by (or by a representative of) a person seeking legal advice from the adviser, or
(c) by a person in connection with legal proceedings or contemplated legal proceedings.

(9) But subsection (8) does not apply to information or other matter which is communicated or given with a view to furthering a criminal purpose.

(10) Schedule 3A has effect for the purpose of determining what is–

(a) a business in the regulated sector;
(b) a supervisory authority.

(11) For the purposes of subsection (2) a person is to be taken to have committed an offence there mentioned if–

(a) he has taken an action or been in possession of a thing, and
(b) he would have committed the offence if he had been in the United Kingdom at the time when he took the action or was in possession of the thing.

(12) A person guilty of an offence under this section is liable–

(a) on conviction on indictment, to imprisonment for a term not exceeding five years or to a fine or to both;
(b) on summary conviction, to imprisonment for a term not exceeding six months or to a fine not exceeding the statutory maximum or to both.

(13) An appropriate body is any body which regulates or is representative of any trade, profession, business or employment carried on by the alleged offender.

(14) The reference to a constable includes a reference to a person authorised for the purposes of this section by the Director General of the National Criminal Intelligence Service.

A3

Money Laundering Regulations 2003, SI 2003/3075 (as amended by Proceeds of Crime Act 2002 and Money Laundering Regulations 2003 (Amendment) Order 2006, SI 2006/308)

2003 No. 3075
FINANCIAL SERVICES
The Money Laundering Regulations 2003

Made   *28th November 2003*
Laid before Parliament   *28th November 2003*
Coming into force in accordance with
regulation 1(2)

ARRANGEMENT OF REGULATIONS

PART I:
GENERAL

1. Citation, commencement etc.

2. Interpretation

PART II:
OBLIGATIONS ON PERSONS WHO CARRY ON RELEVANT BUSINESS

3. Systems and training etc. to prevent money laundering

4. Identification procedures

5. Exceptions

6. Record-keeping procedures

PART IV:
MISCELLANEOUS

26. Supervisory authorities etc. to report evidence of money laundering

27. Offences by bodies corporate etc.

28. Prohibitions in relation to certain countries

29. Minor and consequential amendments

30. Transitional provisions

SCHEDULES

1.   Activities Listed in Annex 1 to the Banking Consolidation Directive

2.   Minor and Consequential Amendments

Whereas the Treasury are a government department designated[1] for the purposes of section 2(2) of the European Communities Act 1972[2] in relation to measures relating to preventing the use of the financial system for the purpose of money laundering;

Now therefore the Treasury, in exercise of the powers conferred on them by –

(i)   section 2(2) of the European Communities Act 1972, and
(ii) sections 168(4)(b), 402(1)(b), 417(1)[3] and 428(3) of the Financial Services and Markets Act 2000[4],

hereby make the following Regulations:

PART I
GENERAL

1. Citation, commencement etc.

(1) These Regulations may be cited as the Money Laundering Regulations 2003.

(2) These Regulations come into force –

(a) for the purposes of regulation 10 in so far as it relates to a person who acts as a high value dealer, on 1st April 2004;
(b) for the purposes of regulation 2(3)(h), on 31st October 2004;
(c) for the purposes of regulation 2(3)(i), on 14th January 2005;
(d) for all other purposes, on 1st March 2004.

(3) These Regulations are prescribed for the purposes of sections 168(4)(b) and 402(1)(b) of the 2000 Act.

(4) The following Regulations are revoked –

(a) the Money Laundering Regulations 1993[5];
(b) the Financial Services and Markets Act 2000 (Regulations Relating to Money Laundering) Regulations 2001[6];
(c) the Money Laundering Regulations 2001[7].

2. Interpretation

(1) In these Regulations –

"the 2000 Act" means the Financial Services and Markets Act 2000;

"applicant for business" means a person seeking to form a business relationship, or carry out a one-off transaction, with another person acting in the course of relevant business carried on by that other person in the United Kingdom;

"applicant for registration" means an applicant for registration as a money service operator, or as a high value dealer;

"the appropriate judicial authority" means –

(a) in England and Wales, a magistrates' court,
(b) in Scotland, the sheriff,
(c) in Northern Ireland, a court of summary jurisdiction;

"authorised person" has the meaning given by section 31(2) of the 2000 Act;

"the Authority" means the Financial Services Authority;

"the Banking Consolidation Directive" means Directive 2000/12/EC of the European Parliament and of the Council of 20th March 2000 relating to the taking up and pursuit of the business of credit institutions as last amended by Directive 2002/87/EC of the European Parliament and of the Council of 16th December 2002[8];

"business relationship" means any arrangement the purpose of which is to facilitate the carrying out of transactions on a frequent, habitual or regular basis where the total amount of any payments to be made by any person to any other in the course of the arrangement is not known or capable of being ascertained at the outset;

"cash" means notes, coins or travellers' cheques in any currency;

"the Commissioners" means the Commissioners of Customs and Excise;

"constable" includes a person commissioned by the Commissioners and a person authorised for the purposes of these Regulations by the Director General of the National Criminal Intelligence Service;

"EEA State" means a State which is a contracting party to the agreement on the European Economic Area signed at Oporto on 2nd May 1992 as it has effect for the time being;

"estate agency work" has the meaning given by section 1 of the Estate Agents Act 1979[9] save for the omission of the words "(including a business in which he is employed)" in subsection (1) and includes a case where, in relation to a disposal or acquisition, the person acts as principal;

"high value dealer" means a person who carries on the activity mentioned in paragraph (2)(n);

"the Life Assurance Consolidation Directive" means Directive 2002/83/EC of the European Parliament and of the Council of 5th November 2002 concerning life assurance[10];

"justice" means a justice of the peace or, in relation to Scotland, a justice within the meaning of section 307 of the Criminal Procedure (Scotland) Act 1995[11];

"money laundering" means an act which falls within section 340(11) of the Proceeds of Crime Act 2002[12] or an offence under section 18 of the Terrorism Act 2000[13];

"the Money Laundering Directive" means Council Directive 91/308/EEC of 10th June 1991 on prevention of the use of the financial system for the purpose of money laundering as amended by Directive 2001/97/EC of the European Parliament and of the Council of 4th December 2001[14];

"money service business" means any of the activities mentioned in paragraph (2)(d) (so far as not excluded by paragraph (3)) when carried on by way of business;

"money service operator" means a person who carries on money service business other than a person who carries on relevant business falling within any of sub-paragraphs (a) to (c) of paragraph (2);

"nominated officer" has the meaning given by regulation 7;

"officer" (except in regulations 7, 10 and 27) has the meaning given by section 1(1) of the Customs and Excise Management Act 1979[15];

"officer in overall charge of the investigation" means the person whose name and address are endorsed on the order concerned as being the officer so in charge;

"one-off transaction" means any transaction other than one carried out in the course of an existing business relationship;

"operator" means a money service operator;

"recorded information" includes information recorded in any form and any document of any nature whatsoever;

"registered number" has the meaning given by regulation 9(2);

"relevant business" has the meaning given by paragraph (2);

"the review procedure" means the procedure under regulation 21;

"satisfactory evidence of identity" has the meaning given by paragraphs (5) and (6);

"supervisory authority" has the meaning given by paragraphs (7) and (8);

"tribunal" means a VAT and duties tribunal.

(2) For the purposes of these Regulations, "relevant business" means –

    (a) the regulated activity of –

        (i) accepting deposits;
        (ii) effecting or carrying out contracts of long-term insurance when carried on by a person who has received official authorisation pursuant to Article 4 or 51 of the Life Assurance Consolidation Directive;
        (iii) dealing in investments as principal or as agent;
        (iv) arranging deals in investments;
        (v) managing investments;
        (vi) safeguarding and administering investments;
        (vii) sending dematerialised instructions;
        (viii)establishing (and taking other steps in relation to) collective investment schemes;
        (ix) advising on investments; or
        (x) issuing electronic money;

    (b) the activities of the National Savings Bank;
    (c) any activity carried on for the purpose of raising money authorised to be raised under the National Loans Act 1968[16] under the auspices of the Director of Savings;
    (d) the business of operating a bureau de change, transmitting money (or any representation of monetary value) by any means or cashing cheques which are made payable to customers;
    (e) any of the activities in points 1 to 12 or 14 of Annex 1 to the Banking Consolidation Directive (which activities are, for convenience, set out in Schedule 1 to these Regulations) when carried on by way of business, ignoring an activity falling within any of sub-paragraphs (a) to (d);
    (f) estate agency work;
    (g) operating a casino by way of business;
    (h) the activities of a person appointed to act as an insolvency practitioner within the meaning of section 388 of the Insolvency Act 1986[17] or Article 3 of the Insolvency (Northern Ireland) Order 1989[18];
    (i) the provision by way of business of advice about the tax affairs of another person by a body corporate or unincorporate or, in the case of a sole practitioner, by an individual;
    (j) the provision by way of business of accountancy services by a body corporate or unincorporate or, in the case of a sole practitioner, by an individual;
    (k) the provision by way of business of audit services by a person who is eligible for appointment as a company auditor under section 25 of the Companies Act 1989[19] or Article 28 of the Companies (Northern Ireland) Order 1990[20];
    (l) the provision by way of business of legal services by a body corporate or unincorporate or, in the case of a sole practitioner, by an individual and which involves participation in a financial or real property transaction

(whether by assisting in the planning or execution of any such transaction or otherwise by acting for, or on behalf of, a client in any such transaction);

(m) the provision by way of business of services in relation to the formation, operation or management of a company or a trust; or

(n) the activity of dealing in goods of any description by way of business (including dealing as an auctioneer) whenever a transaction involves accepting a total cash payment of 15,000 euro or more.

(3) Paragraph (2) does not apply to –

(a) the issue of withdrawable share capital within the limit set by section 6 of the Industrial and Provident Societies Act 1965[21] by a society registered under that Act;

(b) the acceptance of deposits from the public within the limit set by section 7(3) of that Act by such a society;

(c) the issue of withdrawable share capital within the limit set by section 6 of the Industrial and Provident Societies Act (Northern Ireland) 1969[22] by a society registered under that Act;

(d) the acceptance of deposits from the public within the limit set by section 7(3) of that Act by such a society;

(e) activities carried on by the Bank of England;

(f) any activity in respect of which an exemption order under section 38 of the 2000 Act has effect if it is carried on by a person who is for the time being specified in the order or falls within a class of persons so specified;

(g) any activity (other than one falling within sub-paragraph (f)) in respect of which a person was an exempted person for the purposes of section 45 of the Financial Services Act 1986[23] immediately before its repeal;

(h) the regulated activities of arranging deals in investments or advising on investments, in so far as the investment consists of rights under a regulated mortgage contract;

(i) the regulated activities of dealing in investments as agent, arranging deals in investments, managing investments or advising on investments, in so far as the investment consists of rights under, or any right to or interest in, a contract of insurance which is not a qualifying contract of insurance; or

(j) the Official Solicitor to the Supreme Court when acting as trustee in his official capacity.

(4) The following must be read with section 22 of the 2000 Act, any relevant order under that section and Schedule 2 to that Act –

(a) paragraphs (2)(a) and (3)(h) and (i);

(b) regulation 25 (authorised persons operating a bureau de change);

(c) references in these Regulations to a contract of long-term insurance.

(5) For the purposes of these Regulations, and subject to paragraph (6), "satisfactory evidence of identity" is evidence which is reasonably capable of establishing (and does in fact establish to the satisfaction of the person who obtains it) that the applicant for business is the person he claims to be.

(6) Where the person who obtains the evidence mentioned in paragraph (5) knows or has reasonable grounds for believing that the applicant for business is a money service operator, satisfactory evidence of identity must also include the applicant's registered number (if any).

(7) For the purposes of these Regulations, each of the following is a supervisory authority –

   (a) the Bank of England;
   (b) the Authority;
   (c) the Council of Lloyd's;
   (d) the Office of Fair Trading;
   (e) the Occupational Pensions Regulatory Authority;
   (f) a body which is a designated professional body for the purposes of Part 20 of the 2000 Act;
   (g) the Gaming Board for Great Britain.

(8) The Secretary of State and the Treasury are each a supervisory authority in the exercise, in relation to a person carrying on relevant business, of their respective functions under the enactments relating to companies or insolvency or under the 2000 Act.

(9) In these Regulations, references to amounts in euro include references to equivalent amounts in another currency.

(10) For the purpose of the application of these Regulations to Scotland, "real property" means "heritable property".

PART II
OBLIGATIONS ON PERSONS WHO CARRY ON RELEVANT BUSINESS

3. Systems and training etc. to prevent money laundering

(1) Every person must in the course of relevant business carried on by him in the United Kingdom –

   (a) comply with the requirements of regulations 4 (identification procedures), 6 (record-keeping procedures) and 7 (internal reporting procedures);
   (b) establish such other procedures of internal control and communication as may be appropriate for the purposes of forestalling and preventing money laundering; and
   (c) take appropriate measures so that relevant employees are –

      (i) made aware of the provisions of these Regulations, Part 7 of the Proceeds of Crime Act 2002 (money laundering) and sections 18 and 21A of the Terrorism Act 2000[24]; and
      (ii) given training in how to recognise and deal with transactions which may be related to money laundering.

(2) A person who contravenes this regulation is guilty of an offence and liable –

   (a) on conviction on indictment, to imprisonment for a term not exceeding 2 years, to a fine or to both;
   (b) on summary conviction, to a fine not exceeding the statutory maximum.

(3) In deciding whether a person has committed an offence under this regulation, the court must consider whether he followed any relevant guidance which was at the time concerned –

(a) issued by a supervisory authority or any other appropriate body;

(b) approved by the Treasury; and

(c) published in a manner approved by the Treasury as appropriate in their opinion to bring the guidance to the attention of persons likely to be affected by it.

(4) An appropriate body is any body which regulates or is representative of any trade, profession, business or employment carried on by the alleged offender.

(5) In proceedings against any person for an offence under this regulation, it is a defence for that person to show that he took all reasonable steps and exercised all due diligence to avoid committing the offence.

(6) Where a person is convicted of an offence under this regulation, he shall not also be liable to a penalty under regulation 20 (power to impose penalties).

4. Identification procedures

(1) In this regulation and in regulations 5 to 7 –

(a) "A" means a person who carries on relevant business in the United Kingdom; and

(b) "B" means an applicant for business.

(2) This regulation applies if –

(a) A and B form, or agree to form, a business relationship;

(b) in respect of any one-off transaction –

(i) A knows or suspects that the transaction involves money laundering; or

(ii) payment of 15,000 euro or more is to be made by or to B; or

(c) in respect of two or more one-off transactions, it appears to A (whether at the outset or subsequently) that the transactions are linked and involve, in total, the payment of 15,000 euro or more by or to B.

(3) A must maintain identification procedures which –

(a) require that as soon as is reasonably practicable after contact is first made between A and B –

(i) B must produce satisfactory evidence of his identity; or

(ii) such measures specified in the procedures must be taken in order to produce satisfactory evidence of B's identity;

(b) take into account the greater potential for money laundering which arises when B is not physically present when being identified;

(c) require that where satisfactory evidence of identity is not obtained, the business relationship or one-off transaction must not proceed any further; and

(d) require that where B acts or appears to act for another person, reasonable measures must be taken for the purpose of establishing the identity of that person.

5. Exceptions

(1) Except in circumstances falling within regulation 4(2)(b)(i), identification procedures under regulation 4 do not require A to take steps to obtain evidence of any person's identity in any of the following circumstances.

(2) Where A has reasonable grounds for believing that B –

- (a) carries on in the United Kingdom relevant business falling within any of sub-paragraphs (a) to (e) of regulation 2(2), is not a money service operator and, if carrying on an activity falling within regulation 2(2)(a), is an authorised person with permission under the 2000 Act to carry on that activity;
- (b) does not carry on relevant business in the United Kingdom but does carry on comparable activities to those falling within sub-paragraph (a) and is covered by the Money Laundering Directive; or
- (c) is regulated by an overseas regulatory authority (within the meaning given by section 82 of the Companies Act 1989) and is based or incorporated in a country (other than an EEA State) whose law contains comparable provisions to those contained in the Money Laundering Directive.

(3) Where –

- (a) A carries out a one-off transaction with or for a third party pursuant to an introduction effected by a person who has provided a written assurance that evidence of the identity of all third parties introduced by him will have been obtained and recorded under procedures maintained by him;
- (b) that person identifies the third party; and
- (c) A has reasonable grounds for believing that that person falls within any of sub-paragraphs (a) to (c) of paragraph (2).

(4) In relation to a contract of long-term insurance –

- (a) in connection with a pension scheme taken out by virtue of a person's contract of employment or occupation where the contract of long-term insurance –
  - (i) contains no surrender clause; and
  - (ii) may not be used as collateral for a loan; or
- (b) in respect of which a premium is payable –
  - (i) in one instalment of an amount not exceeding 2,500 euro; or
  - (ii) periodically and where the total payable in respect of any calendar year does not exceed 1,000 euro.

(5) Where the proceeds of a one-off transaction are payable to B but are instead directly reinvested on his behalf in another transaction –

- (a) of which a record is kept; and
- (b) which can result only in another reinvestment made on B's behalf or in a payment made directly to B.

6. Record-keeping procedures

(1) A must maintain procedures which require the retention of the records prescribed in paragraph (2) for the period prescribed in paragraph (3).

(2) The records are –

    (a) where evidence of identity has been obtained under the procedures stipulated by regulation 4 (identification procedures) or pursuant to regulation 8 (casinos) –

        (i) a copy of that evidence;
        (ii) information as to where a copy of that evidence may be obtained; or
        (iii) information enabling the evidence of identity to be re-obtained, but only where it is not reasonably practicable for A to comply with paragraph (i) or (ii); and

    (b) a record containing details relating to all transactions carried out by A in the course of relevant business.

(3) In relation to the records mentioned in paragraph (2)(a), the period is –

    (a) where A and B have formed a business relationship, at least five years commencing with the date on which the relationship ends; or
    (b) in the case of a one-off transaction (or a series of such transactions), at least five years commencing with the date of the completion of all activities taking place in the course of that transaction (or, as the case may be, the last of the transactions).

(4) In relation to the records mentioned in paragraph (2)(b), the period is at least five years commencing with the date on which all activities taking place in the course of the transaction in question were completed.

(5) Where A is an appointed representative, his principal must ensure that A complies with this regulation in respect of any relevant business carried out by A for which the principal has accepted responsibility pursuant to section 39(1) of the 2000 Act.

(6) Where the principal fails to do so, he is to be treated as having contravened regulation 3 and he, as well as A, is guilty of an offence.

(7) "Appointed representative" has the meaning given by section 39(2) of the 2000 Act and "principal" has the meaning given by section 39(1) of that Act.

7. Internal reporting procedures

(1) A must maintain internal reporting procedures which require that –

    (a) a person in A's organisation is nominated to receive disclosures under this regulation ("the nominated officer");
    (b) anyone in A's organisation to whom information or other matter comes in the course of relevant business as a result of which he knows or suspects or has reasonable grounds for knowing or suspecting that a person is engaged in money laundering must, as soon as is practicable after the information or

other matter comes to him, disclose it to the nominated officer or a person authorised for the purposes of these Regulations by the Director General of the [Serious Organised Crime Agency];

(c) where a disclosure is made to the nominated officer, he must consider it in the light of any relevant information which is available to A and determine whether it gives rise to such knowledge or suspicion or such reasonable grounds for knowledge or suspicion; and

(d) where the nominated officer does so determine, the information or other matter must be disclosed to a person authorised for the purposes of these Regulations by the Director General of the [Serious Organised Crime Agency].

(2) Paragraph (1) does not apply where A is an individual who neither employs nor acts in association with any other person.

(3) Paragraph (1)(b) does not apply in relation to a professional legal adviser or other relevant professional adviser where the information or other matter comes to him in privileged circumstances.

(4) Information or other matter comes to a professional legal adviser or other relevant professional adviser in privileged circumstances if it is communicated or given to him–

(a) by (or by a representative of) a client of his in connection with the giving by the adviser of legal advice to the client;

(b) by (or by a representative of) a person seeking legal advice from the adviser; or

(c) by a person in connection with legal proceedings or contemplated legal proceedings.

(5) But paragraph (4) does not apply to information or other matter which is communicated or given with the intention of furthering a criminal purpose.

(6) A relevant professional adviser is an accountant, auditor or tax adviser who is a member of a professional body which is established for accountants, auditors or tax advisers (as the case may be) and which makes provision for–

(a) testing the competence of those seeking admission to membership of such a body as a condition for such admission; and

(b) imposing and maintaining professional and ethical standards for its members, as well as imposing sanctions for non-compliance with those standards.

(7) Paragraph (1)(b) also does not apply to a person if–

(a) he is employed by, or is in partnership with, a professional legal adviser or a relevant professional adviser to provide the adviser with assistance or support,

(b) the information or other matter mentioned in paragraph (1)(b) comes to the person in connection with the provision of such assistance or support, and

(c) the information or other matter came to the adviser in privileged circumstances.

8. Casinos

(1) A person who operates a casino by way of business in the United Kingdom must obtain satisfactory evidence of identity of any person before allowing that person to use the casino's gaming facilities.

(2) A person who fails to do so is to be treated as having contravened regulation 3.

PART III
MONEY SERVICE OPERATORS AND HIGH VALUE DEALERS
Registration

9. Registers of money service operators and high value dealers

(1) The Commissioners must maintain a register of operators.

(2) The Commissioners must allocate to every registered operator a number, which is to be known as his registered number.

(3) The Commissioners must maintain a register of high value dealers.

(4) The Commissioners may keep the registers in any form they think fit.

10. Requirement to be registered

(1) A person who acts as an operator or as a high value dealer must first be registered by the Commissioners.

(2) An applicant for registration must –

(a) make an application to be registered in such manner as the Commissioners may direct; and
(b) furnish the following information to the Commissioners –

(i) his name and (if different) the name of the business;
(ii) his VAT registration number or, if he is not registered for VAT, any other reference number issued to him by the Commissioners;
(iii) the nature of the business;
(iv) the address of each of the premises at which he proposes to carry on the business;
(v) any agency or franchise agreement relating to the business, and the names and addresses of all relevant principals, agents, franchisors or franchisees;
(vi) the name of the nominated officer (if any); and
(vii) whether any person concerned (or proposed to be concerned) in the management, control or operation of the business has been convicted of money laundering or an offence under these Regulations.

(3) At any time after receiving an application for registration and before determining it, the Commissioners may require the applicant for registration to furnish them, within 21 days beginning with the date of being requested to do so, with such further information as they reasonably consider necessary to enable them to determine the application.

(4) Any information to be furnished to the Commissioners under this regulation must be in such form or verified in such manner as they may specify.

(5) In this regulation, "the business" means money service business (or, in the case of a high value dealer, the business of dealing in goods) which the applicant for registration carries on or proposes to carry on.

(6) In paragraph (2)(b)(vii), the reference to "money laundering or an offence under these Regulations" includes an offence referred to in regulation 2(3) of the Money Laundering Regulations 1993 or an offence under regulation 5 of those Regulations.

11. Supplementary information

(1) If at any time after a person has furnished the Commissioners with any information under regulation 10 –

  (a) there is a change affecting any matter contained in that information; or
  (b) it becomes apparent to that person that the information contains an inaccuracy;

he must supply the Commissioners with details of the change or, as the case may be, a correction of the inaccuracy (hereafter "supplementary information") within 30 days beginning with the date of the occurrence of the change (or the discovery of the inaccuracy) or within such later time as may be agreed with the Commissioners.

(2) The supplementary information must be supplied in such manner as the Commissioners may direct.

(3) The obligation in paragraph (1) applies also to changes affecting any matter contained in any supplementary information supplied pursuant to this regulation.

12. Determination of application to register

(1) The Commissioners may refuse to register an applicant for registration if, and only if –

  (a) any requirement of –

    (i) paragraphs (2) to (4) of regulation 10 (requirement to be registered);
    (ii) regulation 11 (supplementary information); or
    (iii) regulation 14 (fees);

    has not been complied with; or

  (b) it appears to them that any information furnished pursuant to regulation 10 or 11 is false or misleading in a material particular.

(2) The Commissioners must, by the end of the period of 45 days beginning with the date on which they receive the application or, where applicable, the date on which they receive any further information required under regulation 10(3), give notice in writing to the applicant for registration of –

  (a) their decision to register him and, in the case of an applicant for registration as an operator, his registered number; or

(b) the following matters –

    (i)   their decision not to register him;

    (ii) the reasons for their decision;

    (iii) the review procedure; and

    (iv) the right to appeal to a tribunal.

13. Cancellation of registration

(1) The Commissioners may cancel the registration of an operator or high value dealer if, at any time after registration, it appears to them that they would have had grounds to refuse registration under paragraph (1) of regulation 12 (determination of application to register).

(2) Where the Commissioners decide to cancel the registration of an operator or high value dealer, they must forthwith inform him, in writing, of –

    (a) their decision and the date from which the cancellation takes effect;

    (b) the reasons for their decision;

    (c) the review procedure; and

    (d) the right to appeal to a tribunal.

14. Fees

(1) The Commissioners may charge a fee –

    (a) to an applicant for registration; and

    (b) to an operator or high value dealer annually on the anniversary of his registration by them under these Regulations.

(2) The Commissioners may charge under paragraph (1) such fees as they consider will enable them to meet any expenses incurred by them in carrying out any of their functions under these Regulations or for any incidental purpose.

(3) Without prejudice to the generality of paragraph (2), a fee may be charged in respect of each of the premises at which the operator, high value dealer or applicant for registration carries on (or proposes to carry on) money service business or relevant business falling within regulation 2(2)(n).

Powers of the Commissioners

15. Entry, inspection etc.

(1) Where an officer has reasonable cause to believe that any premises are used in connection with money service business or relevant business falling within regulation 2(2)(n), he may at any reasonable time enter and inspect the premises and inspect any recorded information or currency found on the premises.

(2) An operator or high value dealer must –

    (a) furnish to an officer, within such time and in such form as the officer may reasonably require, such information relating to the business as the officer may reasonably specify; and

(b) upon demand made by the officer, produce or cause to be produced for inspection by the officer at such place, and at such time, as the officer may reasonably require, any recorded information relating to the business.

(3) An officer may take copies of, or make extracts from, any recorded information produced under paragraph (2).

16. Order for access to recorded information

(1) Where, on an application by an officer, a justice is satisfied that there are reasonable grounds for believing –

(a) that an offence under these Regulations is being, has been or is about to be committed by an operator or high value dealer; and
(b) that any recorded information which may be required as evidence for the purpose of any proceedings in respect of such an offence is in the possession of any person;

he may make an order under this regulation.

(2) An order under this regulation is an order that the person who appears to the justice to be in possession of the recorded information to which the application relates must –

(a) give an officer access to it;
(b) permit an officer to take copies of, or make extracts from, any information produced; or
(c) permit an officer to remove and take away any of it which he reasonably considers necessary;

not later than the end of the period of 7 days beginning with the date of the order or the end of such longer period as the order may specify.

(3) Where the recorded information consists of information stored in any electronic form, an order under this regulation has effect as an order to produce the information in a form in which it is visible and legible, or from which it can readily be produced in a visible and legible form, and, if the officer wishes to remove it, in a form in which it can be removed.

17. Procedure where recorded information is removed

(1) An officer who removes any recorded information in the exercise of a power conferred by regulation 16 must, if so requested by a person showing himself –

(a) to be the occupier of premises from which the information was removed; or
(b) to have had custody or control of the information immediately before the removal;

provide that person with a record of what he has removed.

(2) The officer must provide the record within a reasonable time from the making of the request for it.

(3) Subject to paragraph (7), if a request for permission to be granted access to anything which –

(a) has been removed by an officer; and
(b) is retained by the Commissioners for the purposes of investigating an offence;

is made to the officer in overall charge of the investigation by a person who had custody or control of the thing immediately before it was so removed or by someone acting on behalf of such a person, that officer must allow the person who made the request access to it under the supervision of an officer.

(4) Subject to paragraph (7), if a request for a photograph or copy of any such thing is made to the officer in overall charge of the investigation by a person who had custody or control of the thing immediately before it was so removed, or by someone acting on behalf of such a person, that officer must –

(a) allow the person who made the request access to it under the supervision of an officer for the purpose of photographing it or copying it; or
(b) photograph or copy it, or cause it to be photographed or copied.

(5) Where anything is photographed or copied under paragraph (4)(b), the photograph or copy must be supplied to the person who made the request.

(6) The photograph or copy must be supplied within a reasonable time from the making of the request.

(7) There is no duty under this regulation to grant access to, or supply a photograph or a copy of, anything if the officer in overall charge of the investigation for the purposes of which it was removed has reasonable grounds for believing that to do so would prejudice –

(a) that investigation;
(b) the investigation of an offence other than the offence for the purposes of the investigation of which the recorded information was removed; or
(c) any criminal proceedings which may be brought as a result of –

  (i)   the investigation of which he is in charge; or
  (ii) any such investigation as is mentioned in sub-paragraph (b).

18.   Failure to comply with requirements under regulation 17

(1) Where, on an application made as mentioned in paragraph (2), the appropriate judicial authority is satisfied that a person has failed to comply with a requirement imposed by regulation 17, the authority may order that person to comply with the requirement within such time and in such manner as may be specified in the order.

(2) An application under paragraph (1) may only be made –

(a) in the case of a failure to comply with any of the requirements imposed by regulation 17(1) and (2), by the occupier of the premises from which the thing in question was removed or by the person who had custody or control of it immediately before it was so removed;

(b) in any other case, by the person who had such custody or control.

(3) In England and Wales and Northern Ireland, an application for an order under this regulation is to be made by complaint; and sections 21 and 42(2) of the Interpretation Act (Northern Ireland) 1954[25] apply as if any reference in those provisions to any enactment included a reference to this regulation.

19. Entry, search etc.

(1) Where a justice is satisfied on information on oath that there is reasonable ground for suspecting that an offence under these Regulations is being, has been or is about to be committed by an operator or high value dealer on any premises or that evidence of the commission of such an offence is to be found there, he may issue a warrant in writing authorising any officer to enter those premises, if necessary by force, at any time within one month from the time of the issue of the warrant and search them.

(2) A person who enters the premises under the authority of the warrant may –

(a) take with him such other persons as appear to him to be necessary;
(b) seize and remove any documents or other things whatsoever found on the premises which he has reasonable cause to believe may be required as evidence for the purpose of proceedings in respect of an offence under these Regulations; and
(c) search or cause to be searched any person found on the premises whom he has reasonable cause to believe to be in possession of any such documents or other things; but no woman or girl may be searched except by a woman.

(3) The powers conferred by a warrant under this regulation may not be exercised –

(a) outside such times of day as may be specified in the warrant; or
(b) if the warrant so provides, otherwise than in the presence of a constable in uniform.

(4) An officer seeking to exercise the powers conferred by a warrant under this regulation or, if there is more than one such officer, that one of them who is in charge of the search must provide a copy of the warrant endorsed with his name as follows –

(a) if the occupier of the premises concerned is present at the time the search is to begin, the copy must be supplied to the occupier;
(b) if at that time the occupier is not present but a person who appears to the officer to be in charge of the premises is present, the copy must be supplied to that person;
(c) if neither sub-paragraph (a) nor (b) applies, the copy must be left in a prominent place on the premises.

Penalties, review and appeals

20. Power to impose penalties

(1) The Commissioners may impose a penalty of such amount as they consider appropriate, not exceeding £5,000, on a person to whom regulation 10 (requirement

to be registered) applies, where that person fails to comply with any requirement in regulation 3 (systems and training etc. to prevent money laundering), 10, 11 (supplementary information), 14 (fees) or 15 (entry, inspection etc.).

(2) The Commissioners must not impose a penalty on a person where there are reasonable grounds for them to be satisfied that the person took all reasonable steps for securing that the requirement would be complied with.

(3) Where the Commissioners decide to impose a penalty under this regulation, they must forthwith inform the person, in writing, of –

(a) their decision to impose the penalty and its amount;
(b) their reasons for imposing the penalty;
(c) the review procedure; and
(d) the right to appeal to a tribunal.

(4) Where a person is liable to a penalty under this regulation, the Commissioners may reduce the penalty to such amount (including nil) as they think proper.

21. Review procedure

(1) This regulation applies to the following decisions of the Commissioners –

(a) a decision under regulation 12 to refuse to register an applicant;
(b) a decision under regulation 13 to cancel the registration of an operator or high value dealer;
(c) a decision under regulation 20 to impose a penalty.

(2) Any person who is the subject of a decision as mentioned in paragraph (1) may by notice in writing to the Commissioners require them to review that decision.

(3) The Commissioners need not review any decision unless the notice requiring the review is given before the end of the period of 45 days beginning with the date on which written notification of the decision was first given to the person requiring the review.

(4) A person may give a notice under this regulation to require a decision to be reviewed for a second or subsequent time only if –

(a) the grounds on which he requires the further review are that the Commissioners did not, on any previous review, have the opportunity to consider certain facts or other matters; and
(b) he does not, on the further review, require the Commissioners to consider any facts or matters which were considered on a previous review except in so far as they are relevant to any issue to which the facts or matters not previously considered relate.

(5) Where the Commissioners are required under this regulation to review any decision they must either –

(a) confirm the decision; or
(b) withdraw or vary the decision and take such further steps (if any) in consequence of the withdrawal or variation as they consider appropriate.

(6) Where the Commissioners do not, within 45 days beginning with the date on which the review was required by a person, give notice to that person of their determination of the review, they are to be assumed for the purposes of these Regulations to have confirmed the decision.

22. Appeals to a VAT and duties tribunal

On an appeal from any decision by the Commissioners on a review under regulation 21, the tribunal have the power to –

(a) quash or vary any decision of the Commissioners, including the power to reduce any penalty to such amount (including nil) as they think proper; and
(b) substitute their own decision for any decision quashed on appeal.

Miscellaneous

23. Prosecution of offences by the Commissioners

(1) Proceedings for an offence under these Regulations may be instituted by order of the Commissioners.

(2) Such proceedings may be instituted only against an operator or high value dealer or, where such a person is a body corporate, a partnership or an unincorporated association, against any person who is liable to be proceeded against under regulation 27 (offences by bodies corporate etc.).

(3) Any such proceedings which are so instituted must be commenced in the name of an officer.

(4) In the case of the death, removal, discharge or absence of the officer in whose name any such proceedings were commenced, those proceedings may be continued by another officer.

(5) Where the Commissioners investigate, or propose to investigate, any matter with a view to determining –

(a) whether there are grounds for believing that an offence under these Regulations has been committed by any person mentioned in paragraph (2); or
(b) whether such a person should be prosecuted for such an offence;

that matter is to be treated as an assigned matter within the meaning of the Customs and Excise Management Act 1979.

(6) In exercising their power to institute proceedings for an offence under these Regulations, the Commissioners must comply with any conditions or restrictions imposed in writing by the Treasury.

(7) Conditions or restrictions may be imposed under paragraph (6) in relation to –

(a) proceedings generally; or
(b) such proceedings, or categories of proceedings, as the Treasury may direct.

24. Recovery of fees and penalties through the court

Where any fee is charged, or any penalty is imposed, by virtue of these Regulations –

(a) if the person from whom it is recoverable resides in England and Wales or Northern Ireland, it is recoverable as a civil debt; and

(b) if that person resides in Scotland, it may be enforced in the same manner as an extract registered decree arbitral bearing a warrant for execution issued by the sheriff court of any sheriffdom in Scotland.

25. Authorised persons operating a bureau de change

(1) No authorised person may, as from 1st April 2004, carry on the business of operating a bureau de change unless he has first informed the Authority that he proposes to do so.

(2) Where an authorised person ceases to carry on that business, he must inform the Authority forthwith.

(3) Any information to be supplied to the Authority under this regulation must be in such form or verified in such manner as the Authority may specify.

(4) Any requirement imposed by this regulation is to be treated as if it were a requirement imposed by or under the 2000 Act.

(5) Any function of the Authority under this regulation is to be treated as if it were a function of the Authority under the 2000 Act.

PART IV
MISCELLANEOUS

26. Supervisory authorities etc. to report evidence of money laundering

(1) Where a supervisory authority, in the light of any information obtained by it, knows or suspects, or has reasonable grounds for knowing or suspecting, that someone has or may have been engaged in money laundering, the supervisory authority must disclose the information to a constable as soon as is reasonably practicable.

(2) Where a supervisory authority passes the information to any other person who has such knowledge or suspicion or such reasonable grounds for knowledge or suspicion as is mentioned in paragraph (1), he may disclose the information to a constable.

(3) Where any person within paragraph (6), in the light of any information obtained by him, knows or suspects or has reasonable grounds for knowing or suspecting that someone has or may have been engaged in money laundering, he must, as soon as is reasonably practicable, disclose that information either to a constable or to the supervisory authority by whom he was appointed or authorised.

(4) Where information has been disclosed to a constable under this regulation, he (or any person obtaining the information from him) may disclose it in connection with the investigation of any criminal offence or for the purpose of any criminal proceedings, but not otherwise.

(5) A disclosure made under this regulation is not to be taken to breach any restriction on the disclosure of information (however imposed).

(6) Persons within this paragraph are –

    (a) a person or inspector appointed under section 65 or 66 of the Friendly Societies Act 1992[26];

    (b) an inspector appointed under section 49 of the Industrial and Provident Societies Act 1965 or section 18 of the Credit Unions Act 1979[27];

    (c) an inspector appointed under section 431, 432, 442 or 446 of the Companies Act 1985[28] or under Article 424, 425, 435 or 439 of the Companies (Northern Ireland) Order 1986[29];

    (d) a person or inspector appointed under section 55 or 56 of the Building Societies Act 1986[30];

    (e) a person appointed under section 167, 168(3) or (5), 169(1)(b) or 284 of the 2000 Act, or under regulations made as a result of section 262(2)(k) of that Act, to conduct an investigation; and

    (f) a person authorised to require the production of documents under section 447 of the Companies Act 1985, Article 440 of the Companies (Northern Ireland) Order 1986 or section 84 of the Companies Act 1989.

27. Offences by bodies corporate etc.

(1) If an offence under regulation 3 committed by a body corporate is shown –

    (a) to have been committed with the consent or the connivance of an officer; or

    (b) to be attributable to any neglect on his part;

the officer as well as the body corporate is guilty of an offence and liable to be proceeded against and punished accordingly.

(2) If an offence under regulation 3 committed by a partnership is shown –

    (a) to have been committed with the consent or the connivance of a partner; or

    (b) to be attributable to any neglect on his part;

the partner as well as the partnership is guilty of an offence and liable to be proceeded against and punished accordingly.

(3) If an offence under regulation 3 committed by an unincorporated association (other than a partnership) is shown –

    (a) to have been committed with the consent or the connivance of an officer of the association or a member of its governing body; or

    (b) to be attributable to any neglect on the part of such an officer or member;

that officer or member as well as the association is guilty of an offence and liable to be proceeded against and punished accordingly.

(4) If the affairs of a body corporate are managed by its members, paragraph (1) applies in relation to the acts and defaults of a member in connection with his functions of management as if he were a director of the body.

(5) In this regulation –

    (a) "partner" includes a person purporting to act as a partner; and

    (b) "officer", in relation to a body corporate, means a director, manager, secretary, chief executive, member of the committee of management, or a person purporting to act in such a capacity.

28. Prohibitions in relation to certain countries

(1) The Treasury may direct any person who carries on relevant business –

    (a) not to enter a business relationship;

    (b) not to carry out any one-off transaction; or

    (c) not to proceed any further with a business relationship or one-off transaction;

in relation to a person who is based or incorporated in a country (other than an EEA State) to which the Financial Action Task Force has decided to apply counter-measures.

(2) A person who fails to comply with a Treasury direction is to be treated as having contravened regulation 3.

29. Minor and consequential amendments

The provisions mentioned in Schedule 2 to these Regulations have effect subject to the amendments there specified, being minor amendments and amendments consequential on the provisions of these Regulations.

30. Transitional provisions

(1) Nothing in these Regulations obliges any person who carries on relevant business falling within any of sub-paragraphs (a) to (e) of regulation 2(2) to maintain identification procedures which require evidence to be obtained in respect of any business relationship formed by him before 1st April 1994.

(2) Nothing in these Regulations obliges any person who carries on relevant business falling within any of sub-paragraphs (f) to (n) of regulation 2(2) –

    (a) to maintain identification procedures which require evidence to be obtained in respect of any business relationship formed by him before 1st March 2004; or

    (b) to maintain internal reporting procedures which require any action to be taken in respect of any knowledge, suspicion or reasonable grounds for knowledge or suspicion which came to that person before 1st March 2004.

John Heppell

Nick Ainger
Two of the Lords Commissioners of Her Majesty's Treasury

28th November 2003

SCHEDULE 1

Regulation 2(2)(e)

ACTIVITIES LISTED IN ANNEX 1 TO
THE BANKING CONSOLIDATION DIRECTIVE

1. Acceptance of deposits and other repayable funds.

2. Lending.

3. Financial leasing.

4. Money transmission services.

5. Issuing and administering means of payment (eg credit cards, travellers' cheques and bankers' drafts).

6. Guarantees and commitments.

7. Trading for own account or for account of customers in –

   (a) money market instruments (cheques, bills, certificates of deposit, etc.);
   (b) foreign exchange;
   (c) financial futures and options;
   (d) exchange and interest-rate instruments;
   (e) transferable securities.

8. Participation in securities issues and the provision of services related to such issues.

9. Advice to undertakings on capital structure, industrial strategy and related questions and advice as well as services relating to mergers and the purchase of undertakings.

10. Money broking.

11. Portfolio management and advice.

12. Safekeeping and administration of securities.

13. Credit reference services.

14. Safe custody services.

SCHEDULE 2

Regulation 29

MINOR AND CONSEQUENTIAL AMENDMENTS

PART I
Primary Legislation
Value Added Tax Act 1994 (c. 23)

1. – (1) Section 83 of the Value Added Tax Act 1994 is amended as follows.

(2) In paragraph (zz), for "regulation 16 of the Money Laundering Regulations 2001", substitute "regulation 21 of the Money Laundering Regulations 2003".

Northern Ireland Act 1998 (c. 47)

2. – (1) Paragraph 25 of Schedule 3 (reserved matters) to the Northern Ireland Act 1998 is amended as follows.

(2) For "1993" substitute "2003".

PART II
Secondary Legislation
The Cross-Border Credit Transfers Regulations 1999 (S.I. 1999/1876)

3. – (1) Regulation 12 of the Cross-Border Credit Transfers Regulations 1999 is amended as follows.

(2) For paragraph (2) substitute –

" (2) In this regulation 'enactments relating to money laundering' means section 18 of the Terrorism Act 2000, section 340(11) of the Proceeds of Crime Act 2002 and the Money Laundering Regulations 2003.".

The Terrorism Act 2000 (Crown Servants and Regulators) Regulations 2001 (S.I. 2001/192)

4. – (1) The Terrorism Act 2000 (Crown Servants and Regulators) Regulations 2001 are amended as follows.

(2) In regulation 2, for the definition of "relevant financial business" substitute –

" 'relevant business' has the meaning given by regulation 2(2) of the Money Laundering Regulations 2003.".

(3) In regulation 3, for "relevant financial business" substitute "relevant business".

The Representation of the People (England and Wales) Regulations 2001
(S.I. 2001/341)

5. – (1) The Representation of the People (England and Wales) Regulations 2001 are amended as follows.

(2) In regulation 114(3)(b)[31] –

    (i) for "1993" substitute "2003"; and
    (ii) omit ", the Money Laundering Regulations 2001".

The Representation of the People (Northern Ireland) Regulations 2001
(S.I. 2001/400)

6. – (1) The Representation of the People (Northern Ireland) Regulations 2001 are amended as follows.

(2) In regulation 107(3)(b)[32] –

    (i) in paragraph (i), for "1993" substitute "2003";
    (ii) omit paragraph (ii); and
    (iii) in paragraph (iii), omit the words "either of" and "sets of".

The Representation of the People (Scotland) Regulations 2001 (S.I. 2001/497)

7. – (1) The Representation of the People (Scotland) Regulations 2001 are amended as follows.

(2) In regulation 113(3)(b)[33] –

    (i) for "1993" substitute "2003"; and
    (ii) omit ", the Money Laundering Regulations 2001".

The Proceeds of Crime Act 2002 (Failure to Disclose Money Laundering: Specified Training) Order 2003 (S.I. 2003/171)

8. – (1) The Proceeds of Crime Act 2002 (Failure to Disclose Money Laundering: Specified Training) Order 2003 is amended as follows.

(2) In article 2, for "regulation 5(1)(c) of the Money Laundering Regulations 1993" substitute "regulation 3(1)(c)(ii) of the Money Laundering Regulations 2003".

EXPLANATORY NOTE

(This note is not part of the Regulations)

These Regulations replace the Money Laundering Regulations 1993 and 2001 with updated provisions which reflect Directive 2001/97/EC of the European Parliament and of the Council amending Council Directive 91/308/EEC on prevention of the use of the financial system for the purpose of money laundering. A Transposition Note setting out how the main elements of Directive 2001/97/EC will be transposed into UK law is available from the Financial Systems and International Standards Team, HM Treasury, 1 Horse Guards Road, London SW1A 2HQ. The Transposition Note is also on HM Treasury's website (**www.hm-treasury.gov.uk**). A regulatory impact assessment has been prepared and placed in the library of each House of Parliament.

A copy is likewise available from the Treasury and can be found on the Treasury's website.

Where business relationships are formed, or one-off transactions are carried out, in the course of relevant business (defined in regulation 2), the persons carrying out such relevant business are required to maintain certain identification procedures (regulation 4), record-keeping procedures (regulation 6) and internal reporting procedures (regulation 7) and to establish other appropriate procedures for the purpose of forestalling or preventing money laundering (regulation 3(1)(b)). They are also required to train their employees in those procedures and, more generally, in the recognition of money laundering transactions and the law relating to money laundering (regulation 3(1)(c)). A person who fails to maintain the procedures or carry out the training is guilty of a criminal offence (regulation 3(2)). Casino operators must obtain satisfactory evidence of the identity of all people using their gaming facilities (regulation 8).

Regulation 9 requires the Commissioners of Customs and Excise to keep a register of money service operators and a register of high value dealers and regulations 10–11 state the registration requirements placed on such persons. Regulation 12 lists the grounds on which registration may be refused by the Commissioners, including where information which has been supplied is incomplete, false or misleading. Regulation 13 lists the circumstances in which registration may be cancelled by the Commissioners. Regulation 14 allows the Commissioners to charge fees.

Regulations 15 to 19 state the powers of the Commissioners in relation to money service operators and high value dealers, including a power to enter and inspect premises. Where there are reasonable grounds for believing that an offence under the Regulations is being, has been or is about to be committed by a money service operator or high value dealer, the Commissioners may seek a court order requiring any person in possession of certain information to allow them access to it. Regulation 19 allows the Commissioners to enter premises with a warrant, to search persons and to take away documents. Regulation 20 allows the Commissioners to impose a civil penalty in certain circumstances. Regulation 21 provides a mechanism for a formal review by the Commissioners of their decisions. Regulation 22 provides for appeals against the Commissioners' decisions to be heard by a VAT tribunal. Regulation 23 allows the Commissioners to prosecute offences under the Regulations. Regulation 24 allows fees and penalties to be recovered as a civil debt. Regulation 25 requires people who are authorised by the Financial Services Authority ("the FSA") to inform the FSA before they operate bureaux de change.

Regulation 26 requires supervisory authorities (defined in regulation 2) and various other people who obtain information indicative of money laundering to inform a constable. Regulation 28 allows the Treasury to require people who carry on relevant business to refrain from doing business with people in certain non-EEA States.

Notes:

[1] S.I. 1992/1711.
[2] 1972 c. 68. By virtue of the amendment of section 1(2) made by section 1 of the European Economic Area Act 1993 (c. 51) regulations may be made under section 2(2) to implement obligations of the United Kingdom created by or arising under the Agreement on the European Economic Area signed at Oporto on 2nd May 1992 (Cm 2073) and the Protocol adjusting that Agreement signed at Brussels on 17th March 1993 (Cm 2183).

[3] See the definition of "prescribed".

[4] 2000 c. 8.

[5] S.I. 1993/1933, amended by S.I. 1994/1696, S.I. 1998/1129, S.I. 2000/2952, S.I. 2001/3641 and 3649.

[6] S.I. 2001/1819.

[7] S.I. 2001/3641.

[8] OJ L 126, 26.5.2000, p.1; OJ L 35, 11.2.2003, p.1.

[9] 1979 c. 38. Section 1 was amended by the Law Reform (Miscellaneous Provisions) (Scotland) Act 1985 (c. 73), Schedule 1, Pt I, para. 40, the Planning (Consequential Provisions) Act 1990 (c. 11), Schedule 2, para. 42, the Planning (Consequential Provisions) (Scotland) Act 1997 (c. 11), Schedule 2, para. 28 and by S.I. 2001/1283.

[10] OJ L 345, 19.12.2002, p.1.

[11] 1995 c. 46.

[12] 2002 c. 29.

[13] 2000 c. 11.

[14] OJ L 166, 28.6.1991, p.77; OJ L 344, 28.12.2001, p.76.

[15] 1979 c. 2.

[16] 1968 c. 13.

[17] 1986 c. 45.

[18] S.I. 1989/2405 (N.I. 19).

[19] 1989 c. 40.

[20] S.I. 1990/593 (N.I. 5).

[21] 1965 c. 12.

[22] 1969 c. 24 (N.I.).

[23] 1986 c. 60. This Act was repealed as from 1st December 2001 by S.I. 2001/3649, art. 3(1)(c).

[24] Section 21A was inserted by the Anti-terrorism, Crime and Security Act 2001 (c. 24), Schedule 2, Part 3, para. 5.

[25] 1954 c. 33 (N.I.).

[26] 1992 c. 40.

[27] 1979 c. 34.

[28] 1985 c. 6.

[29] S.I. 1986/1032 (N.I. 6).

[30] 1986 c. 53.

[31] Inserted by regulation 15 of the Representation of the People (England and Wales) (Amendment) Regulations 2002 (S.I. 2002/1871).

[32] Inserted by regulation 21 of the Representation of the People (Northern Ireland) (Amendment) Regulations 2002 (S.I. 2002/1873).

[33] Inserted by regulation 14 of the Representation of the People (Scotland) (Amendment) Regulations 2002 (S.I. 2002/1872).

B1

Extracts from the Law Society's Guidance on Money Laundering (Pilot Edition – January 2004)

[. . .]

CHAPTER 3 – MONEY LAUNDERING REGULATIONS 2003 – PARAGRAPHS 3.66–3.121

PART 2 – HOW CAN IDENTITY BE ESTABLISHED?

General principles

3.66 Solicitors must be satisfied that they are dealing with a real person or organisation (natural, corporate or legal), and obtain satisfactory evidence of identity to establish that the client is that person or organisation. For the purpose of the ML Regulations 2003, 'satisfactory evidence of identity' is evidence which is reasonably capable of establishing (and does in fact establish to the satisfaction of the person obtaining it) that the client is the person he or she claims to be.

3.67 Some firms may wish to produce standard forms for use by their staff in relation to evidence of identity.

3.68 In deciding what evidence is satisfactory, and how much evidence is required, a common sense approach should be applied. There will be circumstances when it will be both necessary and permissible to apply commercial judgement to the extent of the initial identification requirements. Decisions will need to be taken on the number of persons to be identified within the client organisation, the identification evidence required, and whether additional evidence is necessary.

3.69 The first step in the identification process is to think about exactly who your client is. In some cases it will be immediately obvious but in others it may be necessary to consider the position and, on occasion, to discuss and agree this with the client(s). For example, if you are acting for one of a group of companies, exactly which company or companies will you be acting for? If another professional firm or a bank asks you for advice, are you acting for them or for their underlying client? If acting on a domestic house purchase, are you acting for one individual or for both partners within a relationship? You must obtain satisfactory evidence of identity in relation to all persons for whom you intend to act. In the case of joint instructions from two or more clients, the identity of all the clients must be checked (but see paragraph 3.120 below in relation to partnerships).

3.70 You must also consider whether your client is instructing you as principal or agent. Where the client is or appears to act for another person then, in addition to obtaining evidence of identity in relation to the client, under Regulation 4(3)(d), you must also take reasonable measures to establish the identity of any principal for whom that client is acting, and under Regulation 6 you must maintain records in relation to that evidence. This obligation to take reasonable measures is rather less than the obligation to obtain satisfactory evidence in relation to the client, but it must still be complied with.

3.71 You may make checks by looking at actual documentary evidence such as passports and certificates of incorporation issued by Companies House, or by making electronic checks of suitable databases such as the FSA register, the Law Society database of practising solicitors, and the electoral register. Where you rely on an electronic check it may be advisable to print out and retain a copy of the evidence with your records. [...]

3.72 You may also ask third parties, such as investigation and information service providers, and credit reference agencies, to obtain the evidence for you as long as you are reasonably satisfied that they are reputable, and that the evidence they produce will be reliable, and that you ensure that your records of the evidence are complete. For example, you may rely on a copy of the details page of a passport as part of the evidence of identity if it has been certified by a reputable lawyer (for details as to who may photocopy UK passports see paragraphs 3.79–3.80).

3.73 When using a combination of electronic and documentary checks, you must ensure that different original sources of information are used. For example, a physical check of a mortgage statement and an electronic check of the same mortgage account come from the same source, so one does not corroborate the other.

3.74 Some clients may object to providing evidence of identity. It may be helpful to explain the reason for requiring evidence of identity in the initial interview or client care letter. More people in the UK are now used to being asked for evidence of identity by their bank or building society, so it will be increasingly rare to find a client who objects to such a request from a solicitor. If a client is unwilling to provide evidence it will be for the solicitor to assess whether this in itself is a cause for concern.

Copying and certifying original identification documents

3.75 As already mentioned, usually you should keep a printed or other copy of any evidence of identification obtained as you may be required to produce the evidence in the future. It may be helpful to make a note on the retained copy as to when the original document was seen and by whom. If reliance is being placed on copies provided by others these should be certified.

3.76 Such a copy may be made in several ways, including fax copying, photocopying, scanning, filming and reproduction in any other medium, including the placing of materials on the Internet.

3.77 Certified copies of original identification evidence should be made by checking the copy against the original and then signing and dating the copy as a true copy of the original. In the case of photographic evidence of an individual's identity the person certifying should confirm that the individual is the person shown in the photograph. When copying a passport or national identity card, only the personal details pages need to be copied and kept as evidence.

3.78 If the client cannot meet you to produce the original identification document, you should think carefully before asking the client to send valuable personal identity documents, such as passports, driving licences and identity cards by normal post because of the dangers of interception and fraud. These dangers can even exist with registered or other guaranteed postal services. The client should be warned of the dangers and given a choice as to another method. You should arrange an appointment when the client can produce the documents required or, if you are not able to meet the client, you should follow the guidance in paragraphs 3.90 to 3.94 below.

3.79 The HMSO guidance note no. 20 dated 5 December 2002 confirms that copies of the personal details page of a UK passport may be made for the purposes of record keeping by the following persons only:

(a) the holder of the passport
(b) notaries, solicitors, UK government departments and British consulates;
(c) financial institutions and other persons and firms who are subject to the ML Regulations 2003; and
(d) any person or firm for the purpose of certifying that identification checks have been made in accordance with the ML Regulations 2003.

3.80 The guidance says that copies must be in black and white only so that they cannot be mistaken for a real passport page. Copying for these purposes includes photocopying, scanning, filming, reproduction in any other medium, including placing material on the Internet. The original document is the evidence of identity. The photocopy of the original is used to record and certify that identification checks have been made. There is no need to apply for a licence or pay a fee to take such copies.

Individuals

3.81 In general, an individual's identity is made up of both full name and current address, including the postcode where available and in most cases you should obtain satisfactory evidence in relation to both name and address, and a combination of checks should be carried out. Where an EEA member state identity card is produced showing name, address, and with a photograph this may be accepted as satisfactory evidence without further corroboration. The previous address should be confirmed if the client has moved recently.

3.82 Where evidence of identity is required in relation to an individual, and that individual is known to a solicitor or qualified EEA or US lawyer who confirms in writing (a) that s/he has known the individual for over two years and (b) the individual's private or trading address, then no further evidence of identity is usually required, unless there are circumstances which increase risk.

3.83   Where you are reasonably satisfied that an individual is nationally or internationally known a record of identification can include a file note of your satisfaction about identity, usually including an address.

Individuals: documentary evidence of personal identity: UK residents

3.84   The following is a list of examples of suitable documentary evidence of name for UK resident private individuals. You should be satisfied that any documents offered are originals to guard against forged or counterfeit documents and that photographs, if any, provide a likeness to the client:

- current signed passport;
- EEA member state identity card (which can also be used as evidence of address if it gives this);
- cheque drawn on an account in the name of the client with a bank in the UK or EEA;
- residence permit issued by Home Office to EEA nationals on sight of own country passport;
- current UK or EEA photo-card driving licence;
- current full UK driving licence – old-style provisional driving licences should not be accepted;
- benefit book or original notification letter from the Benefits Agency confirming the right to benefits;
- photographic registration cards for self-employed individuals and partnerships in the construction industry C1S4 (the card does not contain an issue or expiry date and is renewed only if the individual's appearance changes dramatically);
- firearms or shotgun certificate;
- national identity card containing a photograph of the client; and
- an entry in a local or national telephone directory confirming name and address.

Documentary evidence of address

3.85   The following is a list of examples of suitable documentary evidence of address for UK resident private individuals. Do not use any of these documents if you have already used them as evidence of name:

- confirmation from an electoral register search that a person of that name lives at that address;
- a recent utility bill or statement, or a certificate from a utilities supplier confirming an arrangement to pay for services on pre-payment terms (do not accept mobile telephone bills which can be sent to different addresses);
- local council tax bill for current year;
- current full UK driving licence – old-style provisional driving licences should not be accepted;
- bank, building society or credit union statement or passbook containing current address;
- a recent original mortgage statement from a recognised lender;
- solicitor's letter confirming recent house purchase or land registry confirmation of address;
- local council or housing association rent card or tenancy agreement;

- benefit book or original notification letter from the Benefits Agency confirming the right to benefits;
- EEA member state identity card;
- Inland Revenue self-assessment statement or tax demand;
- house or motor insurance certificate;
- record of any home visit made; and
- an entry confirming name and address in a local or national telephone directory.

Individuals: persons not resident in the UK

3.86 If you meet the client, you should be able to see a passport or national identity card as evidence of name and, if it gives it, an address. You can take copies of the pages containing the relevant information (reference numbers, date and country of issue) in which case you should certify the copy examined against the original and the date of the examination, or record that information in your records as part of the identification evidence. You must be reasonably satisfied that the document is a genuine passport or national identity card, and if in doubt as to whether it is genuine you could ask advice from an embassy or consulate official for the country concerned.

3.87 Where a prospective client is a national of, or resident in, a country on the FATF list of non-co-operative countries and territories, solicitors should consider whether they need to carry out further checks to find out exactly who the client is and what his or her business is before accepting instructions.

3.88 In addition, separate evidence of the client's permanent residential address (or, for business clients, principal business address) should usually be obtained, preferably from a national identity card, an official source, a reputable directory or from a qualified lawyer who confirms that the client is known to him and that he lives or works at the address given. A post box number alone is not normally sufficient evidence of address (although there are some countries, such as Hong Kong and the Gulf States, where post box addresses are commonly used) and if you accept a box number as evidence of address you should satisfy yourself (personally or through an agent) that the address can be physically located by way of a recorded description or other means.

3.89 Evidence of name and address could be obtained from a credit or financial institution in the client's home country or country of residence or through a reputable investigation and information service provider or credit reference agency. For professionals, evidence of name and practising address may be obtained from reputable professional directories.

Individuals: when you do not meet the client

3.90 There may be difficulties in verifying identity if the client is unable to visit your office (for example if he or she is disabled or lives at a distance from you or is overseas). In such cases you must satisfy yourself that your instructions have been given to you by the client or an authorised person on his or her behalf. A client who is unwilling to meet you without a good reason may be cause for concern [...]

3.91   Where you are so satisfied, you should enquire whether it is possible for the client to produce the documentary evidence you require to someone else qualified and willing to take and certify copies on your behalf. This would enable you to obtain evidence from valuable documents such as his or her passport. For a person physically within the UK, copies of evidence should be certified, for example, by a UK solicitor, accountant, doctor or high street bank manager, whose name and address should be noted and checked by reference to a professional directory or, for solicitors, the Law Society database of practising solicitors. The person undertaking the certification must be capable of being contacted if necessary. The certified copies should be kept with your other records of identity.

3.92   For a person not resident within the UK, the copy of the passport, national identity card and documentary evidence of address can be certified by:

- an embassy, consulate or high commission of the country of issue;
- a qualified lawyer or notary; or
- in the case of international students, the registrar of a UK higher education institution.

3.93   Where reliance is placed on certification by a qualified lawyer or notary, you should verify that his or her name and practice address appear in a reputable professional directory, or that the professional is currently on record with the appropriate professional body as practising at the address shown on the certificate or practice notepaper, and you should keep a note of this name and address with the evidence of identity.

3.94   Where it is not possible either to meet the client or for someone else to take and certify copies for you as set out above, you may not wish to ask the client to post valuable identity documents to you so, in practice, you may not see documents such as a passport, driving licence or identity card. You could, however, ask to see a combination of other less valuable documents which might satisfy you as to identity. You might also wish to make some electronic checks or arrange for evidence to be obtained though a reputable investigation and information service provider or credit reference agency. In all cases you must satisfy yourself that you have evidence which is reasonably capable of establishing (and does in fact establish to your satisfaction) that the client is the person he or she claims to be.

Disadvantaged clients

3.95   It is not the intention of the ML Regulations 2003 to exclude those who are already at a disadvantage from access to legal advice and financial services. Some disadvantaged clients may not be able to produce detailed evidence of identity (for example, they may not have a passport or driving licence and their name may not appear on utility bills). You might consider accepting as identification evidence a letter or statement from someone in a position of responsibility who knows the client (for example, a solicitor, doctor, minister of religion, teacher, hostel manager, social worker) which tends to show that the client is who he or she says he or she is and, if applicable, to confirm his or her permanent address.

3.96   Evidence of address might include:

- correspondence from a relevant government agency, including a benefits payment book or giro cheque;
- a tenancy agreement from a local housing association;
- a letter from the householder with whom the client is living who is named on a current council tax bill;
- a letter from the matron of a nursing or residential care home or the client's care worker;
- a letter from a hostel manager confirming temporary residence; or
- a letter from the Home Office confirming refugee status and granting permission to work, or a Home Office travel document for refugees.

Mentally incapacitated clients

3.97   Solicitors unsure as to whether a client is mentally incapacitated should refer to Principle 24.04 of the *Guide to the Professional Conduct of Solicitors 1999*.

3.98   Where solicitors are unable to comply with normal identification requirements because of their clients' mental health problems medical workers, hostel staff, social workers, or Receivers or Guardians appointed by a court, may assist with locating and producing identification documents. It is recognised that confirming the identity of clients whose personal affairs are in some disarray can be difficult, and so solicitors must exercise extra flexibility in the ways identification checks are done, e.g. in some circumstances oral confirmation of identity from a person who knows the client well may suffice.

Asylum seekers

3.99   An applicant's registration card could be used in conjunction with other evidence. The details in the card should, wherever possible, be verified by a passport, identity card or birth certificate. Please note that the registration card does not contain a signature as the Home Office relies on a biometric check (fingerprint held on microchip) to confirm identity.

3.100 Evidence of address can be obtained in the way suggested for disadvantaged clients.

Students and minors

3.101 The normal identification procedures should be used but if they do not provide satisfactory evidence, verification could be obtained in the following ways:

- through the home address of the parents;
- once the student is in residence, confirmation of the UK address from the registrar of the client's higher education institution;
- looking at a tenancy agreement or student accommodation contract; or
- confirmation of a temporary address and documentary evidence from the householder with whom the student is living (for example, by seeing the council tax bill in the householder's name).

3.102 If instructions are given by a family member or guardian, you should check the identity of that adult as well as the minor.

Estates

3.103 When acting for an estate, the firm's client will be the executor(s) or administrator(s) of that estate. Their identities will need to be established using the procedures for individuals or companies set out in this chapter. When acting for more than one executor or administrator it will normally be necessary to establish the identity of at least two. In addition to the will, solicitors should obtain copies of the grant of probate or letters of administration, and in the case of an existing executorship or administration obtain a copy of the death certificate. If a will trust is created, and the trustees are different from the executors the procedures in relation to trusts (see below) need to be followed in relation to the trustees when the will trust comes into operation.

Trusts

3.104 Trusts do not, of course, have separate legal personality. There are many different types of trust. Firms are advised to adopt a risk based approach in determining what evidence should be obtained and the nature of the evidence that is appropriate, recognising that trusts are popular vehicles for money launderers. The classic long established family settlement may raise different issues to an offshore discretionary trust.

3.105 When acting for trusts, the firm's client will be the trustees whose position can be checked by referring to the document establishing the trust (and, if appropriate, documents dealing with the appointment of the current trustees). Their identities need to be established using procedures for individuals or companies summarised elsewhere in this Guidance. When acting for more than one trustee it will be necessary to establish the identity of at least two individual trustees. Whether all the trustees, and/or the identity of any living settlor should also be established will depend on your assessment of the risk which will itself depend on your knowledge of the nature, purpose and original source of the funding for the trust. When acting for trustees who are based in offshore jurisdictions with strict bank secrecy and confidentiality rules or in jurisdictions without equivalent money laundering procedures, you may need to make fuller enquiries of the trustees to obtain details (for example, full name and business or home address) of the settlor.

3.106 When acting for the settlor to form the trust, it will be necessary to establish his or her identity using procedures already mentioned.

3.107 Except where the firm is acting for beneficiaries, there is no need to establish the identity of beneficiaries for the purpose of the ML Regulations 2003, although it would be normal practice for a firm of solicitors to check the identity of beneficiaries before making any distribution.

Employee and Pension Trusts

3.108 Such trusts would normally be low risk. Where the client is the sponsoring employer or settlor of a pensions trust or employee benefits trust, only the identity of that sponsoring employer or the settlor need be verified. Where the client is the trustee(s) of a tax approved pension scheme trust, identification of the sponsoring employer would normally be sufficient.

CORPORATE CLIENTS

3.109 Company structures are attractive to money launderers and firms should take a risk based approach in determining what evidence should be obtained, and the nature of the evidence that is appropriate. Dealing with a listed company presents a different risk to a private company. The following paragraphs set out minimum requirements, and firms may need to seek further evidence in higher risk situations.

Companies listed on the London Stock Exchange or a UK recognised investment exchange

3.110 Where a company is:

- listed on the London Stock Exchange or another recognised UK investment exchange; or
- a member of a UK recognised investment exchange; or
- the subsidiary of such a company;

no further evidence is required of identity beyond evidence of listing (such as a copy of the relevant dated page from the Financial Times or the London Stock Exchange's list of companies (which can be found at **www.londonstock exchange.com**) and, for subsidiaries, a copy of the latest annual return or comparable evidence such as an extract from a reputable online information provider showing the parent/subsidiary relationship.

Corporates listed or traded on any other recognised, designated or approved exchange

3.111 A list of these exchanges is published by the FSA (**www.fsa.gov.uk stock exchanges**) and the JMLSG website: **www.jmlsg.org.uk** also sets out a list. Where a company or corporation is listed or traded on a recognised, designated or approved exchange, or is one whose shares or securities are traded there, or is a subsidiary of such an entity, no further evidence is required of identity beyond evidence of such listing or trading and, for subsidiaries, a copy of the latest annual return or comparable evidence such as an extract from a reputable online information provider showing the parent/subsidiary relationship.

Banks, investment firms and insurance companies carrying on relevant business in the UK or subsidiaries of such entities (see Regulation 2(2) for the definition of relevant business)

3.112 In such cases you may obtain satisfactory evidence of identity by taking a copy of the relevant dated page from the on-line FSA register (**www.fsa.gov.uk**) showing that the bank, investment firm or company is authorised by the FSA to carry on relevant business, and for subsidiaries, a copy of the latest annual return or comparable evidence such as an extract from a reputable online information provider showing the parent/subsidiary relationship.

Banks, investment firms and insurance companies regulated in another EU or FATF member country, or for subsidiaries of such entities

3.113 In such cases you may obtain satisfactory evidence of identity by checking the regulated status of the prospective client with the relevant regulatory or supervisory authority, for example, by taking a copy of the relevant page from the regulator's website, and, for subsidiaries, a copy of the latest annual return or comparable evidence such as an extract from a reputable online information provider showing the parent/subsidiary relationship.

Other corporate clients: general

3.114 For UK companies not within paragraphs 3.109 to 3.111 above, and where reasonably practicable for overseas corporations not within those paragraphs, evidence of identity should be obtained as set out below.

UK companies

3.115 Evidence of identity will be required in relation to the company itself, usually comprising:

- a copy of the certificate of incorporation
- a list of directors
- a list of shareholders
- the registered address

which can be obtained from an official, or recognised independent source including an extract from a reputable online information provider.

3.116 In addition, where it is reasonably practicable, you should obtain evidence of identity in relation to one of its directors or shareholders, one of whom should usually be the person instructing you or alternatively appears to you, on the face of it, to be active in the management or control of the company. Note that lists of Directors and Shareholders should contain details of home addresses for the relevant individuals and so provide the documentary evidence of address (see paragraph 3.85). Where it is not reasonably practicable to obtain such additional identification evidence you might consider establishing a list of any shareholders holding 20% or more of the shares in the company or, if there are none, the principal owners. It may be necessary for further checks to be made about beneficial ownership if the initial information obtained is of the identity of mere nominees. By way of exception where the company is a well established household name there is no need to obtain the additional identification referred to in this subparagraph;

Overseas corporations (unlisted)

3.117 Evidence of identity will be required in relation to the company itself. Where it is obtainable in the relevant country this will usually include the certificate of incorporation, but can also include the lists referred to above in relation to UK companies. In countries where there is no certificate of incorporation, or equivalent, other evidence that reasonably satisfies you that the corporation is in existence should be obtained (for example a copy of the most recent audited accounts).

3.118 You may use an extract from a reputable online information provider, or the services of a reputable directory or information search agency. In addition, where it is reasonably practicable, you should obtain evidence of identity in relation to one of its directors or shareholders, one of whom should usually be the person instructing you or alternatively appears to you, on the face of it, to be active in the management or control of the company. Where it is not reasonably practicable to obtain such additional identification evidence you might consider establishing a list of any shareholders holding 20% or more of the shares in the company or, if there are none, the principal owners.

Subsidiaries (and sister companies) whether in the UK or elsewhere

3.119 Where the new client is a subsidiary of an existing client, in respect of whom an identification check has been carried out recently, evidence of the subsidiary or other relationship will be required and may be sufficient, provided that the record of the identification of the existing client is kept for the correct time period in relation not only for that existing client but also for the new client.

Partnerships, limited partnerships and Limited Liability Partnerships

3.120 For partnerships and limited partnerships you should obtain evidence of identity in respect of the partner who is instructing you and one other partner together with satisfactory evidence of the trading address (possibly obtained from a directory or similar). UK LLPs should obtain evidence in line with the requirements for other corporate clients set out above.

3.121 If preferred, where you are instructed on behalf of a partnership, limited partnership or a LLP formed under the Limited Liability Partnerships Act 2000, of lawyers, chartered or certified accountants or chartered surveyors, satisfactory evidence of identity may be obtained in the form of (a) confirmation of the firm's existence from a reputable directory or information or search agency or from the appropriate professional body (for example a copy of the relevant page from the Law Society's on-line directory of solicitors) and (b) confirmation of the firm's trading address, such as a copy of the relevant page from a reputable directory (such as Chambers, The Legal 500 or Martindale Hubble). For these professional partnerships it is not usually necessary to obtain evidence in relation to individual partners or members of the limited partnership or LLP.

CHAPTER 4 – PRIVILEGE AND CONFIDENTIALITY – PARAGRAPHS 4.1–4.14

The solicitor's duty of client confidentiality

4.1 A solicitor is under a *professional* and *legal* obligation to keep the affairs of clients confidential and to ensure that his or her staff do likewise. This duty of confidentiality is fundamental to the solicitor/client relationship.

4.2 It extends to all matters divulged to a solicitor by a client or (on his behalf) from whatever source.

4.3 Whilst there may be exceptional circumstances in which this general obligation of confidence can be overridden, the common law has long recognised its importance by providing protection to ensure that certain of these communications are immune from disclosure unless statute expressly, or by necessary implication, overrides that protection.

Protecting client confidentiality – legal professional privilege – LPP

4.4 The protection is provided by way of *a privilege against disclosure* and is called legal professional privilege (LPP).

> The policy of legal professional privilege requires that the client should be secure in the knowledge that protected documents and information will not be disclosed at all. [1]

4.5 Both the Government and the courts recognise its importance, describing LPP respectively as,

> *. . .a cornerstone of the legal system. It serves the public interest because it recognises that it is in the interests of justice that a person consulting his legal adviser should be able to do so in confidence, since otherwise he may not feel able to be fully open about his position. This might impede his ability either to protect his rights or to defend himself properly in any subsequent action. [2]*

and as

> *. . .a fundamental human right long established in the common law. It is a necessary corollary of the right of any person to obtain skilled advice about the law. Such advice cannot be effectively obtained unless the client is able to put all the facts before the advisor without fear that they may be afterwards disclosed and used to his prejudice. [3]*

What communications are privileged?

4.6 Not everything that lawyers have a duty to keep confidential is privileged. Only those confidential communications falling under either of the two heads of privilege –'advice privilege' or 'litigation privilege', are protected by LPP.

Who is a 'lawyer' for such purposes?

4.7 This includes solicitors and their employees, barristers, in-house lawyers but not accountants, even if they give legal advice (subject to one very limited exception). However POCA, when dealing with communications in privileged circumstances adopts the narrower term – 'professional legal adviser'. [. . .]

Advice privilege

4.8 Communications between a lawyer (acting in his capacity as a lawyer), and a client, are privileged if they are *confidential* and *for the purpose of seeking legal advice from a lawyer or providing legal advice to a client*. Case law gives some help in showing what is, or is not, covered by advice privilege. For example:

- conveyancing documents are not communications [4]
- neither is a client account ledger maintained in relation to the client's money [5]
- nor an appointments diary or time record on an attendance note, time sheet or fee record relating to a client [6]
- whereas a solicitor's bill of costs and statement of account is privileged [7]
- and notes of open court proceedings [8], or conversations, correspondence or meetings with opposing lawyers [9] are not privileged, as the content of the communication is not confidential.

4.9 Merely because a client is speaking or writing to his or her solicitor does not make that communication privileged – it is only those communications that directly seek or provide advice or 'where information is passed by the solicitor or the client to the other in the course of keeping each other informed so that advice may be sought or given as required' [10]. This will include advice as to what should prudently and sensibly be done in the relevant legal context [11].

Litigation privilege

4.10 Under this head the following are privileged:–

Confidential communications made, *after litigation has started*, or is *'reasonably in prospect'*, between

- a lawyer and a client,
- a lawyer and an agent (whether or not that agent is a lawyer), or
- a lawyer and a third party,

for the *sole or dominant purpose* of litigation, whether

- for seeking or giving advice in relation to it, or
- for obtaining evidence to be used in it, or
- for obtaining information leading to obtaining such evidence.

Pre-existing documents

4.11 An original document which is not brought into existence for either of these privileged purposes and so is not already privileged, does not acquire privileged status merely by being given to a lawyer for advice or otherwise for a privileged purpose.

Fraud or illegality – the crime/fraud exception

4.12 It is proper for a lawyer to advise a client on how to stay within the law and avoid committing a crime [12] or to warn a client that proposed actions could attract prosecution [13] and such advice will be protected by privilege.

4.13 LPP does not however exist in respect of documents which themselves form part of a criminal or fraudulent act or communications which take place in order to obtain advice with the intention of carrying out an offence [14]. It is irrelevant whether or not the lawyer is aware that he is being used for that purpose [15]. If the lawyer suspects that he is unwittingly being involved by his client in a fraud, before he can consider himself released from his duty of confidentiality, the courts require there to be strong prima facie evidence before LPP can be displaced [16]. Whilst he may release himself if such evidence exists, he may also raise the issue with the Court for an order authorising him to make disclosure to the victim [17].

4.14 The general 'crime fraud exception' principle is restated in the Police and Criminal Evidence Act 1984 (PACE) [18] at section 10(2) where items held with the intention of furthering a criminal purpose are declared not to be items subject to LPP. It is important to note that the intention to further a criminal purpose need not be that of the client (or the lawyer) – it is sufficient that a third party intends the lawyer/client communication to be made with that purpose (e.g. where the innocent client is being 'used' by a third party) [19].

Notes:

1. Lord Hoffman in *R* v. *Special Commissioner and Anor, ex p Morgan Grenfell & Co Ltd* [2002] UKHL 21.
2. *'In the public interest?'* Lord Chancellor's Department consultation paper issued following publication of the OFT's report on competition in the professions.
3. *Morgan Grenfell.*
4. *R* v. *Inner London Crown Court ex p Baines & Baines* [1988] QB 579.
5. *Nationwide Building Society* v. *Various Solicitors* [1999] PNLR 53. Such entries are not created for the purpose of giving legal advice to a client but are internal records maintained in part to discharge a solicitor's professional and disciplinary obligations under the Solicitors' Accounts Rules.
6. *R* v. *Manchester Crown Court, ex p. Rogers* [1999] 1 WLR 832.
7. *Chant* v. *Brown* (1852) 9 Hare 790.
8. *Parry* v. *News Group Newspapers* (1990) 140 New Law Journal 1719.
9. *Parry.*
10. In *re Konigsberg (a bankrupt)* [1989] 1 WLR 1257.
11. See generally the judgment of Taylor LJ in *Balabel* v. *Air India* [1988] Ch at 330.
12. *Bullivant* v. *Att-Gen of Victoria* [1901] AC 196.
13. *Butler* v. *Board of Trade* [1971] Ch 680.
14. *R* v. *Cox & Railton* (1884) 14 QBD 153.
15. *Banque Keyser Ullman* v. *Skandia* [1986] 1 Lloyds Rep 336.
16. *O'Rourke* v. *Darbishire* [1920] AC 581.
17. *Finers* v. *Miro* [1991] 1 WLR 35.
18. It is also reflected in numerous other criminal statutes – including POCA section 330 (failure to disclose) and section 333 (tipping off) – [...].
19. *R* v. *Central Criminal Court ex p Francis & Francis* [1989] 1 AC 346.

CHAPTER 5 – CIVIL LIABILITY – PARAGRAPHS 5.1–5.23

Introduction to liabilities under civil law

5.1 The principal focus of recent legislation on money laundering has been to ensure that businesses, which can include solicitors, have in place effective AML systems and controls in order to reduce opportunities for money laundering and to provide for the forfeiture of the profits of crime. That legislation does not seek to recompense the victim of criminal activity but to take away the proceeds. By contrast, under civil law in England & Wales, a victim of crime may have a claim against those who became involved in or provided assistance in the process of laundering money. Such a claim may be attractive where the victim is seeking a 'deep pocket' from which a recovery can be made, particularly in situations where the wrongdoer cannot be found or is not able to repay. Recent examples include the high profile frauds such as the BCCI, Maxwell and Polly Peck affairs, all of which involved claims against professionals. This trend is likely to continue. Solicitors should therefore be alive to the possibility of a civil claim.

5.2   There are no civil claims that equate directly to the criminal offences of theft and handling stolen property but there are established legal principles that can be used to recover money or property. In particular, a victim may have claims against third parties involved in money laundering for constructive trusteeship; money had and received; and tracing in equity or conspiracy.

5.3   The law of constructive trust and the circumstances in which liability can arise are complicated. This chapter aims to give guidance on how civil liability for breach of a constructive trust can arise and offers practical guidance on how to reduce the risk of liability. This Guidance is no substitute for appropriate legal advice.

Constructive trusteeship

5.4   'Trusteeship' here does not connote an orthodox trust involving a trust deed or a settlor and beneficiaries. Rather, in certain circumstances the courts will impose on an intermediary a liability to repay, as constructive trustee, the monies claimed by a claimant. For liability to arise, there must be 'trust' monies. A trust relationship arises whenever a person, the trustee, is compelled in equity to hold property for the benefit of some person or persons, the beneficiary, or for some purpose other than his own. *In certain situations (but by no means all) there will be a fiduciary relationship between a solicitor and his client.* [1] *Further, negligence or breach of contract by a fiduciary will not necessarily amount to breach of a fiduciary duty – it is breach of a fiduciary obligation (often by disloyalty or infidelity by the fiduciary) that gives rise to a constructive trust.*

5.5   Conventionally, liability as a constructive trustee can arise in two situations:

    (a)   where a person 'receives and becomes chargeable' with trust property – commonly called *'knowing receipt'*;
    (b)   where a person 'assists with knowledge of a fraudulent and dishonest design on the part of the trustees' – historically referred to as 'knowing assistance', but more accurately referred to as *'dishonest assistance'*.

5.6   There are differences between these two heads of liability. The main difference concerns 'knowledge' for the purposes of founding liability and in particular whether or not an element of dishonesty is required. An intermediary will be trustee of funds laundered after acquiring the requisite degree of knowledge.

Knowing receipt

5.7   Liability for 'knowing receipt' is receipt-based. The cause of action is restitutionary and is available only where the defendant received or applied the monies in breach of trust *for his own use and benefit*. Dishonesty is not an essential ingredient of the claim. The claimant must show:

(a) a disposal of his assets in breach of fiduciary duty or breach of trust;
(b) the beneficial receipt by the defendant of assets which are traceable as representing the assets of the claimant; and
(c) knowledge on the part of the defendant that the assets received are traceable to a breach of fiduciary duty which makes it unconscionable for the defendant to retain the benefit of those assets.

5.8   Element (b) is perhaps the most significant, since in many cases a solicitor will not be in receipt of the monies for his own benefit. A solicitor receiving money into client account and therefore effectively acting as agent for the client and paying it away as part of a transaction does not receive the trust monies for his own benefit. He must also account to the client for interest earned on those monies whilst in his hands. The position is different where the solicitor receives the money and applies it in payment of fees – this would constitute beneficial receipt of the monies.

5.9   Element (c) requires a defendant to have knowledge that the funds received are traceable to a breach of trust. The level of knowledge required has given rise to a substantial body of case law – in particular, whether actual knowledge is required or whether constructive knowledge is enough. That case law suggests that knowledge could derive from:

(a) actual knowledge;
(b) wilfully shutting one's eyes to the obvious;
(c) wilfully and recklessly failing to make such inquiries as an honest and reasonable man would have made;
(d) knowledge of circumstances which would indicate the facts to an honest and reasonable man;
(e) knowledge of circumstances which would put an honest and reasonable man on inquiry.

The first three categories are regarded as constituting actual knowledge, the latter two as constructive knowledge. However, more recently the courts have moved away from the distinction between actual and constructive knowledge, preferring instead to adopt a test of whether the recipient's state of knowledge was such as to 'make it unconscionable for him to retain the benefit of the receipt.' [2]

5.10   As a general rule, solicitors are entitled to act on the basis that their customers are honest. In relation to a bank it has been stated that:

> Account officers are not detectives. Unless and until they are alerted to the possibility of wrongdoing, they proceed, and are entitled to proceed, on the assumption that they are dealing with honest men. [3]

Dishonest assistance

5.11   This head of liability is also commonly referred to as 'knowing assistance' or 'accessory liability.' The elements of liability are:

(a) a breach of trust or fiduciary duty by someone other than the defendant in which the defendant assisted;

(b)   where in doing so the defendant acted dishonestly;

(c)   resulting in loss.

5.12   There are any number of ways in which a breach of trust or of fiduciary duty might arise. The breach of trust can be innocent rather than dishonest[4], although in the context of money laundering this is unlikely.

5.13   Assistance is essentially a factual issue, involving an examination of the accessory's conduct and state of knowledge. The case of *Agip (Africa) Ltd* v. *Jackson* [5] concerned a firm of accountants but illustrates that assistance for these purposes is likely to include activities that give rise to liability under section 328 POCA. In this case the defendant accountants formed companies in the Isle of Man with nominal share capital and served as directors. The companies opened bank accounts, received and made payments and were then liquidated. These were considered to be types of assistance for the purpose of this liability.

5.14   It is now clear that the accessory must have acted dishonestly [6] in the sense that his conduct falls below what is required of an honest solicitor in the circumstances. Honesty is judged objectively and inferences can be drawn where, for example, someone deliberately closes his eyes or ears, or deliberately fails to ask questions in case he learns something he would rather not know. [7]

5.15   Suspicion falls a long way short of knowledge required to establish constructive trust liability. In a recent court decision a judge made clear that the bank's suspicions about its customer, based on intelligence but not hard evidence, were not sufficient to give rise to constructive trust liability even though a report to NCIS was considered necessary. [8] However, each case must be judged on its own facts and there are risks which are difficult to quantify until this issue is finally determined in court.

5.16   Care is needed when acting for Politically Exposed Persons (PEPs) which includes senior political figures, their immediate family and close associates. A broad definition of PEPs is that they are individuals who are or have been entrusted with prominent public functions. Such persons may abuse their public powers. Business relationships with individuals holding important public positions and with persons or companies clearly related to them may expose a service provider to significant legal and/or reputational risks. Particular care should be taken if the amounts involved are in excess of the expected legitimate wealth of the person in question and where that person is from a country where corruption is said to be prevalent.

Practical issues

5.17   It is obviously difficult to prove a defendant's state of knowledge. A disclosure report to NCIS will provide useful evidence and it has been suggested that the fact that a disclosure report has been made could increase the risk of constructive trust claims. This risk cannot be completely ruled out. It is the Law Society's view that a solicitor's risk of constructive liability will be lowered rather than increased by making an immediate disclosure to NCIS. This is because the disclosure report is likely to be seen as a badge of honesty. Similarly, assessing money laundering risk and reacting appropriately are likely to be regarded as badges of honesty and reduce the risk of constructive trust liability.

5.18 The courts may give directions to trustees as to the administration of the trust. It is unlikely that a firm acting in accordance with such directions would be liable as constructive trustees. The case of *Finers* v. *Miro* [9] is an example of where this procedure was followed. This procedure should only be used in cases of real need. This is because the danger for solicitors making such applications is that they have to furnish the Court with evidence that they are constructive trustees. This could be relied on by the victim of the wrong in mounting a claim against a solicitor. An alternative is that solicitors consider seeking a binding declaration under Civil Procedure Rules, Part 40.20.

5.19 Two further notes of caution should also be considered:

(a) A solicitor should not as a matter of knee-jerk reaction report a matter to NCIS, simply in order to provide protection against a claim in constructive trust. If in fact there is no reasonable basis for the solicitor's suspicions of money laundering then a report to NCIS should not be made.

(b) Even where an NCIS report is appropriately made, appropriate consent to continue dealings does not by itself absolve solicitors of the need to satisfy themselves that they are conducting themselves as an honest person would.

Negligence

5.20 Delays between making a report to NCIS and receiving appropriate consent can lead to solicitors fearing that their client's matter may be damaged or lost, which in turn might lead to fears of a negligence claim.

5.21 The only reported case of which we are aware of a civil action instituted by a customer against an intermediary as a result of delays in processing instructions is *A* v. *Bank of Scotland* [2002] 1 WLR 751. In that case the delay was exceptional and arose after the bank obtained an order freezing the customer's bank account. The bank was concerned about tipping off liability. The guidelines in this case and in the case of *C* v. *S* [1999] 2 All ER 343 promulgated by the Court of Appeal for dealing with the risk of tipping off liability could be equally relevant to situations where there is a perceived risk of civil action.

5.22 The absence of reported decisions about cases involving claims against intermediaries may suggest that the risks of civil action consequent upon delay should not be overstated. The risk will be minimised by making NCIS aware as soon as possible of concerns over a possible civil action or complaint. These concerns should be explained to NCIS over the telephone and the disclosure report should be submitted by fax under a covering letter which explains the concerns and the reasons for it. NCIS should be told of any developments which affect the risk of a complaint or civil action and should be pressed on a regular basis to deal with the disclosure [. . .]. NCIS will fast track the disclosure and try to ensure that it is processed within a shorter timescale than usual. If despite your efforts appropriate consent is not provided within the timescale you require you should consider seeking legal advice, and whether you should notify your insurers. Insurance companies have their own nominated officer, and if possible solicitors should contact the nominated officer to explain the reasons for the notification. In case of doubt, particularly in relation to the tipping-off offence, contact Professional Ethics.

5.23   [. . .]

Notes:

1.   *Bristol & West Building Society* v. *Mothew* [1996] 4 All ER 698 at 710 where this issue is examined at some length.
2.   *BCCI* v. *Akindele* [2000] 4 All ER 221 at 235.
3.   *Macmillan Inc* v. *Bishopsgate Investment Trust plc (No 3)* [1995] 1 All ER 747 at 783.
4.   *Royal Brunei Airlines* v. *Tan* [1995] 2 AC 378.
5.   [1990] Ch 265.
6.   *Royal Brunei Airlines* v. *Tan* [1995] 2 AC 378.
7.   *Twinsectra Ltd* v. *Yardley* [2002] 2 AC 164.
8.   *The Governor and Company of the Bank of Scotland* v. *A Limited* [2000] All ER (D) 864.
9.   [1991] 1 All ER 182.

ANNEX 11

MONEY LAUNDERING

APPENDIX 1

INTRODUCTION CERTIFICATE

For Completion by Intermediaries Regulated in the UK, the EEA or in non-EEA Countries with Equivalence Status

FULL NAME OF APPLICANT:

DATE OF BIRTH:
(*if applicant is an individual*)

ADDRESS OF APPLICANT:
(*including [postcode/zip code]*)

INTRODUCER:

ADDRESS OF INTRODUCER:

REGULATOR:

WE CERTIFY THAT:

A.   we have verified the identity and address of the applicant stated above in accordance with the anti-money laundering laws of the jurisdiction in which we are regulated and that documentary evidence has been obtained and checks have been undertaken to confirm the client's name and address shown above is true and correct, and

EITHER:

B.1   certified copies of the documentary evidence obtained in respect of the applicant stated above are attached to this certificate.

OR:

B.2   copies of the documentary evidence obtained in respect of the applicant stated above will be retained in our records and, upon request, certified copies of such documentary evidence will be made available to you.

(please circle B1 or B2)

WE CERTIFY THAT we have no knowledge, suspicion or reasonable grounds to believe that the applicant stated above is or has been involved in criminal conduct or otherwise engaged in money laundering. Should we subsequently have knowledge or suspicion that the applicant may be involved in any such activities, subject to any legal constraints we shall inform you as soon as reasonably practicable.

Signed   Full Name:

....
Authorised Signatory

Job Title: ....   Date: ....

NOTES TO A *REGULATED PERSON* OR *FIRM* ON COMPLETING THE CLIENT INTRODUCTION CERTIFICATE

1.   The full name and address of the Client must be given at the top of the Certificate. [Where the client is a Trust, a separate Certificate must be completed in respect of each Trustee or settlor whose identity has been verified.]

2.   Part A should be completed where the *Introducer* has fully verified the identity and address of the client in accordance with the Regulations/EU directive or equivalent provisions. The Certificate may be used by you as evidence of the identity and address of the client(s) and should be retained on file for the required period. Where this Certificate has been completed by the Introducer you are not obliged to undertake any further verification of identity.

3.   Part B.1 or B.2 should be completed to state whether the client is acting on his/her own behalf or as trustees or nominee on behalf of one or more third

parties. If a trust/nominee relationship applies it is important that the client confirms that the identity of the person who has provided the funds together with any named beneficiary have been verified. If there are anonymous principals, these should be declared in Part C.

4. Part C should be completed where the Introducer has not confirmed the identity of the client. A reason should be given, for example, transaction exempt from the Introducer viewpoint.

5. The Certificate must be signed by the Introducer and details of the Introducer's firm, etc., inserted as shown. If an incomplete Certificate is received, it should be returned immediately to the Introducer for completion.

6. The information given in the draft certificate may be submitted by the Introducer in a variety of forms as long as the document(s) include all the information detailed in the certificate overleaf and it has been completed in accordance with above.

7. The Certificate should be completed by an intermediary which is regulated by an "overseas regulatory authority" which exercises "regulatory functions". These terms are defined in the money laundering regulations to include functions similar to the Financial Services Authority and the Bank of England.

Law Society Guidance on *Bowman* v. *Fels* [2005] EWCA Civ 226

References here to 'the Guidance' refer to the pilot money laundering guidance booklet published in January 2004, and references to 'POCA' are to the Proceeds of Crime Act (2002).

This Annex forms an important addendum to Chapter 2 of the Guidance, as it clarifies how the Proceeds of Crime Act (2002) ('POCA') applies to the work of solicitors.

1. INTRODUCTION

1.1   The *Bowman* v *Fels* Court of Appeal judgment ('the judgment') arose as a result of County Court litigation involving a property dispute between ex-cohabitees. Shortly before the County Court hearing a party's legal adviser reported the other side to NCIS for money laundering. This resulted in the legal adviser seeking to adjourn the hearing because of a belief that 'appropriate consent' would not be forthcoming by the hearing date. The court was concerned about the potential impact of the report upon the usual course of the court proceedings.

1.2   The Law Society intervened in the case to clarify the impact of POCA upon the work of solicitors, particularly regarding the interpretation of 'arrangements' under section 328. The Bar Council and NCIS also intervened. The judgment imposes important limitations on the reporting requirements under POCA for solicitors.

1.3   The case had in fact settled but, with the agreement of the parties, the Court of Appeal wanted to give a judgment as it was aware that the orderly conduct of litigation was being affected by POCA, and this was a matter of importance not only for courts and lawyers, but also for the public.

1.4   This Annex is intended to act as an introduction to the impact of this case, but it cannot be a substitute for reading the judgment in full. Nominated officers within solicitors' firms will wish to inform themselves of the full judgment, available from **www.bailii.org/ew/cases/EWCA/Civ/2005/226.html** and with this guidance about its practical implications.

1.5   Solicitors concerned about whether they need to report may obtain individualised guidance from the Law Society's Professional Ethics money laundering helpline: 0870 606 2577, although they may require legal advice.

2. LITIGATION

2.1   This Annex replaces the previous version of Annex 3, the Law Society's Guidance about the case of *P* v *P* (2003) EWHC Fam 2260, which appeared in the pilot money laundering guidance booklet published in January 2004 ('the Guidance'). Annex 4 was guidance issued by the National Criminal Intelligence Service ('NCIS'), which has also been withdrawn. The judgment effectively overturns the decision in *P* v *P*. It also supersedes paragraphs 4.55–4.58 of the guidance, 'acting in confiscation proceedings'.

2.2   Sections 327–329 of POCA are money laundering offences which apply to all citizens in the UK, see paragraphs 2.13–2.18 of the Guidance.

2.3   There is a defence to these offences if an 'authorised disclosure' is made under section 338, see paragraphs 2.19–2.22 of the Guidance. If an authorised disclosure is made before a prohibited act under section 327–329, appropriate consent is required, see paragraphs 2.23–2.27 of the Guidance.

2.4   The *Bowman* v *Fels* judgment excludes certain activities from the scope of the section 328 arrangements offence, which is considered at paragraph 2.17 of the Guidance. The judgment describes the excluded activities as 'litigation from the issue of proceedings and the securing of injunctive relief or a freezing order up to its final disposal by judgement' (see paragraph 83 of the judgment). The Law Society's view is that this extends to dealing with the final division of assets in accordance with a judgment or settlement, including the actual handling of the assets which are 'criminal property'.

2.5   This exclusion also covers consensual resolution of issues in a litigious context (see paragraph 99–102 of the judgment). The Law Society's view is that the logic of the exclusion in relation to both litigation and consensual resolution must also apply to Alternative Dispute Resolution ('ADR').

2.6   The qualifications of the person performing the excluded activity is not a consideration, as the court were anxious for reasons of policy as well as statutory interpretation, that activities involving the resolution of rights and duties of individuals according to law should not be affected by POCA (see paragraph 62 and 99–102 of the judgment).

2.7   In practical terms this means that those conducting litigation, including preparatory stages (including pre-action), or diversion from the court system, such as settlements, negotiations, out of court settlements, and ADR, and Tribunal representation, are not involved in section 328 'arrangements' and therefore do not need to make authorised disclosures. The Law Society's view is that logically solicitors will also not be committing section 327 or section 329 offences in these circumstances (see paragraph 95 of the judgment).

2.8   Sham litigation created for the purposes of money laundering remains within the ambit of section 328 (see judgment paragraph 102).In these circumstances solicitors should also bear in mind their ethical duties, e.g. Principle 12.02 which outlines when instructions must be refused, and Principle 21.01 regarding duty not to mislead the court.

Note:

See www.guide-online lawsociety.org.uk, or telephone the Law Society's Professional Ethics helpline between 11am–1pm or 2pm–4pm: 0870 606 2577.

2.9   Also, it is important to note that whilst the litigation and related processes may fall outside of the ambit of the offences, the property itself remains 'criminal property' for the purposes of section 340(3) of POCA, see paragraph 2.10 of the Guidance. Therefore any future dealings with the property after the terms of any judgment or settlement have been carried out will require a re-examination of whether a report to NCIS is required.

2.10   In circumstances where individuals have suspicions, then even if no report can be made, firms ought to consider what procedures they should have in place to record those suspicions bearing in mind the obligations which apply to those firms falling within the ML Regulations 2003. Regulation 3 requires all persons carrying on relevant business to 'establish such procedures of internal control and communication as may be appropriate for the purposes of forestalling and preventing money laundering', see paragraph 3.16 and Chapter 6 of the Guidance. If appropriate, those procedures should include an internal communication system which ensures that the Money Laundering Reporting Officer has sufficient information to address issues posed by future dealings with property which has been identified by staff of the firm as 'criminal property', see paragraph 2.10 of the Guidance.

2.11   However, solicitors may need to advise their clients about their own position if ownership of criminal property by them falls outside a court order or other type of settlement covered by the exclusion, as considered above at paragraph 2.3. The section 329 offence of acquisition, use and possession, may be particularly relevant in these circumstances, see paragraph 2.18 of the Guidance.

3. TRANSACTIONAL WORK

The judgment does not directly deal with transactional work, but it has important implications for transactional lawyers, particularly with regard to their potential criminal liability under section 328 and the making of a disclosure as a defence under section 328(2) of POCA. This guidance should be read in conjunction with paragraph 2.17 of the Guidance.

Section 328 – the arrangements offence

3.1.   Although the Court did not directly consider the conduct of transactional work, its approach to what constitutes an arrangement under section 328 provides some assistance in interpreting how that section applies to transactional work.

3.2.   In the light of part 10 of the judgment, especially paragraphs 64 and 67, the interpretation of 'arrangement' under section 328, adopted without argument in paragraph 48 of the judgment in *P* v *P*, can no longer be regarded as good law.

3.3.   Although the Court did not seek to lay down definitive guidance on issues of interpretation outside the context of litigation, the judgment provides support for a restricted understanding of the concept of becoming concerned in an arrangement. The judgment, at paragraphs 67 and 68, provides support for the view that:

* entering into or becoming concerned in an arrangement involves an act done at a particular point in time, and
* a person does not enter into or become concerned in an arrangement under section 328 and no offence under this section is committed until such an arrangement is made, and
* no preparatory or intermediate step taken in the course of transactional work which does not itself involve the acquisition, retention, use or control of property will constitute the making of an arrangement under section 328.

3.4.   Where a solicitor engaged on transactional work forms a relevant suspicion, he will have to consider:

  3.4.1.   whether an arrangement within the terms of section 328 exists and, if so, whether he has entered into or become concerned in that arrangement or may do so at some point in the future;

3.4.2. if there is no existing arrangement under section 328, whether an arrangement within the terms of section 328 will or may come into existence at some date in the future.

3.5. The word 'arrangement' is not defined in Part 7 of POCA, but under section 328 it is an arrangement which [the alleged offender] 'knows or suspects facilitates (by whatever means) the acquisition, retention, use or control of criminal property. . .'. A solicitor may be involved in bringing such an arrangement into existence, but for the arrangement to come within the terms of section 328, it must be a concluded arrangement which does in fact facilitate in the way described in the section. The arrangement itself, which a person can be said to 'enter into' or 'become concerned in', must exist and have practical effects relating to the acquisition, retention, use or control of property.

3.6. The operative phrase in section 328 – 'enters into or becomes concerned in an arrangement' – needs to be considered as a whole. To enter into such an arrangement is to become a party to it; to become concerned in an arrangement suggests some wider degree of practical involvement in an existing arrangement such as taking steps to execute or put into effect an arrangement. Both 'enters into' and 'becomes concerned in' describe doing an act that is the starting point of an involvement in an existing arrangement.

3.7. Solicitors conducting transactional work may anticipate that at some future date an arrangement under section 328 will come into existence and that they may become concerned in it. At that time the solicitor would commit a criminal offence if he does not make an authorised disclosure (unless he is prevented from reporting by common law LPP), see section 5.

3.8. A solicitor making an authorised disclosure would need to seek consent to doing the 'prohibited act' of entering into or, more likely, becoming concerned in the arrangement. Until an arrangement under section 328 does exist, the solicitor can continue in the normal way with any preparatory steps relating to the transaction.

3.9. An agreement by the solicitor's client and another party to bring about an arrangement that would fall within the terms of section 328 is not, in itself, an arrangement under section 328. The test is whether it does in fact, in the present and not the future, have the effect of facilitating the acquisition, retention, use or control of criminal property by or on behalf of another person.

4. FAILURE TO REPORT OFFENCES

This guidance should be read in conjunction with Part 2, of Chapter 2 of the Guidance regarding POCA sections 330–332, paragraph 2.39 onwards.

Section 330 'regulated sector'

4.1 Where a solicitor, when undertaking work covered by the Money Laundering Regulations, has knowledge or suspicion of money laundering or reasonable grounds for suspicion the solicitor should consider the obligation under section 330 to make a money laundering disclosure. Transactional work undertaken by solicitors is almost always covered by the Regulations whereas usually litigation and pure legal advice work is not covered by the Regulations and, therefore, also falls outside section 330. As part of the 'regulated sector' transactional lawyers need to be aware of the section 330 offence which applies even if the solicitor withdraws from the matter. A key consideration is whether the information which causes them to know or suspect or have reasonable grounds to suspect, that another person is engaged in money laundering falls within the professional legal adviser exemption under 330(6). It is also important to note that this exemption does not apply where the intention behind the communication is to further a criminal purpose, see paragraphs 2.40 – 2.43 of the Guidance and paragraphs 5.11 & 5.12 below.

Sections 331–332: nominated officers in the regulated sector, and failure to disclose outside the regulated sector

4.2. The *Bowman* v *Fels* judgment confirmed that common law LPP was not overridden in sections 327 – 329 of POCA. Common law LPP remains intact even if a professional legal adviser passes information to their Nominated Officer, see paragraph 2.55 of the Guidance. In respect of information which is not subject to common law LPP, but falls within the 330(6) exemption, again the Law Society remains of the view that if the person passing the information to the Nominated Officer is a professional legal adviser, then the Nominated Officer has a reasonable excuse. On 1 July 2005 Section 330 was amended, and these amendments confirm that professional legal advisers can speak openly with their Nominated Officers without affecting clients' rights to confidentiality. See Law Society guidance on the Serious Organised Crime & Police Act 2005, available from **www.lawsociety.org.uk** or Professional Ethics: 0870 606 2577.

5. LEGAL PROFESSIONAL PRIVILEGE

5.1. Whilst the *Bowman* v *Fels* judgment concentrated upon litigation, and similar work, the judgment makes references to how Parliament could not have intended the authorised disclosure defence to the principal offences (sections 327–329 of POCA) to override the common law doctrine of legal professional privilege ('common law LPP') as described at 4.8–4.10 of the Guidance (see paragraphs 89 and 90 of the judgment). Whenever solicitors have to consider whether to make a report in relation to the section 327–329 offences they need to consider whether the information on which their knowledge or suspicion is based is subject to common law LPP.

5.2. Solicitors considering reporting under section 330 need to consider whether the information on which their knowledge or suspicion is based, or which gives them reasonable grounds for such knowledge or suspicion, came to them in 'privileged circumstances' as defined in section 330(10) ('330(6) exemption'). These differ from the circumstances governing common law LPP and are set out at 4.27–4.29 of the Guidance.

5.3. Given the enhanced importance of LPP as a result of the judgment, MLROs should make themselves fully aware of chapter 4 of the Guidance about LPP.

5.3.1. The judgment has confirmed that common law LPP is not overridden by the authorised disclosure defence to the section 327–329 offences. Therefore before such a disclosure is made any solicitor who forms knowledge or suspicion of money laundering will have to consider whether common law LPP applies. If it does, no disclosure can be made without a client waiver of LPP and before that waiver can be obtained a solicitor would need to consider the tipping off offences, see section 6.

5.3.2. It is important to note that common law privilege and the 330(6) exemption differ particularly in relation to the protection given to 'advice'.

5.4. When advice is given or received in circumstances where litigation is neither contemplated nor reasonably in prospect, common law LLP will normally only apply to communications between a solicitor and his client for the purpose of obtaining or providing legal advice, or which form part of the chain of correspondence between solicitor and client for the purpose of obtaining legal advice. Therefore, save in limited circumstances, communications between solicitors and third parties will not fall within common law LPP. An exception where common law LPP might apply is where the third party is merely acting as a conduit or post box (see *Jones* v *Great Central Railway* [1910]) AC 4).

5.5.   In contrast, the 330(6) exemption applies, to any information received by a professional legal adviser from a client or a representative of a client for the purpose of giving or obtaining legal advice. A 'representative' is not defined in POCA but the Law Society takes a wide interpretation. For example, information communicated by a client's tax adviser to the professional legal adviser may fall within the 330(6) exemption when in the professional legal adviser's hands. The tax adviser is not however a professional legal adviser and therefore falls outside the 330(6) exemption and may of course commit an offence himself under s330 POCA if he fails to make a disclosure under the section.

5.5.1.   Following the Court of Appeal's decision in *Three Rivers District Council* v *The Governor and Company of the Bank of England* (No 5) [2003] QB 1556 (which is unaffected by the House of Lords decision referred to elsewhere) communications by a solicitor with employees of a corporate client may not be protected by common law LPP if the employee cannot be considered to be 'the client' for these purposes. The Court of Appeal concluded that some employees may be clients, some may not. However, even if a junior employee might not be a client for the purposes of common law LPP they may fall within the meaning of 'representative' for the purposes of the 330(6) exemption.

5.5.2.   Under Common law, privileged information can be shared or disclosed within law firms, without losing the protection of LPP, e.g. with secretaries, other fee earners, the MLRO. This can also include those with a common interest, e.g. in certain circumstances co-defendants (see *Gotha City* v *Sotheby's (no.1)* [1998] 1 WLR 114)). However, except where litigation is in contemplation, arguably the 330(6) exemption only applies to information received by a professional legal adviser from a client or a representative of a client, or from a person seeking legal advice, in the circumstances outlined in section 330(10)(a) and (b). For example, during the course of a transaction a vendor may provide copies to the purchaser of legal advice received by the vendor, but require that it be kept confidential and stipulate that in disclosing it, privilege in the information is not waived. Since the 330(6) exemption only applies to information provided by a client or his or her representative, to a professional legal adviser, whilst it will apply if the vendor or his lawyer gives it to the purchaser who then passes it to the purchaser's professional legal adviser, it will not apply if it is simply put in a data room and the purchaser's professional adviser inspects it.

What is legal advice in a transaction?

5.6.   Whereas the range of those whose communications fall within the 330(6) exemption may be broader than within common law LPP, under both heads the communications must relate to legal advice. A definition of the scope of common law advice privilege has recently been approved by the House of Lords in *Three Rivers District Council and others* v *Governor and Company of the Bank of England* [2004] UKHL 48 at 111 as covering 'all communications between a solicitor and his client relating to a transaction in which the solicitor has been instructed for the purpose of obtaining legal advice . . . notwithstanding that they do not contain advice on matters of law and construction, provided that they are directly related to the performance by the solicitor of his professional duty as legal adviser of his client'.

5.7.   By way of example, in a conveyancing transaction, common law advice privilege will be limited to all such communications with, and instructions from, the client and any advice given to the client, (including any working papers and drafts prepared by the solicitor)[1] for the purpose of giving that advice, provided they are directly related to the performance by the solicitor of his professional duty as legal adviser of his client. Thus before making a disclosure to NCIS under s.338, the solicitor must ensure that his knowledge or suspicion does not arise from information imparted within this definition.

5.8.   Adapting the *Three Rivers* definition to the wording of s.330 (10), the exemption under the section will cover all communications between a professional legal adviser and his client or his client's representative relating to a transaction in which the professional legal adviser has been instructed for the purpose of obtaining legal advice, notwithstanding that they do not contain advice on matters of law and construction, provided that they are directly related to the performance by the professional legal adviser of his professional duty as legal adviser of his client.

5.9.   In the conveyancing example given above, the 330(6) exemption will cover, in addition to the 'common law' items, communications with third parties, such as surveyors, tax advisers or accountants, provided to the professional legal adviser to enable him to advise his client and directly related to the performance by the professional legal adviser of his professional duty as legal adviser of his client.

5.10.   Thus, a conveyancing solicitor does not commit an offence under s.330 if he fails to disclose, if his knowledge, suspicion, or reasonable grounds for knowledge or suspicion, arose from communications of such a nature with his client or a representative of his client:

Note:

Solicitors' costs

Solicitors concerned about their receipt of costs, including payment on account, should have regard not only to paragraph 2.30 of the Guidance which describes the 'adequate consideration' defence to the section 329 offence, but also this judgment which confirms that legal professional privilege excludes the reporting requirement under the other principal offences, namely sections 327 and 328.

Crime/Fraud exception

This section replaces paragraphs 4.12 – 4.14 of the Guidance.

5.11.   Neither common law LPP nor the 330(6) exemption apply to communications made with the intention of furthering a criminal purpose. For this exception to apply in either context, the solicitors should have prima facie evidence of such an intention, which as indicated at 4.14, need not be that of the client.

5.12.   As indicated in the Guidance at paragraphs 4.37–4.40, during the Parliamentary passage of the POCA bill the Law Society expressed concern that solicitors might be prosecuted under POCA even though they were unaware of the

---

1 It will not of course cover documents sent to the other side in a transaction, or any documents of title, including conveyances, transfers, mortgages etc. for these are either not confidential and/or not communications.

criminal intention of a third party. In these circumstances the solicitor would lose the exemption as a 'professional legal adviser' because of the exception in subsection 330(11) which provides that the 'professional legal adviser' exemption does not apply to information '. . ..communicated or given with the intention of furthering a criminal purpose. The Law Society believes that a solicitor should not make a report unless there is prima facie evidence that he is being used in the furtherance of a crime.

Note:

The question of protecting client confidentiality is a key consideration for professional legal advisers considering reporting under either the principal money laundering offence provisions (to which common law LPP applies) or under the section 330 failure to report offence (to which the 330(6) exemption applies). In either case solicitors should refer to section 6 regarding tipping off.

6. TIPPING OFF

This guidance should be read in conjunction with paragraph 2.61 of the Guidance.

6.1.　The judgment's clarification of the importance of common law LPP in relation to the principal offences under sections 327/328/329 also affects how solicitors conducting transactions should approach the exemption for professional legal advisers to the tipping off offences in POCA under sections 333 & 342.

6.2.　Solicitors who are acting in transactions in circumstances where they have knowledge or suspicion of money laundering, and so are going to risk being concerned in an arrangement at some future date, have a legal duty to give legal advice to clients whom they act for, including about the possibility of their client committing money laundering offences if the transaction proceeds without 'appropriate consent' having been obtained, see paragraphs 2.23–2.27 of the Guidance.

6.3.　In considering that legal duty solicitors will need to consider the tipping off offence in section 333, and the similar offence in 342. Both of these offences have exemptions for professional legal advisers. That exemption was explored in *P* v *P*. The judgment in *Bowman* v *Fels* further supports the statutory exemption: professional legal advisers have a discretion to give advice to their clients about money laundering reports, although there remains no absolute duty to do so. Depending upon the circumstances, solicitors may prefer to withdraw.

6.4.　*Bowman* v *Fels* makes clear that common law LPP attaches to a communication with the client on this point (unless it falls within the crime/fraud exception). Thus a solicitor will need a waiver from common law LPP before making a disclosure. In the event that this is not given, the solicitor should withdraw. In these circumstances the Law Society does not consider the guidance given in *P* v *P* about the timetable for the use of exemption is helpful.

6.5.　It should be noted that this exemption does not apply if, in discussing the issue with the client, the solicitor has a criminal intention.

7. WHAT APPROACH SHOULD TRANSACTIONAL LAWYERS TAKE?

7.1.　For these purposes transactional lawyers include those involved in non-contentious work, e.g. conveyancing, company mergers and acquisitions.

7.2.　This has also been set out in the form of a flow chart at Appendix 1. Anyone following the flow chart should also read the guidance below, which expands on the options.

7.3. Having outlined the particular issues which transactional lawyers may face in light of the decision in Bowman v Fels, it may assist to set out an approach which they can usefully adopt.

Stage 1

7.4. An 'arrangement' within the terms of section 328 must come into existence at a particular point in time. If a suspicion is formed, the first issue for any transactional lawyer to consider is whether an arrangement is already in existence. (See paragraphs 3.4 to 3.8 above.) For example, the client may instruct a conveyancing solicitor to act on his behalf in the purchase of property, including the drafting of the contract and transfer documents. At the time that the solicitor is instructed, there will already be in existence an agreement between vendor and purchaser, but not yet an arrangement for the purposes of section 328.

7.5. Where the solicitor considers that an arrangement falling within section 328 is already in existence, any steps that he takes in furtherance of that arrangement would probably amount to the solicitor becoming concerned in the arrangement. The solicitor would therefore need immediately to consider making a disclosure under section 328.

7.6. Where there is no pre-existing arrangement, the transactional work carried out by the solicitor may nevertheless involve bringing into existence an arrangement under section 328. Thereafter, the solicitor may become concerned in the arrangement by, for example, executing or implementing it. He may, therefore, commit an offence under section 328 and perhaps also under section 327 or 329. In order to provide himself with a defence to a possible money laundering charge, the solicitor would be obliged to make an authorised disclosure, (Boxes B–D), provided common law LPP does not apply.(See section 2 and stage 2 below.)

7.7. The solicitor would also need to consider whether, as would very probably be the case, the work on which he is engaged is 'relevant business' so that the obligations placed on a person within the 'regulated sector' apply to him. If so, the solicitor would also need to consider whether he should make a money laundering disclosure under section 330, unless the 'professional legal adviser' exception in section 330(6) and (10) of POCA applies, (Box E).

Stage 2

7.8. Having determined which, if any, of the relevant sections of POCA apply, the next issues for any solicitor to consider are:

    (i)   whether common law LPP applies where it is suspected that an offence under sections 327–329 may be committed; and/or

    (ii) if the solicitor has determined that they are acting in the regulated sector, whether the 330(6) exemption applies for the purposes of section 330. (See Box 2)

7.9. If neither common law LPP or the 330(6) exemption applies, then there is nothing to constrain a solicitor from making a report.

7.10. Where a report is made and consent needs to be sought, as stated at paragraph 7.5 above, the solicitor will need to consider whether they can conduct further work prior to receiving that consent, dependent upon whether there is already an arrangement in existence, (Boxes 3 and 4).

7.11.   If either the common law LPP or the 330(6) exemption applies, the next issue to consider is whether there is prima facie evidence that the solicitor is being used in the furtherance of a crime (Box 5). The scope of the crime/fraud exception and the nature of the test to be applied is discussed, see paragraphs 5.11 & 5.12. If the solicitor concludes that there is prima facie evidence, the effect is that there is no common law LPP or 330(6) exemption, so a report can be made. However, the solicitor has the option of simply withdrawing from the transaction rather than making an authorised disclosure. (Box 7)

7.12.   If the conclusion is that common law LPP or the 330(6) exemption do apply and are not overridden by the crime/fraud exception the solicitor has two options: (Box 8)

(i)   He can either approach his client(s) for a waiver of privilege such that he can obtain consent to carry out the prohibited act (Box 10); or,

(ii)   alternatively, he can withdraw from the transaction. (Box 9)

7.13.   Section 6 above relates to the tipping off offence. Where the solicitor is acting for a client(s) who is not the suspected party, but is engaged in a transaction which involves criminal property, then the solicitor may feel less concerned about tipping off and more comfortable discussing the risk of not tipping off when issues of waiver of common law LPP and whether to report, and possibly joint reports to NCIS with the client(s) . If, however, the solicitor suspects that the client is implicated in the underlying criminal conduct, careful consideration would need to be given to the tipping off offence and whether it is still appropriate, in those circumstances, to discuss these matters openly with the suspected party/client. (Box 10)

7.14.   If the matter is raised with the client(s) and the client(s) agrees to waive LPP, the solicitor is free to make a report on his own, or as a joint report together with the client, and seek consent if required. Provided that there is no pre-existing arrangement, the solicitor should be free to continue his preparatory activities, but the arrangement (or other prohibited act under sections 327–329 of POCA) should not be finalised without appropriate consent. (Box 11)

7.15.   Of course, the client(s) may refuse to waive LPP (Box 12) either because he does not agree with the solicitor's suspicions or because, whilst he accepts the solicitor's suspicions, for his own purposes he does not wish a report to the authorities to be made about the transaction. It is of course possible at this stage that the client(s) may provide further information which removes the solicitor's suspicions, and as a consequence no report is required. However, if the client(s) refuses consent to waive common law LPP the solicitor is again put in the position of determining whether he is being used in furtherance of a crime such that common law LPP or the 330(6) exemption do not apply. If the solicitor does not have prima facie evidence that the crime/fraud exception applies, he will have no option but to withdraw from the transaction, and provided the 330(6) exemption also applies no report can be made either under the principal offences or section 330. (Box 13)

7.16.   Where the client(s) has refused to waive privilege but accepts that in proceeding with the transaction he may be committing an offence, the solicitor may more readily be able to conclude that he is being used in furtherance of a crime such that common law LPP or the 330(6) exemption will not apply to prevent a report being made. In those circumstances, it would usually be inappropriate to make a report with the client's knowledge as the risks of tipping off are heightened. (Box 14)

7.17.   If a solicitor is acting for more than one client in relation to a matter all clients would need to agree to waive privilege before the solicitor could report to NCIS.

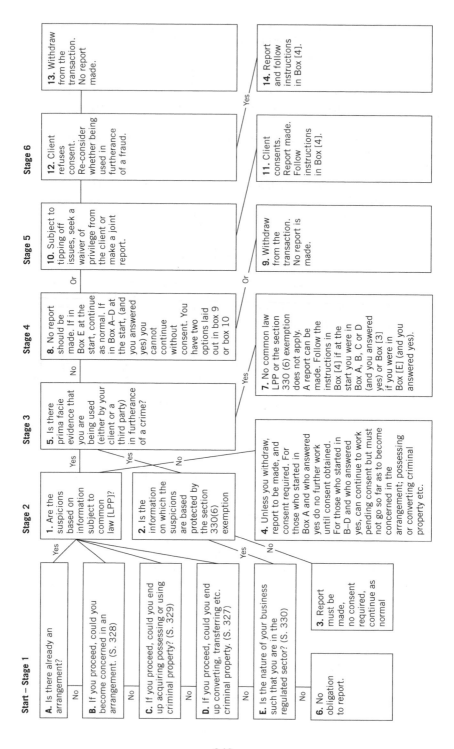

Start – Stage 1

Stage 2

Stage 3

Stage 4

Stage 5

Stage 6

A. Is there already an arrangement?

No

B. If you proceed, could you become concerned in an arrangement. (S. 328)

No

C. If you proceed, could you end up acquiring possessing or using criminal property? (S. 329)

No

D. If you proceed, could you end up converting, transferring etc. criminal property. (S. 327)

No

E. Is the nature of your business such that you are in the regulated sector? (S. 330)

No

6. No obligation to report.

Yes

1. Are the suspicions based on information subject to common law [LPP]?

Yes

2. Is the information on which the suspicions are based protected by the section 330(6) exemption

Yes

3. Report must be made, no consent required, continue as normal

No

4. Unless you withdraw, report to be made, and consent required. For those who started in Box A and who answered yes do no further work until consent obtained. For those who started in B–D and who answered yes, can continue to work pending consent but must not go so far as to become concerned in the arrangement; possessing or converting criminal property etc.

Yes

5. Is there prima facie evidence that you are being used (either by your client or a third party) in furtherance of a crime?

No

Yes

7. No common law LPP or the section 330 (6) exemption does not apply. A report can be made. Follow the instructions in Box [4] if at the start you were in Box A, B, C or D (and you answered yes) or Box [3] if you were in Box [E] (and you answered yes).

8. No report should be made. If in Box E at the start, continue as normal. If in Box A–D at the start, (and you answered yes) you cannot continue without consent. You have two options laid out in box 9 or box 10

Or

9. Withdraw from the transaction. No report is made.

10. Subject to tipping off issues, seek a waiver of privilege from the client or make a joint report.

Or

11. Client consents. Report made. Follow instructions in Box [4].

12. Client refuses consent. Re-consider whether being used in furtherance of a fraud.

Yes

13. Withdraw from the transaction. No report made.

14. Report and follow instructions in Box [4].

B3

Law Society's anti-money laundering guidance for solicitors undertaking property work (December 2005)

INTRODUCTION

1. Solicitors conducting conveyancing are at risk of money laundering because property transactions can involve any stage of the money laundering process, see paragraph 1.13 of the Guidance. As the property itself can be 'criminal property' for the purposes of POCA, solicitors can still be involved in money laundering even if no money changes hands, see paragraph 3 below.

2. Conveyancing transactions can be attractive to money launderers who are trying to disguise the audit trail of the proceeds of their crimes. However, a criminal may also want to buy a property simply to live in themselves. This would also involve an offence or offences of money laundering under the wide definition in section 340(11) of POCA. Solicitors who defend clients charged with criminal offences should be particularly alert to the danger of money laundering if their firms also undertake property work.

3. Solicitors should also be aware that information about tax evasion or welfare benefit fraud may come to light in conveyancing matters. The notional proceeds of tax evasion, that is an amount of money equal to the saving in tax, are 'criminal property' under section 340(3) and (6). Although the law on notional criminal property is unclear and it is uncertain how such property can be identified, solicitors are advised to act cautiously and treat assets, including bank balances, acquired in whole or in part after the date of any obtaining of a pecuniary advantage by tax evasion, as being or including criminal property. Depending on the date when notional property is obtained through tax evasion, real property may be regarded as 'criminal property' either at the time of the purchase or later if mortgage payments in respect of that property are made from a bank account that should be treated as itself being or including criminal property. Any subsequent sale of the property for the 'suspected party' would amount to money laundering. In such cases, the client may not even realise that their conveyancing instructions amount to money laundering. Solicitors should remain alert to situations of this kind and should speak to their client and, if appropriate, should make a money laundering report, see paragraph 31 onwards below.

4. Conveyancers should be alert to instructions which are a deliberate attempt to avoid assets being dealt with in the way intended by a court, or through the usual legal process, for example solicitors may sometimes suspect that instructions are being given to avoid the property forming part of a bankruptcy, or forming part of assets subject to confiscation. Although money laundering reports may not necessarily arise, in such circumstances solicitors should consider their duties in

conduct, in particular Principle 12.02 which prevents solicitors acting if instructions would involve the solicitor in a breach of the law or a breach of the principles of professional conduct.

5. The case of *Bowman* v *Fels* (2005) EWCA Civ 226 has drastically altered how conveyancers should deal with knowledge or suspicion of money laundering which they form in the course of their work, especially how they should balance their duties to inform clients with the reporting obligations under POCA. This has in turn affected solicitors' duties to their Lender clients. This recent change centres upon the increased importance of legal professional privilege, and an increased reliance on the defence to the tipping off offences which applies to professional legal advisers.

MONEY LAUNDERING REGULATIONS 2003

6. Conveyancing, and indeed any legal work connected to ' real property', is 'relevant business' for the purposes of the ML Regulations (2003) ('the Regulations'). The Regulations require the appointment of a Nominated Officer (Money Laundering Reporting Officer, MLRO), training of relevant employees, record-keeping, and client identification, see paragraph 3.16 of the Guidance. Chapter 3 of the Guidance provides guidance on methods of compliance with the Regulations, including how to identify clients who solicitors don't meet in person, see paragraphs 3.91–3.94 and paragraph 15 below.

Note:

The Regulations came into force for solicitors on 1 March 2004. If a solicitor formed a 'business relationship' with a client before that date there will not usually be a need to identify the client, however solicitors are advised to exercise caution and check clients' identity if they have not undertaken any work for the client for some time.

7. Identification checks should be undertaken 'as soon as reasonably practicable' after contact is first made between solicitors and their clients, see paragraph 3.29 of the Guidance. Given the money laundering risk posed by conveyancing, and the speed of some transactions, it may be preferable to make the necessary checks prior to starting work, and usually before accepting any money. In most cases the person or entity who needs to be identified will be the solicitors own client, but in some circumstances solicitors will consider Regulation 4(3)(d) and identify parties providing funding, see note to paragraph 18 below and Money Laundering Regulations 4 and 5.

Note:

Solicitors may be asked by others subject to the Regulations and involved in the transaction, to confirm they have undertaken identity checks, e.g. house building companies acting as Estate Agents regularly ask solicitors acting for purchasers to provide such confirmation. Solicitors are advised to ensure that if they provide information they do not accept liability for the compliance with the Regulations by others.

8. Commonly solicitors who undertake conveyancing also act for a Lender. However, the Lender client will usually not need to be identified if the exception from the identification requirement in Regulation 5(2) applies, see paragraph 3.42 of the Guidance and Money Laundering Regulations 4 and 5.

Note:

In some circumstances, solicitors' conducting fixed fee conveyancing may not fall within the definition of 'business relationship' in the Regulation 2(2) because the total amount of any payments may be capable of being ascertained at the outset, see paragraph 3.33 of the Guidance. However, even if fixed fee conveyancing is defined as ' one off', the client identification requirement will still apply unless the transaction involves less than approximately 15,000 Euro in total, see paragraph 3.44 of the Guidance.

9. In addition to the identification checks required under Regulation 4, Regulation 3 requires 'systems' to prevent money laundering. For conveyancers compliance with this Regulation is likely to be achieved if the solicitor is reasonably comfortable about what they are being asked to do by the client and why. Some firms will choose to ask all clients for some basic information before accepting instructions, but this is not an absolute requirement and other firms will take a different approach. The important point is that higher risk transactions are identified and acted upon. Usually the most effective way of ensuring this is a sufficient level of training and awareness amongst staff, ongoing supervision by the MLRO, and detailed record-keeping about additional questions posed and responses received in particular cases.

10. Chapter 6 of the Guidance encourages solicitors to take a risk based approach which should avoid solicitors' wasting resources on low risk matters and allow greater focus of resources on higher risk transactions. Higher risk work may require broader checks to be made beyond basic identification, the extent of which will depend upon the level of risk. However, conveyancing instructions automatically include obtaining significant information about both the client and the proposed transaction, especially if instructions are also received from a Lender. For example, a solicitor conducting conveyancing is already likely to know about their client's occupation, especially if they also act for the Lender. This information will help the solicitor judge whether the amount of private funding available to the client makes sense, or whether they need to ask more questions. All information which is already available should be considered before other enquiries are made, especially as this will avoid repetition and enable the solicitor to determine what additional questions to ask. If additional enquiries are to be made it is usually helpful to consider whether there are any reasons for concern about the provenance of funds used either in the original purchase of a property about to be sold, and/or to be used in a current property purchase, i.e. is there any reason to know or suspect that those funds could constitute 'criminal property'.

11. Solicitors should consider whether it is preferable to collect in all of the money needed for the purchase before exchange of contracts takes place to avoid unexpected matters arising at a later stage when they can be much more difficult to deal with. This method is likely to be of most use if a solicitor is uncertain about the information they have been given by a client including what the client has said about where the monies are coming from.

12. Solicitors acting for purchasers will usually make sufficient checks about their client, and transfer the funds to the seller's solicitors. In effect, the purchaser's solicitors act as a filter, which gives the seller's solicitor additional comfort. For this reason solicitors acting for sellers should try and avoid accepting money direct from the purchaser if possible, although in some instances this will be unavoidable, e.g. if the purchaser is unrepresented.

WARNING SIGNS

13. Both sales and purchases of domestic, commercial, and agricultural property can have money laundering implications under POCA, and so solicitors conducting such transactions need to remain alert. Solicitors should take care not to be deterred from making the necessary checks because instructions are given urgently as this may be a tactic designed to draw the focus away from making the necessary checks.

14. Attention should also be paid to the Law Society's green warning card, Property Fraud II (see Annex 15 of the Guidance), the blue warning card (see Annex 5 of the Guidance), and paragraphs 6.14–6.34 of the Guidance. The additional comments below may also be of assistance to conveyancers specifically.

15. Many conveyancers receive instructions from clients whom they never meet and who may live and/or work a considerable distance away from their solicitor, perhaps because the client is introduced by an intermediary or because of online conveyancing. The anti money laundering requirements are not intended to restrict the development of innovative business practices. However, where solicitors do not meet their clients, they should consider how they check their client's identity and minimise any increased risk of money laundering. If an intermediary is involved they may be able to provide information which could allay concerns. Regulation 4(3)(b) also refers to the need to take into account the greater potential for money laundering which arises when the client is not physically present when being identified.

OWNERSHIP ISSUES

16. In the absence of any logical explanation properties owned by nominee companies, multiple owners may be used as sophisticated money laundering vehicles designed to disguise the true owner and / or confuse the audit trail. Solicitors also need to be alert to quick or unexplained changes in ownership.

17. For example, a solicitor may know or suspect that a third party is providing the funding for a purchase, but that the property is being registered in somebody else's name. There may be legitimate reasons for this, such as a family arrangement, but it is important that solicitors are alert to the possibility that they are being misled about the true ownership and consider Regulation 4(3) (d).

METHODS OF FUNDING

18. Many properties are bought with a combination of deposit, mortgage, and/or equity from a current property. Usually solicitors will have information about how their clients intend to fund the transaction, and will expect to be updated if those details change, e.g. if a mortgage offer falls through and new funding is obtained. Obtaining this information will help firms with their risk assessment, and decision whether they need to know more. As well as assisting with anti-money laundering procedures, this information may prevent difficulties linking payments received into client account with particular clients.

Note:

Third parties often assist others with purchases, e.g. relatives of a first time buyer. Solicitors may be asked to receive funds direct from those third parties. Whether, and to what extent, any checks need to be undertaken in relation to the third parties will be a matter of judgement for the solicitor dependant upon the level of risk and whether there are suspicions that in fact the client is not the true owner, Regulation 4(3)(d). Relevant risk factors may be what is known about the actual client and/or the third party – including the relationship between them, the proportion of the funding being provided by the third party, and whether any warning signs are apparent. In some circumstances identification checks of the third parties, and / or information about provenance of funds they are providing, should be obtained. Solicitors should also consider their obligations to Lenders in these circumstances as there is generally a requirement to advise Lenders if the purchasers are not funding the balance of the price from their own resources.

CASH PAYMENTS

19. Most commonly purchase funds are made up of some private funding, with the majority of the purchase price being provided by way of a mortgage. Transactions are likely to be a higher risk if they do not involve mortgages. However, concerns over such transactions may be allayed by the solicitor simply asking the client for an explanation, and assessing whether in their view the explanation is valid, e.g. money received from an inheritance, or from the sale of another property. In such higher risk situations it may be prudent for the solicitor to ask some questions about the provenance of the private funding. 'Provenance' is not limited to the whereabouts of the monies, but goes beyond that to how the client has come by the money. However, solicitors are not required to become detectives, but to prevent money laundering.

20. Payments made through the mainstream banking system are not guaranteed to be of clean 'provenance', although the fact that a client has successfully opened and maintained an account with a mainstream financial institution may be one of the factors solicitors take into consideration in their risk assessment. If payments may be made from an individual's personal funds, or collected from a number of individuals or other sources, solicitors should consider whether they would feel more comfortable proceeding only after asking some questions about where the money has come from and also consider Regulation 4(3) (d). For example, large amounts of money provided by clients who only have relatively low incomes may be a cause to ask more questions. It is good practice to make a file note both of the questions posed and the responses received. However, if there are concerns about money laundering the circulation of these notes will need to be carefully managed, e.g. not provided to clients if they ask for their files.

21. Large payments made in actual cash can also give rise to money laundering suspicions. Firms can avoid this difficulty by having a clear office policy on not accepting cash at the office or direct into their bank account, see paragraph 6.2 of the Guidance. However, clients may attempt to circumvent such a policy, and avoid paying a bank fee, by depositing cash direct into the solicitor's client account at a branch of the solicitor's bank. If possible solicitors should try and avoid this by controlling the manner and circumstance of the disclosure of their client account details, and when doing so making it clear that an electronic method of transfer of the funds is expected. Having said that, it is accepted that account details are readily available on client account cheques. Solicitors may also wish to arrange with their bank that such cash deposits should never be accepted by the bank. Ultimately if a cash deposit is received solicitors will have to consider what they know about their clients and the overall circumstances to assess whether or not they are suspicious of money laundering.

22. Solicitors may form knowledge or suspicion that, cash has changed hands directly, between a seller and purchaser, e.g. where money has changed hands at a rural auction. If a solicitor is openly informed about this payment, they may be

requested to bank the cash payment into their client account. This places the solicitor in a difficult position as the source of the cash is not their own client, which can make checking more difficult. The auction house may be able to assist because of checks they must make themselves under the Regulations, but ultimately the solicitor may feel more comfortable not banking the cash into their account and would prefer their client to do so. Again, this is where a firm's cash policy can be helpful. If the solicitor is not openly informed but forms knowledge or suspicion that there has been a direct payment between a seller and purchaser's solicitors, the solicitor will need to consider whether there is any reason for concern, or whether the documentation will include the true purchase price, so that there are no concerns about tax evasion, see paragraph 30 below.

23. On the other hand solicitors may feel that, although their instructions are that money has changed hands directly, in fact it has not done so. The motivation for such a misrepresentation could be to encourage a mortgage Lender to lend more than they would ordinarily do so, because they are under the impression that private funds will also be put into the purchase when in fact this is not the case. Solicitors in this situation who act for the Lender need to consider their duties to their Lender, see paragraph 24 onwards below.

LENDER ISSUES

24. Solicitors may form knowledge or suspicion that a lay client is attempting to mislead a Lender client to improperly inflate a mortgage advance, e.g. misrepresentations about the potential borrower's income, or that a seller and purchaser are conspiring to overstate a sale price, see paragraph 25 below. Transactions which are not 'arms length' may warrant particularly close consideration, see paragraph 4 above. However, until the improperly obtained mortgage advance is received there will not be any 'criminal property' for the purposes of reporting obligations under POCA.

25. Where a solicitor acting for purchaser suspects that their client maybe making a misrepresentation to a mortgage they must either dissuade their client from doing so, or terminate their retainer. Even if the solicitor no longer acts in these circumstances they may still be under a duty to advise the mortgage company (see footnote).

26. If knowledge or suspicion is formed that a mortgage advance has already been improperly obtained a solicitor may advise the mortgage Lender that they were misled. In fact if a solicitor is acting in a remortgage and forms knowledge or suspicion about a previous mortgage there may be a duty to advise the Lender, especially if the remortgage is with the same Lender. It may also be necessary to consider reporting to NCIS as there is 'criminal property', namely the improperly obtained mortgage advance. If the client has purposefully decided to make a misrepresentation on their mortgage application it is likely that the crime/fraud exception to legal professional privilege would apply, meaning that no waiver to confidentiality will be needed before a report is made, but solicitors will need to consider matters on a case by case basis, and if necessary seek guidance from Professional Ethics or take independent legal advice.

27. Naturally solicitors will be concerned about whether speaking to their lender client conflicts with the tipping off offences. A key element of these offences is likelihood of prejudicing an investigation, and this may be a small risk when making disclosures to reputable Lenders. Also if the Lender is the solicitor's client the exception in s.333(3)(a) and s.342(4)(a) may apply, relating to professional legal advisers giving advice to their clients, see paragraph 2.61 of the Guidance, and the guidance about the case of *Bowman* v *Fels*.

UNUSUAL INSTRUCTIONS

28. It may be important to know why instructions have been received. Asking for that information may help deter potential money launderers.

29. Transactions which abort without good apparent cause and/or which lead a solicitor to be unexpectedly asked to transfer funds back to their source, may be suspicious. Firms may wish to have a policy on only sending money back to clients, or to the original source. Such a policy also avoid a breach of Rule 15 of the Solicitors' Accounts Rules (note (ix)), see paragraph 6.24 of the Guidance and Money Laundering Regulations 4 and 5.

TAX ISSUES

30. Tax evasion of any type, by whatever means, whether committed by a client or the other party to a transaction, can lead to a solicitor committing a section 328 arrangements offence, see paragraph 2.17 of the Guidance. Abuse of the new Stamp Duty Land Tax procedure may also give rise to money laundering implications, e.g. through misleading apportionment of the purchase price. If a client gives a solicitor instructions which offend the Stamp Duty Land Tax procedure the solicitor must consider their position under Principle 12.02. If a solicitor discovers the evasion after it has occurred they may have a reporting obligation, see paragraph 31 onwards below.

REPORTING ISSUES

31. If a solicitor continues to act in a conveyancing matter which has a money laundering element, this may amount to the commission of a section 328 arrangements offence, see paragraph 2.17 of the Guidance. However a defence is available if a report is made and 'appropriate consent' obtained, see paragraph 2.23 of the Guidance.

32. The recent case of *Bowman* v *Fels* has drastically altered how conveyancers should approach this area and careful attention should be paid to the full Law Society guidance about the implications of this case. Essentially, if a conveyancer forms knowledge or suspicion of money laundering he should first consider whether the information on which that knowledge or suspicion is based was received in legally privileged circumstances; if it was, he cannot make a report to NCIS without the client's authority. In *Three Rivers District Council and others* v *Governor and Company of the Bank of England* (2004) UKHL 48 at 111 common law privilege was described as covering ' all communications between a solicitor and his client relating to a transaction in which the solicitor has been instructed for the purpose of obtaining legal advice, notwithstanding that they do not contain advice on matters of law and construction, provided that they are directly related to the performance by the solicitor of his professional duty as legal adviser of his client.' Communications to which the crime/fraud exception applies will not be covered by legal professional privilege and conveyancers must be particularly careful in this regard see paragraphs 5.11 and 5.12 of the *Bowman* v *Fels* guidance.

33. Section 6 of the *Bowman* v *Fels* guidance covers the exception to the tipping off offences for professional legal advisers. Solicitors who cannot make reports because of legal professional privilege need to consider whether they would prefer not to act, or use this exception to speak to clients about reporting. Weighing up the options can be very difficult, and will need to be approached by MLROs on a case by case basis, although Professional Ethics can help. (The Professional Ethics helpline telephone number is 0870 606 2577.)

34. Solicitors conducting conveyancing transaction often feel they could benefit from speaking to the solicitor acting for the other side in a transaction. The exceptions to the tipping off offences applies to communications with clients, which may either be the lay client or Lender client. The exceptions also apply to disclosures made to 'any person in connection with the giving by the adviser of legal advice to the client', see paragraphs 5.6–5.10 of the *Bowman* v *Fels* guidance. In any event a key element of the tipping off offences is 'likely to prejudice an investigation', and it may be unlikely that speaking to another solicitor who is also under a duty not to tip off would fulfil this test.

35. In urgent cases where appropriate consent is required faster than the usual statutory timetable, perhaps because suspicions are formed when a transaction is at an advanced stage and a Notice to Complete has been received the NCIS fast track procedure may be used, see paragraphs 7.18 – 7.21 of the Guidance. Reliance cannot be placed on others already having made a report. However, a key advantage achieved by the judgment is that a solicitor who makes a report would be able to continue work on the transaction short of transferring funds or taking some other irrevocable step without committing a section 328 offence, see section 3 of the *Bowman* v *Fels* guidance, especially paragraph 3.3. However, for other professional reasons solicitors who report pre-exchange should not exchange until 'appropriate consent' has been received.

In case of difficulties solicitors are advised to call the Professional Ethics helpline: 0870 606 2577

Money Laundering Task Force

Conveyancing and Land Law Committee

Footnote to paragraph 25: Although usually principles of client confidentiality would usually mean that the lay client would need to waive their confidentiality before the mortgage company could be informed, in these circumstances because there was not a valid retainer because of the crime/fraud exception, which means that the solicitor can tell the mortgage company without their client's permission. If knowledge or suspicion is formed during the course of the retainer with the mortgage company the solicitor will have a duty to advise the Lender because the information is relevant to the Lender's decision to make the loan.

Law Society's anti-money laundering guidance for solicitors conducting private client work (February 2006)

INTRODUCTION

1. This work draws heavily on work already published by the Law Society to help solicitors comply with the UK's anti money laundering regime, which is available from **www.lawsociety.org.uk**, or from Professional Ethics: 0870 606 2577. Family lawyers will have a particular interest in the guidance on *Bowman* v *Fels* (2005) EWCA Civ 225, which is referred to below.

2. Private client work which involves learning about, or dealing with, a client's assets can lead a solicitor to form knowledge or suspicion, or gives rise to reasonable grounds for suspicion, of money laundering. However, whether a money laundering report is required in any individual situation will require a detailed examination of the relevant criminal offences within Part 7 of POCA as most recently interpreted by the case of *Bowman* v *Fels*. Full guidance on *Bowman* v *Fels* (2005) EWCA Civ 226 is available, and solicitors conducting private client work should carefully consider their approach in the light of this judgment.

3. Solicitors could be at risk of money laundering if their work involves assisting with the management or distribution of assets which include suspected 'criminal property', whether they take a principal role themselves or act for others, e.g. trust work, administration of estates, Powers of Attorney, Court of Protection work, or wealth management. Such work can risk commission of a principal money laundering offence under sections 327–329 of POCA, see paragraphs 2.13–2.18 of the Law Society's Money Laundering Guidance – pilot January 2004 – ('the Guidance') available from **www.lawsociety.org.uk**. However, a defence may be available if a report is made to the National Criminal Intelligence Service ('NCIS'), or after 1 April to the Serious and Organised Crime Agency ('SOCA'), and if relevant, 'appropriate consent' is obtained or can be deemed through lapse of time, see paragraph 2.23–2.27 of the Guidance. However, because of the judgment in *Bowman* v *Fels*, before a solicitor reports to NCIS/SOCA a key consideration will be whether their knowledge or suspicion of money laundering is based on information received in legally professionally privileged circumstances.

4. If a solicitor takes a principal role in a matter, for example by acting as an executor or trustee, it may mean that there are fewer alternative ways to deal with a money laundering situation than when acting for others, e.g. termination of the retainer may not be possible.

5. Solicitors undertaking private client work should remain alert to the warning signs outlined in chapter 6 of the Guidance. For example, private client instructions which fall outside a solicitor's expertise need careful consideration, see paragraph

6.16–6.19 of the Guidance. Solicitors may benefit from discussing the issues with Professional Ethics before accepting instructions, or at a later stage if reasons for suspicion emerge: Tel 0870 606 2577.

MONEY LAUNDERING REGULATIONS 2003

6. Whenever a solicitor is conducting any 'relevant business' for a client, they will need to comply with the Money Laundering Regulations 2003, see paragraph 3.6–3.15 of the Guidance. Suggested identification methods for individuals, estates, and trusts are also covered in chapter 3 of the Guidance.
7. Although will writing is not 'relevant business' for the purposes of the Money Laundering Regulations 2003 as no trust exists until death, ancillary services provided by solicitors when drafting wills may be 'relevant business'. For example, tax advice is covered by the definition of relevant business in Regulation 2(2)(i). Similarly trust services are covered in Regulation 2(2)(m), see paragraph 3.12 of the Guidance, and administration of estates is likely to fall within the meaning of 'financial transaction' within Regulation 2(2)(l), see paragraph 3.9 of the Guidance. However, obtaining a Grant of Probate may fall outside the definitions.

Note:

Whether or not work being undertaken is covered by the Money Laundering Regulations 2003 solicitors should take a risk based approach when considering what anti money laundering procedures they wish to implement, bearing in mind the level of money laundering risk posed by the nature of the work they are being asked to undertake. When taking clients' instructions it may already be necessary, or at least helpful, to obtain information about the purpose of those instructions, e.g. the reason for forming or winding up a trust, or for the execution of a Power of Attorney. Aside from providing clients with the best possible service, assessing the information provided, and if appropriate asking more questions, may help resolve any money laundering concerns. Making careful notes of questions posed and answers received may assist if a solicitor's conduct is questioned later.

RISK AREAS

Administration of estates

8. Administration of estates is likely to fall within the definition of 'financial transaction' within Regulation 2(2)(l), (see paragraph 3.9–3.12 of the Guidance). Therefore, as well as being aware of the principal offences, see paragraphs 2.13–2.31 of the Guidance, solicitors need to be aware of the section 330 failure to report (regulated sector) offence; see paragraphs 2.40–2.43 of the Guidance.
9. When a solicitor is either acting as executor, or for executors, there is no blanket requirement that a solicitor should be satisfied as to the provenance of all of the funds which form a part of the estate they are administering. However, solicitors should be alive to factors which can increase the money laundering risk of the work they are undertaking and act accordingly, see chapter 6 of the Guidance. For example, where estate assets have been earned in a foreign jurisdiction, solicitors should be aware of the wide definition of 'criminal conduct' in section 340 (2) (b), namely the provision in POCA relating to overseas criminal conduct, see paragraph 2.7 (Also, see footnote). Suspect territories in particular should prompt solicitors to make more checks, see paragraphs 6.31–6.34 of the Guidance.

Note:

It does not matter when the underlying criminal offence occurred as the definition of 'criminal conduct' in s.340(2) has unlimited retrospective effect.

10. The wide nature of the offence of 'acquisition, use and possession' in section 329 offence of POCA may lead to a money laundering offence being committed at an early point in the administration. The section 328 arrangements offence may also be relevant. This is one reason why solicitors need to be alert from the outset, and throughout, so that any reporting can be considered as soon as knowledge or suspicion is formed to avoid problems with delayed appropriate consent, see paragraph 2.26 of the Guidance. However, a key advantage achieved by the *Bowman* v *Fels* judgment is that a solicitor who makes a report is able to continue work on the matter short of transferring funds or taking some other irrevocable step.

11. An extreme example of when administration of an estate may constitute a money laundering offence would be where a solicitor dealing with administration knows or suspects that the deceased was accused or convicted of acquisitive criminal conduct during their lifetime, perhaps because their firm acted in the relevant criminal litigation.

12. Where a solicitor forms knowledge or suspicion that the deceased improperly claimed welfare benefits during their lifetime, for example because the capital of the deceased took them over the financial threshold for the relevant benefit they claimed, there will be 'criminal property' included in the estate, and so usually a money laundering report may be required. More information on the financial thresholds for benefits can be obtained from **www.dwp.gov.uk**, However, a practical solution to consider in these circumstances is whether any outstanding liability to the Department of Work and Pensions can be repaid prior to collation of the assets or administration, as this may rid the estate of any 'criminal property' and so avoid the risk of committing a money laundering offence by administering the estate. The extent of the liability should be established from the Department of Work and Pensions.

Note:

The definition of 'criminal property' in section 340(3)(a) does not have a financial minimum which applies to solicitors. Any proceeds of criminal conduct, including deemed proceeds from obtaining a pecuniary advantage, maybe defined as criminal property, however small the amount.

14. It may be helpful to consider the general warning signs for money laundering in chapter 6 of the Guidance if there is concern about beneficiaries. In high risk circumstances, such as terrorism, solicitors may wish to refer to the Bank of England consolidated sanctions list, see paragraph 2.36 of the Guidance and **www.bankofengland.co.uk**.

15. Whilst administering an estate a solicitor may form knowledge or suspicion that beneficiaries are not intending to pay the correct amount of tax, or are avoiding some other financial penalty, e.g. creditors, or the Assets Recovery Agency. For example, beneficiaries may be reluctant to disclose gifts they have received from the deceased less than seven years before death. Dependant on the circumstances these types of matters may not in fact constitute money laundering because no criminal conduct has yet occurred, and therefore there is no 'criminal property', but a solicitor should carefully consider their position in conduct terms under Principle 12.02 because they may be in breach of the law or Professional Conduct rules. Further help can be obtained from Professional Ethics: 0870 606 2577.

Grant of Probate

16. Simply obtaining a grant of probate may not fall within the definition of 'financial transaction' in Regulation 2(2)(l), see paragraph 3.9–3.12.

Deceased non-UK domiciled persons

17. A UK grant of probate may be required before UK assets can be released, whilst for overseas assets the relevant local laws will apply. Solicitors should remain alert to money laundering warning signs, e.g. where the deceased or their business interests are based in a suspect territory. Information about non cooperative territories is available from www.fatf-gafi.org, and information about countries where corruption/bribery is a problem is available from **www.transparency.org**. In appropriate circumstances it may be helpful to ask the lawyer dealing with the matter in the home country for information about the deceased to gain some reasonable assurances that there are no suspicious circumstances surrounding the provenance of their estate. The issue of the tax payable on the estate may depend upon the relevant jurisdiction, see paragraph 14 above regarding the future potential tax evasion.

Trusts

18. Trust work is covered by Regulations 2(2)(m). Guidance on possible methods of identification is given at paragraphs 3.104–3.107 of the Guidance.

19. Although trusts are most commonly used for legitimate reasons, they can also be used as money laundering vehicles. Discretionary trusts and complex offshore trusts are most vulnerable to money laundering. When setting up trusts, solicitors should remain alive to the warning signs of money laundering, and consider whether the purpose of the trust could be money laundering. Information about the purpose of the trust, including why any unusual structure or jurisdiction has been used, can help allay concerns. Similarly information about the provider of the funds, and those who have control over the funds, may also assist, see *Re: the Esteem settlement, Groupo Torras SA* v. *Al–Sabah* (2004) WTLR 1.

20. Whether solicitors act as trustees themselves, or for trustees, the nature of work may already require information which will assist in assessing money laundering risk, e.g. location of assets, identity of trustees, see paragraph 3.105 of the Guidance. Again, any involvement of suspect jurisdictions, especially those with strict bank secrecy and confidentiality rules, or in jurisdictions without equivalent money laundering procedures, may mean that further enquiries are helpful, see paragraphs 6.31–6.34 of the Guidance.

21. Solicitors may form knowledge or suspicion of money laundering in relation to money or property which either already forms a part of trust property, or is intended to do so. Such knowledge or suspicion may arise from information about the circumstances of historic events, e.g. where there has been a sale of a property overseas and tax was not paid on that sale. In these circumstances solicitors should consider whether their instructions may involve them in a section 328 arrangement offence, and if so what options are open to them in accordance with the *Bowman* v *Fels* guidance.

Charities

22. Whether the Money Laundering Regulations 2003 apply to work undertaken for charities depends upon whether 'relevant business' is being undertaken, see chapter 3. Where the work will constitute 'relevant business' the charity will need to be identified, see paragraphs 3.9–3.15. Identification will need to be to an objective and subjective standard, see paragraph 3.28 of the Guidance. In cases where a charity is not the solicitor's client, but is involved in some way in the solicitor's instructions, the solicitor may still wish to make some checks.

Note:

The Charity Commission provides some information about registered charities in England and Wales, www.charity-commission.gov.uk or tel: 0870 333 0123, The information available includes the charities' objects, contact details, the names of its trustees, its broad areas of activity as well as overall financial information including when annual returns have been filed and accounts. Charities which are household names may pose a lower risk. However, not all charities in England and Wales are required to register, or the charity may be based in a country which does not have a registration system. Solicitors may make enquiries about the level of regulation in the host country, or seek advice from Professional Ethics.

23. In common with trusts, whilst the majority of charities are used for legitimate reasons, they can also be used as money laundering/terrorist financing vehicles. Solicitors who act for charities may need to consider the purpose of the charity itself. Remaining alert to the warning signs of money laundering may assist with this, see Chapter 6. An extreme example of the misuse of charities may be terrorist purposes, and where there is concern, reference should be made to the Bank of England terrorist lists see paragraph 14 above.

24. Where a solicitor is acting for a charity and is due to receive money on their behalf from an individual or company donor, the solicitor needs to be alert to unusual circumstances including significant sums. Where the charity is due to receive a bequest from an estate similar considerations apply.

Powers of Attorney/Receivership

25. Execution of a Power of Attorney for clients does not itself constitute a 'financial transaction' for the purposes of Regulations 2(2) (l), see paragraph 3.9 of the Guidance. However, a solicitor acting for an attorney, or as an attorney themselves, is likely to be undertaking 'relevant business'. Similarly solicitors acting for receivers appointed by the Court of Protection, or who are appointed as receivers themselves, are likely to be undertaking 'relevant business'.

26. All these areas of work can give rise to money laundering issues. For example, where a solicitor acts as an attorney they may learn financial information about the donor, such as their non payment of tax, or wrongful receipt of welfare benefits. Whether this is a matter which is reportable to NCIS/SOCA as money laundering will depend upon a detailed analysis of the *Bowman* v *Fels* guidance, especially whether knowledge or suspicion has been formed from information received in legally professionally privileged circumstances. Where the Court of Protection has an interest because of a receivership or registered enduring power of attorney, consideration will need to be given as to whether the Master needs to be informed. Informing the Master is unlikely to be tipping off because it is

unlikely to prejudice an investigation, which is a necessary criterion for either of the tipping off offences, see paragraph 2.57–2.61 of the Guidance.

27. Principle 24.03 of the Guide to the Professional Conduct of Solicitors contains information for solicitors regarding Powers of Attorney, e.g. if a solicitor forms knowledge or suspicion that a donee is acting improperly, for example not dealing with the donor's assets in the donor's best interests, the solicitor should seek confirmation of instructions from the donor.

28. If a solicitor forms knowledge or suspicion that a donee has already completed an improper financial transaction, that may amount to a money laundering suspicion, and a money laundering report to NCIS/SOCA may be required, dependant on whether legal professional privilege applies. However, solicitors may find it hard to decide whether they have a suspicion if the background is a family dispute, and it can help to discuss matters with Professional Ethics: 0870 606 2577.

Reporting Issues

29. The case of *Bowman* v *Fels* has drastically altered how private client solicitors undertaking private client work should approach their reporting obligations because of the increased importance of legal professional privilege. Administration of estates or other types of private client work should lead solicitors to consider in detail the *Bowman* v *Fels* guidance referred to above.

30. Legal professional privilege is a key consideration and recent case law has defined privilege in transactional work widely, see paragraph 5.6 onwards in the *Bowman* v *Fels* guidance. For example instructions to prepare wills are likely to be covered by legal professional privilege (unless there is a criminal intention behind the instructions), and after death but before publication of wills, rights to legal professional privilege vest in the Personal Representatives.

Solicitors in need of guidance should contact:

Professional Ethics tel: 0870 606 2577

Footnote to Paragraph 9: Once section 102 of the Serious Organised Crime and Police Act 2005 comes into force, usually a money laundering offence will not be committed if a solicitor knows or believes on reasonable grounds that the relevant criminal conduct occurred outside the UK and was not, at the time it was committed, a crime in that country or territory. Up to date information about this future change to POCA can be obtained on this subject from Professional Ethics: 0870 606 2577.

C1

Client identification form

Client Name

Date of Birth

Address

Postcode

[Client No.]

I certify that I have carried out the appropriate client verification procedures as follows:

<u>**Individuals (including partnerships and unincorporated businesses)**</u>   **Tick** ☐

I have obtained the client's/clients':

(a)   full name
(b)   current permanent address
(c)   date of birth

by reference to at least one document from each of the following lists:

List A (evidence of name and date of birth)

(a)   current valid full passport
(b)   national identity card or resident's permit
(c)   current photocard driving licence
(d)   firearms certificate
(e)   state pension or benefit book
(f)   inland revenue tax notification

List B (evidence of address)

(a) home visit
(b) electoral roll check
(c) recent utility or local authority council tax bill
(d) recent bank/building society statement
(e) recent mortgage statement
(f) current driving licence (not if used in List A)
(g) local council rent card or tenancy agreement.

I confirm having seen the original documents and that any photograph of the client bore a good likeness to the client. A copy of each document is attached to this form.

<u>Corporate</u>   **Tick** ☐

I confirm that I have carried out a company search and attach a copy to this form. I also confirm that the identity of a director/shareholder instructing the firm has been obtained in accordance with the procedures for individuals and a copy of each document is attached to this form.

<u>Trusts, nominees and fiduciaries</u>   **Tick** ☐

I confirm that I have received a certified copy of the trust (and the grant of probate or copy of the will creating the trust in the case of a deceased settlor). The trustees have been identified in accordance with the procedures for individuals or companies noted above.

I also confirm that as far as I am aware the client(s) is/are acting in his/her/their own name(s) and not as agent for any other person.*

(*delete if necessary. If a client is acting as agent for another person, a separate identification record is required for the other person/principal)

Signed ....   **Date** ....

[Note: this form provides a basic precedent for a client identification form. It should be developed to suit the needs of individual firms. Reference should be made to **Appendix B1**, the Law Society **Money Laundering Guidance** on 'How can identity be established'.]

C2

Precedent for a basic money laundering manual

1. WHAT IS MONEY LAUNDERING?

Money laundering is the process by which the identity of 'dirty money' is changed so that the proceeds of crime appear to originate from a legitimate source. It is important that solicitors and their employees take steps to ensure that their services are not used by those seeking to legitimise the proceeds of crime. Solicitors must be aware that they may be involved in the money laundering process.

It is the policy of *[Firm name]* that we will take no avoidable risks and will co-operate fully with the authorities where necessary. No matter how much you want to help your client, you must not be a party to any form of dishonesty. You must be alert to the possibility that transactions on which we are instructed may involve money laundering. You must therefore follow the firm's policy in order to reduce the risk of:

(a) our clients suffering loss as a result of innocent involvement in money laundering transactions;
(b) our reputation being harmed if we are a party to a money laundering transaction; and
(c) a possible civil claim against the firm by the true owner of any property involved in a money laundering transaction.

2. THE FIRM'S POLICY

Recent legislation (in particular the Proceeds of Crime Act 2002, the Serious Organised Crime and Police Act 2005 and the Money Laundering Regulations 2003) has made significant changes to our responsibilities relating to money laundering. These changes are reflected in this manual.

3. THE CRIMINAL OFFENCES

The law relating to money laundering changed in February 2003 as a result of the Proceeds of Crime Act 2002. The Money Laundering Regulations 2003 came into force on 1 March 2004. Amendments were introduced by the Serious Organised Crime and Police Act 2005. These amendments were brought into force at various dates in 2005 and 2006.

There are a number of criminal offences relevant to a solicitor's practice. The offences divide into three categories:

A. Offences where the firm is involved in a client matter or transaction

It is an offence:

(a) to acquire, use or possess criminal property;
(b) to conceal, disguise, convert, transfer or remove from the UK criminal property; or
(c) to enter into or become concerned in an arrangement which facilitates the acquisition, retention, use or control of another person's criminal property,

in all cases where we know or suspect that this is the case.

Criminal property is defined as constituting or representing a person's benefit from criminal conduct. Criminal conduct for these purposes means any conduct which constitutes a crime in the UK or if undertaken abroad, would have constituted a crime if committed in the UK. (Although a defence was introduced by the Serious Organised Crime and Police Act 2005 in relation to overseas criminal property, this defence has limited application in practice. Consequently, you must follow the procedures noted in this manual where funds or other assets are sourced from abroad. Those responsible in the firm will ascertain whether or not the limited defence relating to overseas property is available.) The very wide definition of criminal property will include, for example, the benefit of tax evasion. The offence of 'facilitating the acquisition, retention, use or control' (noted in (c) above) does not require the firm to be in possession of any money or other asset which constitutes a person's criminal property. Advising a client on the structure of a transaction to evade tax (as opposed to avoid tax lawfully) may be an offence.

Examples of what might amount to suspicion for these purposes are to be found below in the next section of this manual.

A defence is available where you disclose your knowledge or suspicion to a nominated officer (i.e. a person nominated by the firm to receive internal disclosures). The firm's nominated officer is *[name]*. In his/her absence disclosure should be made to the firm's deputy nominated officer, *[deputy's name]*.

If you have any knowledge or suspicion which requires reporting, you may initially discuss your concerns with your *[group partner or firm's nominated officer]*. If after such discussion you still have concerns a formal disclosure report should be made to the nominated officer using the Internal Reporting Form (a copy of which is attached to this document as Appendix 1).

Note that any disclosure you make must generally be made before the prohibited act (i.e. the act of facilitation or otherwise). If you only become aware of information giving rise to knowledge or suspicion whilst committing the prohibited act (for example, you may have placed money in client account innocently and thereafter discover information which makes you suspicious) you must make your disclosure as soon as possible after you become suspicious. If the disclosure is made after you have committed the prohibited act you will only have a defence **if you can show that there was a good reason for your failure to make the disclosure before the act.**

(A similar offence relating to the laundering of 'terrorist property' appears in the Terrorism Act 2000.)

B. Offences following a disclosure report made to the firm's nominated officer

It is an offence to disclose to any person (including your client) that a report has been made to the firm's nominated officer in circumstances where this is likely to prejudice an investigation. (Further, even if no disclosure report has been made, an offence is committed if you know or suspect that a money laundering investigation is or is likely to be conducted and you disclose any information which is likely to prejudice the investigation.)

Once a report has been made to the nominated officer it may be an offence to continue to act for the client without the consent of the nominated officer. The nominated officer can only give consent if (s)he has disclosed details to the Serious Organised Crime Agency (SOCA) and SOCA have, in turn, given consent for the firm to continue to act.

Consequently, once a disclosure has been made to the nominated officer, (s)he must be involved in every decision relating to that client matter and you must not communicate any information concerning the subject matter of the disclosure to the client or to any other person (including your work colleagues) without the express consent of the nominated officer. **Failure to comply with this procedure could lead to a criminal offence being committed.**

C. Offences involving a failure to disclose knowledge or suspicion of money laundering

It is an offence for a person who knows or suspects or who has reasonable grounds for knowing or suspecting that another is engaged in money laundering not to disclose that information where the information came to him in the course of business in the regulated sector.

The disclosure should be made to the firm's nominated officer using the same procedures as noted above.

This offence does not require the firm to be acting for a particular client, nor for the firm to be in possession, etc. of criminal property, nor involved in an arrangement which facilitates the acquisition, retention, use or control of criminal property. Further, the offence is not limited to knowledge or suspicion of our client – it applies to any knowledge or suspicion of money laundering offences committed by any person.

The obligation to report arises simply if the information comes into your possession in the course of our business in the regulated sector. The definition of the regulated sector has been extended significantly. The sector now covers the bulk of our work for clients. Consequently it is the policy of the firm to assume that all client work falls within the regulated sector and that accordingly all knowledge or suspicion of money laundering must be reported to the nominated officer where the information arises in the course of our business.

The definition of money laundering for these purposes includes the three crimes noted above in category (A). In particular it should be appreciated that the crimes involving 'acquisition, use and possession' and 'concealing etc.' can be committed by the perpetrator of the crime. A person guilty of theft or tax evasion will also have committed a money laundering offence if he is in possession of criminal property.

There is a similar obligation to report knowledge or suspicion (or reasonable grounds for knowledge or suspicion) that another is engaged in certain terrorist offences where that information comes into your possession in the course of business in the regulated sector (Terrorism Act 2000).

Note:

The Court of Appeal's decision in *Bowman* v *Fels* [2005] EWCA Civ 226 has made changes to the way in which the legislation is to be interpreted. First, generally speaking, the money laundering offences do not apply to most litigation (including consensual resolution of issues in a litigious context). Secondly, the interpretation of the word 'arrangement' (see 3A(c) above) is restricted to the act of facilitation – preparatory acts which do not themselves assist in the acquisition, use, retention or control of criminal property will not give rise to liability. Thirdly, the Court of Appeal's decision has preserved the concept of legal professional privilege. If information is privileged we cannot disclose the information to SOCA unless a waiver of privilege is obtained.

You should continue to report to [*the firm's nominated officer*] any knowledge or suspicion, even if you believe *Bowman* v *Fels* makes the report unnecessary. [*The firm's nominated officer*] with the assistance of others will decide upon the impact of the judgment in *Bowman* v *Fels*.

4. THE DANGER SIGNS TO WATCH FOR

Unusual settlement requests: Settlement by cash of any large transaction involving the purchase of property or other investment should give rise to caution. Payment by way of a third party cheque or money transfer where there is a variation between the account holder, the signatory and a prospective investor should give rise to additional enquiries.

Fictitious buyer: Especially if the buyer is introduced to the Firm by a third party (e.g. a broker or an estate agent) who is not well known to you. Beware of clients you never meet – they may be fictitious. Wherever a meeting with the client is not possible, special care is needed.

Unusual instructions: Care should always be taken when dealing with a client who has no discernible reason for using the Firm's services, e.g. clients with distant addresses who could find the same service nearer their home base; or clients whose requirements do not fit into the normal pattern of the Firm's business and could be more easily serviced elsewhere. Similarly care should be taken if you are instructed to remit the net proceeds of sale to the estate agent who was instructed.

Misrepresentation of the purchase price: Make sure that the true cash price for a property which is to be actually paid is the price shown in the contract and the transfer, and is identical to the price shown in the mortgage instructions.

A deposit paid direct: A deposit, perhaps exceeding the normal 10 per cent, paid direct, or said to be direct, to the seller should give rise to concern.

Incomplete contract documentation: Contract documents not fully completed by the seller's representative, e.g. dates missing or the identity of the parties not fully described.

Changes in the purchase price: Adjustments to the purchase price, particularly in high percentage mortgage cases, or allowances off the purchase price for, e.g. works to be carried out.

Unusual transactions: Those which do not follow their normal course or the usual pattern of events.

Large sums of cash: Always be cautious when requested to hold large sums of cash in client account, either pending further instructions from the client or for no other purpose than for onward transmission to a third party. It is the firm's policy not to accept sums of cash in excess of *[£500]* unless prior approval of the firm's nominated officer has been obtained.

The secretive client: A personal client who is reluctant to provide details of his or her identity. Be particularly cautious about the client you do not meet in person.

Suspect territory: Caution should be exercised whenever a client is introduced by an overseas bank, other investor or third party based in countries where production of drugs or drug trafficking may be prevalent.

Mortgage fraud: It is possible that a member of staff may unwittingly assist in a mortgage fraud. This is especially true of staff who deal with any form of conveyancing, whether domestic or commercial. We must therefore be very vigilant to protect our mortgagee clients and ourselves. If you turn a blind eye to any form of dishonesty over mortgages, no matter how small, you could be personally implicated in the fraud. It is important to stress that the penalties are criminal as well as civil.

5. IDENTIFICATION: GENERAL POINTS

5.1.   In the light of the requirements contained in the Money Laundering Regulations 2003 it is the firm's policy to verify the identity of all new clients and all existing clients at the start of a new matter unless they have been identified already.

5.2.   Documentary evidence must be obtained in accordance with the procedure set out below. It is important that the original of any document is examined and copied. The fee earner should endorse the copy with the words 'original seen' followed by the fee earner's signature.

5.3.   Particular care must be taken when acting on the instructions of someone on behalf of the true client or where our client is clearly an agent for a third party. In those circumstances our procedures must ensure that reasonable measures are taken to establish the identity of both parties.

5.4.   The identification procedures must be carried out as soon as reasonably practicable after first contact is made between the firm and client. It is not necessary for the firm to wait until the verification process is complete before commencing work for the client. However, if it proves impossible to satisfactorily complete the process **we must cease to act for the client.**

5.5. No client money should be accepted from the client for payment into client account until the verification process has been satisfactorily completed.

5.6. A Client Identification form should be completed and *[kept with the file/submitted to   ]* (see Appendix 2).

5.7. The copy of evidence taken to confirm a client's identity *[must be kept with the file/submitted to   ]* (the Firm's policy is to keep all client files for a minimum of *[6]* years).

6. IDENTIFICATION: PROCEDURES

The method for identifying clients will depend upon the type of client. The procedure below and the documentary evidence referred to are not to be taken as an exhaustive list of requirements. A judgement must be made by fee earners as to whether alternative or additional information should be sought. If in doubt you should seek advice from the nominated officer.

A. *Companies*

In the case of a corporate client we need to be satisfied that the company exists and that we are dealing with that company. The existence of the company can be determined by making a company search which reveals the following information:

(a) name and registered address
(b) registered number
(c) list of directors
(d) members or shareholders
(e) nature of the company's business
(f) certificate of incorporation
(g) if a subsidiary, the name of the holding company.

If the company is listed or traded on a recognised investment exchange or is a wholly-owned subsidiary of such a company, there is no need to obtain a list of directors or shareholders.

If the company is not listed, and does not have directors or shareholders whose identities have already been verified, you should seek identification of those individuals instructing the firm in accordance with the procedures noted for individuals below.

B. *Individuals*

The following information should be obtained for individuals:

(a) full name
(b) current permanent address (including postcode)
(c) date of birth.

At least one document from each of the following lists should be produced:

List A (evidence of name and date of birth)

(i)   current valid full passport
(ii) national identity card or resident's permit
(iii) current photocard driving licence
(iv) firearms certificate
(v)   state pension or benefit book
(vi) inland revenue tax notification

List B (evidence of address)

(i)   home visit
(ii)   electoral roll check
(iii) recent utility or local authority council tax bill
(iv)   recent bank/building society statement
(v)   recent mortgage statement
(vi)   current driving licence (not if used in List A)
(vii) local council rent card or tenancy agreement.

*[Additional documents are listed in the Law Society's Guidance – see **Appendix B1**. This list may be added to depending upon the firm's typical client profile]*

Where joint instructions are received, identification procedures should be applied to each client. If joint clients have the same name and address (e.g. spouses) the verification of the address for one client only is sufficient.

C. *Partnerships and other unincorporated businesses*

If the business is regulated by an independent public body, the evidence of the name, address and existence of the business should be obtained from that body.

In other cases, evidence of identification should be obtained from the individuals or partners by reference to the procedure for individuals as noted above.

D. *Trusts, nominees and fiduciaries*

Where the trust is regulated by an independent public body (e.g. the Charities Commission) the evidence of the existence of the trust and the identity of the trustees should be sought from that body.

In other cases a certified copy of the trust (and the grant of probate or copy of the will creating the trust in the case of a deceased settlor) must be obtained. The trustees must also be identified in accordance with the procedures for individuals or companies noted above.

Particular care must be taken where the trust is offshore since these trusts present a high risk of money laundering.

E. Non-UK Clients

Non-UK individual clients should produce passports or national identity cards together with separate evidence of the client's permanent address obtained from the best source available. PO Box numbers are not sufficient evidence of an address.

Non-UK corporate clients should produce equivalent information to that obtained by making a UK company search. The results of company searches made abroad will depend upon the filing requirements in the local jurisdiction.

F. Clients where there is no face-to-face contact

Where contact with the client is not face-to face but by post or telephone, it is still necessary to obtain evidence of identity in accordance with the above procedures. Such evidence can be produced by way of an original document or by way of a certified copy provided that the copy is certified by a reputable institution, such as a bank or firm of lawyers, who should verify the name used, the current permanent address and the client's signature. The name and address of the institution providing the certification should be noted and checked by reference to a professional directory. This procedure may be appropriate where the client is a foreign national resident abroad.

If you are unable to obtain satisfactory evidence of identity in accordance with the above procedures you must contact the firm's nominated officer who will advise on any alternative steps which may be taken or consider whether instructions must be terminated.

7. DEPARTMENTAL INSTRUCTIONS

*[If appropriate include under this heading typical circumstances where different departments of the firm might find themselves at risk. Details can be found in **Chapter 12** in the main text of this book]*

8. HELP

Money laundering is real and it will affect us. **If you have any concerns regarding the firm's policy and/or your responsibilities contact *[name of nominated officer]* or in his/her absence *[name of deputy]*.**

9. CONCLUSION

To minimise the risks of liability:

Verify the identity and bona fides of your client: Meet the client or clients where possible and get to know them.

Question unusual instructions: Make sure that you discuss them fully with your client, and note all such discussions carefully on the file.

Discuss any aspects of the transaction which worry you with your client: For example, if you suspect that your client may have submitted a false mortgage application or references, or if you know or suspect the Lender's valuation exceeds the actual price paid, discuss this with your client and, if you believe they intend to proceed with a fraudulent application, you must refuse to continue to act for the buyer and the mortgagee.

Check that the true price is shown in all documentation: Check that the actual price paid is stated in the contract, transfer and mortgage instructions. Ensure that your client understands that, where you are also acting for the Lender, you will have to report all allowances and incentives to the Mortgagee.

Do not witness pre-signed documentation: No deed should be witnessed by a solicitor or staff unless the person signing does so in the presence of a witness. If a deed is pre-signed, ensure that it is re-signed in the presence of a witness.

Verify signatures: Consider whether signatures on all documents connected with a transaction should be examined and compared with signatures on any other documentation.

Make a Company Search: Where a private company is the seller or the seller has purchased from a private company in the recent past and you suspect that there may be a connection between the company and the seller or the buyer which is being used for improper purposes, then consideration would be given to ascertain the names and addresses of the officers and shareholders which can then be compared with the names of those connected with the transaction and the seller and buyer.

APPENDIX 1

MONEY LAUNDERING INTERNAL REPORTING FORM
*[For a precedent, see **Appendix C3** to this book]*

APPENDIX 2

CLIENT IDENTIFICATION FORM
*[For a precedent, see **Appendix C1** to this book]*

C3

Internal reporting form

1. Name of client/s:

   Aliases/Trading names:

2. Address (including postcode,
   telephone, fax, e-mail and contact name):

3. Date of Birth:

4. Summary of instructions:

5. If not acting as principal:

   (a) Name of Principal:

   (b) Address of Principal (including postcode,
   telephone, fax, e-mail and contact name):

6. Evidence of identity (please attach):

7.   Value of transaction:

8.   Name and address of introducer (if any):

9.   Is the client named above the person you know or suspect is involved in money laundering? YES/NO

10.   If your answer to 9 is NO:

        (a)   Name of person you know or suspect is involved in money laundering:

        (b)   Address of person you know or suspect is involved in money laundering:

11.   Source and destination of funds:

        (a)   source of cash/bank/other securities

        (b)   destination

12.   The whereabouts of the laundered property:

13.   If you are unable to answer 12, do you have information which might assist in identifying the whereabouts of the laundered property? If so, please state this information:

14.   **Reason for suspicion:**

15.   **Does Professional Privilege apply? YES/NO**

16.   **If Professional Privilege does apply is a waiver of privilege necessary?   YES/NO**

        If NO, give reasons:

Signed .... **Date**..

To be completed by nominated officer only:

Report to SOCA?   YES/NO

If No, give reasons:

Date Business completed ....

Record destruction date ....

        **(If a report has been made to SOCA this record must not be destroyed at the 'date
        of destruction' without first referring to SOCA)**

C4

SOCA reporting forms and guidance notes

Guide to completing disclosure forms

The guidance notes explain what information is required in the Standard form template and are to be read in conjunction with the form itself. If you are not completing the form using one of the electronic methods outlined above, the form should be completed on the computer-generated template, which is available to download from the SOCA website, but if this is not possible it should be typed onto a paper copy. A number of fields within the computer-generated template can be completed by selecting options from dropdown menus.

It is important that the relevant information is completed within the appropriate fields and not merely placed within the 'Reasons for Suspicion' field.

There are a number of fields that should be completed in order for a report to be accepted by SOCA. These fields are: Your Ref (even if none), Disclosure Type, New or Update, Source ID, Source Outlet ID, Today's Date, (Main Subject) Surname or Company Name and Reasons for Suspicion. Following this, according to the additional information you have available, a number of fields within each section must be completed if you are filling in that section and are identified below in bold italics.

For a more detailed explanation of the template itself, please contact the SOCA SAR Team at PO Box 8000, London, SE11 5EN.

SUSPICIOUS ACTIVITY REPORT

- Main subject (person or company)
- Address
- ID Information
- Disclosed account details
- Individual transactions with counterparty account details
- Associated subject (person and company)
- (Associated subject) address
- (Associated subject) ID information
- Reason for suspicion

Your ref: The reference number or alphanumeric identifier that you allocate to the SAR within your own filing system

Sheet no: The number of pages used to complete the SAR?

Disclosure type: This field should contain the type of offence under which you report (i.e. Crime, Drugs or Terrorism)

Disclosure date: The date on which the original report is made within your institution New or Update: New is any new suspicious activity or any further activity on a previously reported account/activity or arrangement. An update is any further information that is not a transaction, on a previously reported account/activity or arrangement, e.g. a new address of a subject

Existing disclosure ID: If you have entered 'Update' in the previous field, please enter here any reference number SOCA may previously have supplied relating to the subject in question

Constructive trust: Fill this check box if the report relates to an issue of constructive trust Further information: Fill this check box to indicate that you retain further information relating to the report that may be of interest to SOCA or another financial investigator. For example, if your disclosure relates to a mortgage application, it may not always be necessary to provide the full documentation. In this case, indicate its existence here and provide a concise description in the 'Reasons for Suspicion' field. DO NOT SEND THE FURTHER INFORMATION WITH YOUR FORM.

Source ID: The name of your institution

Source outlet ID: The name (or sort code) of the branch office from which the report originates

Today's date: Date report submitted to SOCA (Automatic date field)

MAIN SUBJECT (PERSON OR COMPANY)

This information describes the individual (or company) on whom you wish to report.

Surname: Subject's family name

Forenames: Subject's forenames

Title: Title of subject (Mr, Mrs, Dr etc)

Date of birth: Date of birth of subject

Gender: Gender of subject

Occupation: Occupation of subject

Employer: Subject's employer

Or:

Company Name: Company name of subject

Company No: Company registration number of subject

Type of business: Type of business of subject

VAT no: VAT number of subject

Country of Registration: Country of registration of subject

ADDRESS

Number, street, city/town, county, country: Full address of subject

Post code: Post Code of address of subject

Type: Type of address of subject (i.e. home, accommodation, trading etc)

Current: Is the address of the subject current, Yes or No

ID INFORMATION

ID Information: Describes the type of identification offered or taken (e.g. driving licence)

Unique information ID: Give details of the identification taken (e.g. driving licence number)

Extra information/description: Give any further information relating to the identification taken, which may be relevant or of use (e.g. if passport, the country of issue)

Other information: Give any further details that help to identify the subject

DISCLOSED ACCOUNT DETAILS

This information describes an account with which the subject or suspicious activity is connected.

FI ID: The name of the financial institution that holds the subject's account

Sort Code: The sort code of the branch office that holds the subject's account

Opened: Date account opened

Closed: Date account closed (if applicable)

Turn' Cd: Turnover credit

Turn' Db: Turnover debit

Acct. Name: Account name

Acct No: Account number

Acct Bal: Account balance

Bal Date: Date of the balance

Turn Pd: Turnover period

INDIVIDUAL TRANSACTIONS WITH COUNTERPARTY ACCOUNT DETAILS

This section contains details of the transaction, or series of transactions that have aroused your suspicion, and details of the counterparties involved.

Date: The date of the transaction

Amount: The amount of the transaction

Currency: The currency concerned in the transaction (e.g. GBP, USD, DEM etc)

Cr/Db: This field stipulates whether the transaction constitutes a credit or debit in relation to the account identified above

Type: The type of transaction conducted (e.g. cash, cheque, electronic transfer, mortgage etc)

Notes: This field is available for further information relating to the transaction identified above

FI ID: The name of the institution that holds the counterparty account, if applicable

Sort Code: The sort code of the branch office that holds the counterparty's account

Acct. Name: The name of the counterparty

Acct. No: The counterparty's account number

ASSOCIATED SUBJECT (PERSON AND COMPANY)

This information describes the person(s) or companies with which the subject or suspicious activity. It is a person or company that is linked to the main person/company in some direct way and is involved in the suspicious activity. Include the financial institution responsible for that account if it is involved in your suspicions.

Surname: The associated subject's family name

Forenames: The associated subject's forenames

Title: Title of associated subject (Mr, Mrs, Dr etc)

Date of birth: Date of birth of associated subject

Gender: Gender of associated subject

Occupation: Occupation of associated subject

Employer: Associated subject's employer

Reason for association: Give details of the connection between the Main Subject and associate subject

Or:

Company name: The name of the associate company

Company no: Company number of associated subject

Type of business: Type of business of associated subject

VAT no: VAT number of associated subject

Country of registration: Country of registration of associated subject

Reason for association: Give details of the connection between the Main Subject and associate subject

Or:

(Associated) subject already exists as main subject of a previous report and is provided for use if you have previously reported on the associated subject.

Existing disclosure ID: The reference number which SOCA may have provided in relation to previous reports, relating to the associated subject

Your Ref: The reference number or alphanumeric identifier that you allocated within your own file system to the previous report on the associated subject

Reason for association: Details of the connection between the Main Subject and associate subject

(ASSOCIATED SUBJECT) ADDRESS

Number, street, city/town, county, country: Full address of associated subject

Post code: Post code of address of associated subject

Type: Type of address of associated subject (i.e. home, accommodation, trading etc)

Current: Is the address of the associated subject current, Yes or No

(ASSOCIATED SUBJECT) ID INFORMATION

ID information: Describes the type of Identification offered or taken (e.g. driving licence)

Unique information ID: Give details of the Identification taken (e.g. driving licence number)

Extra information/description: Give any further information relating to the Identification taken, which may be relevant or of use (e.g. if passport, country of origin)

General information: Give any further details that help to identify the subject

REASON FOR SUSPICION

This section requires a clear and thorough explanation of the grounds for your suspicion. (Submissions that do not provide reasons for suspicion cannot be accepted as a SAR by SOCA).

For further information contact the SOCA UK Financial Intelligence Unit (UKFIU) SAR Team at PO Box 8000, London, SE11 5EN

APPENDIX C4

Serious Organised Crime Agency
PO Box 8000
London
SE11 5EN
Tel: 020 7238 8282
Fax: 020 7238 8286

SOURCE REGISTRATION DOCUMENT

IMPORTANT - THE DETAILS IN THIS FORM MUST BE PROVIDED WITH YOUR FIRST DISCLOSURE TO SOCA OR FOLLOWING ANY SUBSEQUENT CHANGE TO THOSE DETAILS.

Institution Name:

Institution Type:

Regulator:

Regulator ID:

Contact Details (1): Forename:

Surname:

Position:

Address:

Telephone Details:

Facsimile Details:

E-mail Address:

Contact Details (2): Forename:
(where applicable)

Surname:

Position:

Address:

Telephone Details:

Facsimile Details:

E-mail Address:

Version 2.1 - Appendix 2

Serious Organised Crime Agency
PO Box 8000
London
SE11 5EN
Tel: 020 7238 8282
Fax: 020 7238 8286

DISCLOSURE REPORT DETAILS: STANDARD REPORT:

Reporting Institution: [ ]

Your Ref: [ ]

Disclosure Reason:

PoCA 2002: ○   Terrorism Act 2000: ○

Branch/Office: [ ]

Consent Required: ☐

Disclosure Date: [ ]-[ ]-[ ]
         D D   M M M   Y Y Y Y

Type: New ○   OR   Update ○

Existing Disclosure ID/s: (where applicable) [ ] [ ] [ ]

Please use whichever sheets you feel are necessary and indicate below how many of each you are submitting.

REPORT SUMMARY:

Number of 'Subject Details' sheet appended relating to a Main Subject: [ ]

Number of 'Additional Details' sheets appended relating to Main Subject: [ ]

Number of 'Subjects Details' sheets appended relating to Associated Subject/s: [ ]

Number of 'Additional Details' sheets' appended relating to Associated Subject/s: [ ]

Number of 'Transaction Detail' sheet/s appended: [ ]

Number of 'Reason For Disclosure Sheets' appended: [ ]

Once completed please collate your sheets in the above mentioned order and then sequentially number your sheets at the bottom of each page. This will ensure that the information is processed in the correct sequence.

Total number of pages submitted including this Header: [ ]

Page 1 of [ ]

SUBJECT DETAILS:　　　　　　　　　　　　　　　　Version 2.0 - Appendix 3 ■

| Subject Type: | Main Subject: ○ | **OR** | Associated Subject: ○ | (number [ ] of [ ]) |

Individual's Details:

Subject Status:　　　　Suspect : ○　　　　**OR**　　　　Victim: ○

Surname: [ ]

Forename 1: [ ]

Forename 2: [ ]

Occupation: [ ]

DoB: [ ] - [ ] - [ ]　　　　　　　　Gender:　Male ○　Female ○
　　　D D　　M M M　　Y Y Y Y

Title:　　Mr ○　Mrs ○　Miss ○　Ms ○　Other [ ]

Reason for Association of this subject to the Main Subject (for use only with Associated Subject details)

[ ]

OR

Legal Entity's Details

Subject Status:　　　　Suspect : ○　　　　**OR**　　　　Victim: ○

Legal Entity Name: [ ]

Legal Entity No: [ ]　　VAT No: [ ]

Country of Reg: [ ]

Type of Business: [ ]

Reason for Association of this subject to the Main Subject (for use only with Associated Subject details)

[ ]

■　　　　　　　　　Page [ ] of [ ]　　　　　　　　■

280

ADDITIONAL DETAILS: Version 2.0 - Appendix 4

Do these details refer to the Main Subject: ○   OR   to an Associated Subject ○

(Please indicate the Associate's number where applicable) ☐

Subject Name:

Premise No/Name: Current: ☐   Type:

Street:

City/Town:

County: Post Code:

Country:

Premise No/Name: Current: ☐   Type:

Street:

City/Town:

County: Post Code:

Country:

Premise No/Name: Current: ☐   Type:

Street:

City/Town:

County: Post Code:

Country:

Information Type: Unique
                                Information
                                Identifier:

Extra Information
/ Description

Information Type: Unique
                                Information
                                Identifier:

Extra Information
/ Description

Page ☐ of ☐

281

■ **TRANSACTION DETAILS: (Complete if applicable)** ■

MAIN SUBJECT ACCOUNT SUMMARY   Version 2.0 - Appendix 5

Institution Name:

Account Name:

Sort Code: Account No /Identifier:

Business Relationship Commenced: (DD-MMM-YYYY)   -   -   Acct Bal:

Business Relationship Finished: (DD-MMM-YYYY)   -   -   Bal Date: (DD-MMM-YYYY)   -   -

Turnover Period: Credit Turnover:

                                                    Debit Turnover:

TRANSACTION/S

Activity Type: Activity Date: (DD-MMM-YYYY)   -   -

Amount: Currency: Credit: ◯ or Debit: ◯

Other party name: Account No/ Identifier:

Institution Name or Sort Code:

Activity Type: Activity Date: (DD-MMM-YYYY)   -   -

Amount: Currency: Credit: ◯ or Debit: ◯

Other party name: Account No/ Identifier:

Institution Name or Sort Code:

Activity Type: Activity Date: (DD-MMM-YYYY)   -   -

Amount: Currency: Credit: ◯ or Debit: ◯

Other party name: Account No/ Identifier:

Institution Name or Sort Code:

Activity Type: Activity Date: (DD-MMM-YYYY)   -   -

Amount: Currency: Credit: ◯ or Debit: ◯

Other party name: Account No/ Identifier:

Institution Name or Sort Code:

■   Page   of   ■

REASON FOR DISCLOSURE: Version 2.0 - Appendix 6

Main Subject Name:
(cross reference purposes)

Report Activity Assessment
(Please use only where you know or suspect what the offence behind the reported activity may be)

Drugs: ☐   Missing Trader, Inter Community (VAT) ☐   Immigration: ☐   Tobacco/Alcohol Excise Fraud: ☐
Fraud

Personal Tax Fraud: ☐   Corporate Tax Fraud: ☐   Other Offences:

Reason for Disclosure:

Page ☐ of ☐

Guidance Notes for the completion of the SOCA Regulated Sector

Suspicious Activity Report

Proceeds of Crime Act 2002 – Limited Intelligence Value Report

SCOPE AND PURPOSE

This document provides guidance for the completion of authorised and protected disclosures, under sections 337 and 338 of the Proceeds of Crime Act (2002), categorised as 'Limited Intelligence Value Reports'. This guidance should be read alongside the Limited Intelligence Value Report (Appendix 7) which has been issued by SOCA. Both the Form and Guidance have been completed following consultation with organisations representing the Regulated Sector. **Please note that Limited Intelligence Value Reports should only be made under the Proceeds of Crime Act (PoCA). Any reports being made under the Terrorism Act (2000) should be Standard Reports.**

The Form has not been prescribed by the Secretary of State and therefore is not mandatory. However the Form was agreed by NCIS (a SOCA pre-cursor agency) and organisations representing the Regulated Sector as the preferred format for all reports. The Form has been designed to reflect the different needs of the sectors as well as SOCA's requirement to handle the disclosures as efficiently and effectively as possible.

Although none of the fields in the form is mandatory, since the format is not prescribed, those submitting disclosures should take account of regulatory and sectoral approved guidance. SOCA's feedback to reporting institutions will assess the quality of reporting against relevant guidance.

HOW TO OBTAIN THE NEW FORMS AND GUIDANCE

Those organisations which currently use the Money.web system or Bulk File submission should continue to submit reports electronically, using the existing input screens or reporting format. Additionally SAR Online, a new internet based reporting mechanism will be available from April 2006.

Organisations not able to use Money.web, Bulk File Submission or SAR Online, are advised to obtain a copy of the preferred Forms. Those reporters who wish to complete reports on their own computer should download the Form(s) from the SOCA website (www.soca.gov.uk).

If you wish **to complete a report by hand** you will need to request a special version of the Form by telephoning 020 7238 8282. **Please do not complete the version of the Form downloaded from the main SOCA website (www.soca.gov.uk) by hand.**

SENDING YOUR REPORT TO SOCA

Those organisations which currently use the money.web system or Bulk File submission method, should continue to submit reports in the same way.

Other organisations will need to submit reports by fax to 0207 238 8286 or by post to PO Box 8000, London SE11 5EN. Please do not email completed disclosures to SOCA without encryption.

REPORT STRUCTURE

These Guidance Notes are provided to explain the various fields within the Report and assist you in its completion and should be read alongside the Report Forms themselves.

The Form has been designed to be read by Image Character Recognition (ICR) technology. Therefore any amendments or additions outside the structure of the Form will significantly hamper SOCA's capability to process the disclosure efficiently.

LIMITED INTELLIGENCE VALUE REPORTS

SOCA recognises that POCA results in reports being required in some circumstances where, individually, there is likely to be limited intelligence value to law enforcement, although wider analysis of such reports may provide useful data. The table below provides guidance on the types of circumstance that are appropriate for abbreviated information to be provided in the form of a Limited Intelligence Value report. SOCA reserves the right, in all cases, to ask for the Standard Report form at to be used and will monitor disclosures submitted to ensure that Limited Intelligence Value reporting is not exploited as a 'short cut' where its use is not justified.

Type	Detail	Comments
1 Certain classes of crimes committed overseas	This is intended to apply where the suspicious activity takes place outside the UK and:- • Is not a criminal offence in the jurisdiction where committed, and • Relates either to local differences in regulation or social and cultural practices.	A Limited Intelligence Value Report is not appropriate to report money laundering relating to serious tax evasion or occasions where the underlying offence is a serious crime such as terrorism, offences relating to drugs, paedophilia etc. In these circumstances, a full report is appropriate. Please note that s102 of SOCAP 2005 (not yet enacted) will remove certain crimes from reporting obligations. This will have the effect of defining the types of crime reportable in the context of jurisdictions etc.

Type	Detail	Comments
2 Minor irregularities where there is nothing to suggest that these are the result of dishonest behaviour.	Balance discrepancies and minor credit balances not returned because of the administrative costs involved, or other small discrepancies which are judged to have resulted from a mistake rather than dishonest behaviour.	If reporting institutions are satisfied that no criminal property is involved (as defined by s340 (3) of the Proceeds of Crime Act, 2002), they may conclude that a report is not required. However where reporting institutions feel obliged to make a disclosure, a Limited Intelligence Value report is appropriate.
3 The subject of the report cannot be deduced from the information to hand and the proceeds have disappeared without trace.	This would include bank raids, driving away from a petrol station without paying, shoplifting, retail shrinkage and various cheque and credit card frauds.	Section 330 of POCA (as amended) means that such reports should not be made unless the Suspect, or the means to identify the Subject, is known.
4 Accountants, auditors and tax advisers. Multiple instances of suspicion arising during one audit: 'Aggregation of incidents to form one report'	Multiple incidents may be aggregated within a single Limited Intelligence Value Report provided that:- • One or more of the other categories in this table for limited intelligence value reporting is met, for example number three (above): bank raids, driving away from a petrol station without paying, shoplifting, retail shrinkage and various cheque and credit card frauds; • The reason for the aggregate report is summarised; • Aggregate reports relate to a single audit only.	The Act refers to reports being made 'as soon as practicable'. SOCA accepts that this will not always mean 'immediately' and is content to receive aggregate Limited Intelligence Value Reports within one month of the completion of an audit, provided that during the assignment no time sensitive information is discovered (that may, for example, allow the recovery of proceeds of crime if communicated immediately). Reporters should note that a Standard Report is appropriate should the issue of a Hansard (CoP9) Letter by the

Type	Detail	Comments
		Inland Revenue, taken with such other information as may be available, cause (or provide reasonable grounds for) knowledge or suspicion of money laundering.
5 Law enforcement prosecutor, regulator or other Government agency already aware of an offence that also happens to be an instance of suspected money laundering	This category is intended to capture a range of regulatory/procedural offences. Examples include health and safety offences, environmental offences, and failure to file annual returns with the Companies Registrar.	Provided the caveat of 'no additional information' is adhered to, a Limited Intelligence Value report is appropriate. However, any knowledge or suspicion of money laundering relating to serious crime or tax evasion, including cases covered by the Hansard procedure, should be reported in a Standard Report.
6 Section 167 (3) Customs and Excise Management Act 1979	This makes the submission of an incorrect VAT or Customs return, however innocent, a criminal offence.	It is the position of SOCA that a disclosure is not required for innocent error in these circumstances. Where the person knows of the omission and does not rectify the situation there will be a duty to report. Where reporting institutions feel obliged to make a disclosure, a Limited Intelligence Value report is appropriate.
7 Reporting institution served with a Court Order, which prompts suspicion.		A Limited Intelligence Value report is appropriate except where the suspicion and report relate to matters not covered by the Court Order letter, in which case a report on the

Type	Detail	Comments
		Standard Form should be submitted.
8 Where the benefit from criminal conduct is in the form of cost savings, such as breaches of employment law and the illegal copying or distribution of software licences within a company.		However if there are funds or criminal property to arrange the transfer of, and which may require consent to carry out a prohibited act, then a Standard form must be completed.

COMPLETION INSTRUCTIONS

Source Registration Document (Module 1)

In order to record disclosures and correspond accurately and in a timely manner with the regulated sector, SOCA needs accurate contact details of each reporting organisation. A **Source Registration Document** has been constructed to capture this information as concisely as possible. SOCA already holds such details for organisations which have previously disclosed, therefore **this sheet should only be used by organisations that have never previously reported and then only when making their first report**. It will not be required for each subsequent disclosure. **However, all organisations should use the source registration document to update SOCA about any changes to their contact details in order that SOCA's records can be accurately maintained**.

Institution Name — Please provide details of the Registered and/or Trading name of the company or individual making the report.

Institution Type — Please provide details of the type of company or individual making the report, e.g. Money Transmission Agent, Bank, Estate Agent etc.

Regulator — Please provide details of your regulator, where applicable, (e.g. FSA, Gaming Board of Great Britain etc)

Regulator ID — Please provide details of your regulator's Identity Number, where known to you.

Contact Details (1) — This will be SOCA's primary point of contact with you.

Forename — Please provide full details of your Forename/s.

Surname — Please provide full details of your Surname.

Position — Please provide details as to the position you hold within your employer, where applicable.

Address	Please provide your full postal address details (inc Post Code).
Telephone Details	Please provide details of your principal contact number.
E-mail Address	Please provide details where applicable. The ability to use this medium will enhance the speed of delivery of our correspondence with you.
Contact Details (2) (where applicable)	This will be SOCA's point of contact with you in the absence of the above detailed individual, if applicable.
Name	As above.
Position	As above.
Address	As above.
Telephone Details	As above.
E-mail Address	As above.

LIMITED INTELLIGENCE VALUE REPORT (MODULE 7)

Reporting Institution Please provide details of the company or individual making the report. If a Money Laundering Reporting Officer (MLRO) is completing the form it is not essential at any point to mention by name the person making the initial disclosure.

Your Reference Please provide details of your own reference number relevant to the disclosure in question. **This is an important field as the information supplied will be quoted by us SOCA in any correspondence with you relating to this disclosure**. We are shortly to explore a system change so that our automated response letters will quote only your reference number (alongside our own Intelligence Reference Number).

Branch/Office This information will enable SOCA to ascertain which of your outlets is reporting the activity, assisting SOCA decide which law enforcement agency to allocate the disclosure to.

Disclosure Date The date upon which you submit your report to SOCA. The format DD/MMM/YYYY has been used to prevent any transposition of Day and Month. Please insert two digits in the DD field to state the day, three letters in the MMM field (for example, JAN for January) and four digits to show the year in the YYYY field.

SUBJECT DETAILS

This is the Person/Legal Entity about whom/which the report is being made. Normally, reporters will be in a position to complete one of these fields, although in some circumstances this is not the case. For example you may be reporting a fraud where the perpetrator is unknown

This section of the sheet can be used to refer to an Individual or a Legal Entity. However only one of these sections should be completed. This sheet should not be used for both an individual and a Legal Entity at the same time.

Subject Status   Please indicate *only one* box from 'Suspect' or 'Victim'.

Suspect should be ticked if you know or suspect or have reasonable grounds for knowing or suspecting that this person is engaged in money laundering.

Victim is the person or entity who/which is harmed by or loses as a result of the criminal activity which you are reporting. To ensure that any intrusion against a victim's privacy is minimised, the victim's details should not, ideally, be included in subject fields. **The personal details of victims should only be included if, in the judgement of the nominated officer, the details are essential to understanding the activity being reported.**

PLEASE COMPLETE EITHER THE INDIVIDUAL'S DETAILS SECTION OF THE SHEET OR THE LEGAL ENTITY SECTION. PLEASE DO NOT COMPLETE BOTH.

Surname   Please provide details, as appropriate.

Forename 1   Please provide details, as appropriate.

Date of Birth   This is an important field. Date of birth information helps law enforcement to positively identify individuals when cross-matching personal data. The format DD/MMM/YYYY has been used to prevent any transposition of Day and Month. Please insert two digits in the DD field to state the day, three letters in the MMM field (for example, JAN for January) and four digits to show the year in the YYYY field.

Gender   Please select from options provided.

Title   Please select from options provided. If the correct title is not shown, please specify the relevant title within the 'Other' field.

Appropriate options are provided with the Field Values List.

OR

Legal Entity Name   Please provide details as appropriate, e.g. a Company or Charity Name.

Legal Entity Number Please provide details as appropriate, e.g. a Company or charity Number.

VAT Number   Please provide details as appropriate.

REASON FOR DISCLOSURE

This area is free text and should include any information not already provided which you feel is relevant to your Report. It should provide details of the reason(s) why you have knowledge or suspicion or reasonable grounds for knowledge or suspicion that another person is engaged in money laundering and why you feel that a Limited Value Report is suitable.

REASON FOR DISCLOSURE CONTINUATION SHEET (MODULE/ APPENDIX 8)

Where required, please use this section to continue your reasons for knowledge or suspicion, where the space provided within Appendix 7 is insufficient. Multiples of this module can be utilised as required.

Please ensure that you complete the Main Subject Name at the top of any of these modules completed in order that we may cross reference this module to the rest of your report.

Version 2.1 - Appendix 7

Serious Organised Crime Agency
PO Box 8000
London
SE11 5EN
Tel: 020 7238 8282
Fax: 020 7238 8286

SOCA
SERIOUS ORGANISED CRIME AGENCY

PROCEEDS OF CRIME ACT 2002 - LIMITED INTELLIGENCE VALUE REPORT

Reporting Institution	
Your Ref:	
Branch/ Office:	

Disclosure Date:

☐ - ☐ - ☐

D D - M M M - Y Y Y Y

SUBJECT DETAILS:

Individual's Details: Subject Status: Suspect : ○   **OR**   Victim: ○

Surname:

Forename:

DoB: ☐ - ☐ - ☐   Gender: Male ○   Female ○

D D   M M M   Y Y Y Y

Title: Mr ○   Mrs ○   Miss ○   Ms ○   Other [ ]

Legal Entity Details: Subject Status: Suspect : ○   **OR**   Victim: ○

Legal Entity Name:

Legal entity No: VAT No:

REASON FOR DISCLOSURE:

APPENDIX SEVEN

292

REASON FOR DISCLOSURE CONTINUATION:

Version 2.0 - Appendix 8

Main Subject Name:
(cross reference purposes)

Reason for Disclosure Continuation:

Page ☐ of ☐

Index